The
Politics of Truth

*For Stuart
and
Catherine Hall*

The Politics of Truth

From Marx to Foucault

Michèle Barrett

Polity Press

First published in 1991 by Polity Press
in association with Blackwell Publishers

Editorial office:
Polity Press
65 Bridge Street
Cambridge CB2 1UR, UK

Marketing and production:
Blackwell Publishers
108 Cowley Road
Oxford OX4 1JF, UK

106615 6 S

ISBN 0 7456 0502 8
ISBN 0 7456 0503 6 (pbk)

British Library Cataloguing in Publication Data
A CIP catalogue record for this book is available from the British
Library.

Typeset in 11 on 13 pt Plantin
by Graphicraft Typesetters Ltd, Hong Kong
Printed in Great Britain by
T.J. Press Ltd., Padstow, Cornwall
This book is printed on acid-free paper.

14.2.94

Contents

Preface

The main preoccupation of this book is the concept of 'ideology'. I do not take ideology to mean ideas, or even values, but have addressed the more powerful meaning that it has in critical social theory. A consensual definition of ideology, in Marxisant and broader circles, would be something like 'mystification that serves class interests'. Originally, I intended to review the criticisms of this concept, which have come from a variety of different directions, and reflect upon the ways in which a Marxist theory of ideology could be adapted to a world where class is not the only social division of interest. My own investment in this was that I had previously argued that one could not explain the oppression of women without taking very seriously indeed the role of ideology and culture in the creation, as well as reproduction, of that inequality. Yet, as critics asked, can one do this within the framework of a theory that had been developed in relation to social class?

My presumption was that in the course of a thorough treatment of these questions, I would emerge with a reformulation of the theory of ideology that enabled me to use it (rather as John Thompson has suggested) in the critical sense characteristic of Marxism, but applying it to any form of social domination or exploitation rather than restricting it to mystifications related to social class. But maybe Foucault was right when he said: 'to work is to try to think something other than what one thought before'. In any event, I became considerably more sceptical as to whether one can, with any success, retain much force or resonance in the concept once its explanatory associations with class and its economic determinism have been stripped away, and for this reason I conclude on a fairly lukewarm note as to the value of the concept of ideology itself for contemporary social analysis.

Not that the questions to which a theory of ideology addresses itself are ones about which one might feel lukewarm. On the contrary, they are among the most interesting and, indeed, the most politically important issues that we have to deal with. But to think about them we need to move away from the Marxist conception of ideology, and partly because of what is constraining and narrowing in that tradition. Later in the book I discuss some of the more general weaknesses of Marxism, in particular its 'universalism', and propose some rethinking of the issue of 'relativism'. Another major problem with the Marxist tradition, in terms of what a modern theory of what 'ideology' deals with, is that we look in vain there for a theory of subjectivity. Later in the book, too, I take up these themes, particularly in relation to the psychoanalytic project to contribute such a theory.

The title of this book, as many readers will recognise, is borrowed from Foucault. In a stylishly epigrammatic moment he contrasted 'the economics of untruth' with 'the politics of truth': *the economics of untruth* being Marxism's account of ideology, used to show 'the relation between what goes on in people's heads and their place in the conditions of production', and *the politics of truth* being his own approach to the relationships between knowledge, discourse, truth and power. In using Foucault's preferred term rather than entitling this book 'The Economics of Untruth' I am nailing my colours to the mast of a more general post-Marxism and on this subject I will add a note to those readers who will undoubtedly interpret this 'politically'.

Classical Marxism is not the only route to socialism: to criticise Marxism, even definitively, is not a form of conservatism. E. P. Thompson has quoted William Morris advising someone that 'you ought to read Marx ... up to date he is the only completely scientific Economist on our side'. As Thompson says, Marx is on our side, not vice versa; Marx did not invent socialism, and it will not be brought about by the 'scientific' status of Marxism but by the choices, values and struggles of men and women.

Acknowledgements

I would like to thank City University, London, and especially my colleagues in Sociology there, for giving me sabbatical leave for writing. I am also grateful to participants in my 'Modern Social Theory' class at City University for very useful discussions of the issues dealt with in the book. Students and colleagues at Cornell ensured that my semester there in 1988 was immensely productive for this book and I am grateful to them and to the Society for the Humanities there for inviting me. Chapter 5 of the book draws on a paper written for a conference at Stonybrook, State University of New York, and I am grateful to the Humanities Institute there for inviting me. I also benefited from discussions with students on my 'Ideology' course at Carleton University, in 1985, and colleagues in Ottawa.

Many individuals have helped me with the book, either by reading draft sections, discussing the issues with me or (unbeknownst to them) airing relevant views in my hearing. My thanks to Peter Beilharz, Zillah Eisenstein, John Fletcher, Catherine Hall, Stuart Hall, Ernesto Laclau, Biddy Martin, Francis Mulhern and Anne Phillips.

David Held and others at Polity were very encouraging and I am grateful to them for all their help.

Mary McIntosh and William Outhwaite continue to read what I propose to publish, however little they may agree with it, and for this and their continued friendship I thank them very much. Ruthie Petrie has been unfailingly supportive to me in my work and I am deeply grateful for the terrific encouragement, advice and help, intellectual, emotional and practical, that she has given me.

Part I

Classical Marxism and Theories of Ideology

1

Marx: Inheriting Contradictions

Anybody looking at the substantial literature about Marx's theory of ideology will soon discover a startling variety of interpretations of what Marx actually thought on this subject. I say startling, because the range of disagreement is far wider than one normally encounters in 'secondary sources' about a major thinker and the questions around which the disputes revolve are absolutely fundamental ones. There are a number of causes of this confusion and one of them is undoubtedly the fact that the 'quotable quotes' – passages where Marx addresses ideology directly, or takes the risk of defining it – are found only in his earliest works where the position he outlines is very contentious. So some of these disputes hinge not so much on what Marx said about ideology, but about what he might have said – or really *meant* to say – on the basis of differing interpretations of his theories as a whole. Also, there are several distinct – and in some respects contradictory – uses of the concept of ideology to be found in Marx, and of course these have been taken up selectively by the various commentators. This is not simply an issue of doctrinal disputes between political disciples, nor of academic pedantry from professional Marxologists. For Marx mobilised, in some eloquent and illuminating passages scattered across his works, an approach to 'ideology' that has caught the imagination of generations of people with a critical perspective on capitalist society. But, and it is a very big but, one can plausibly lay at the door of these persuasive, yet in many ways unsatisfactory, ideas some of the fundamental weaknesses of Marxism in the contemporary western political world.

Many general criticisms can be made of Marxist theory as a guide to analysis and action in a world dramatically altered since the key ideas were formulated over a century ago. Sometimes these involve a criticism of the ideas and arguments themselves, sometimes they rest on a straightforward recognition that the social world has changed in significant ways over that period of time. Marx's ideas on ideology have in the past been taken up and used, time and time again, to explain intractable or inconvenient aspects of political consciousness. But now it is increasingly recognised that the model does not work very well, or at least that it has been stretched too far. This is not just a matter of objecting to patronising castigations of people as suffering from brainwashing by 'capitalist ideology', although this old bogey has a lot of life in it still. It is more that the whole framework of a theory of ideology, any theory of ideology, has become a focus for some searching new work in social theory generally. The entire field of social theory is being recast in such a way as to take more seriously questions of culture and of subjectivity. The Marxist approach to ideology, conventionally understood in shorthand as something like 'mystification that serves class interest', is perhaps one of the key targets of contemporary thought in the post-structuralist vein. I shall be arguing that we need an infinitely more complex consideration of how subjectivity, particularly political subjectivity, is constituted and operates; how identifications of various kinds are formed, expressed and change over time; and how questions of agency and motivation can be addressed with the seriousness they deserve.

It is, however, essential to go back over Marx's own work on this question, because the debates surrounding his ideas genuinely constitute the 'classical tradition' of thought on ideology.[1] As we shall see, the changes of emphasis and the inconsistencies of Marx's arguments on certain key topics – such as whether ideology is necessarily an illusion, or distortion, or not, or whether it is economically determined or not – played an important part in ensuring that there was a long-running saga of debates in subsequent Marxist theory. And although the Marxist debates about ideology have since, and particularly since the inter-war period in Europe, filtered into a wider field of social and political theory, the concept of ideology cannot properly be understood without a knowledge of its historical development.

Let us begin, then, by looking at the changing definitions of ideology in Marx's writings. The first one we encounter is probably the most problematic: it is found towards the beginning of Marx and Engels's *The German Ideology*, a book originally written in 1845–6.

Marx I   Men are the producers of their conceptions, ideas, etc. – real, active men, as they are conditioned by a definite development of their productive forces and of the intercourse corresponding to these, up to its furthest forms. Consciousness can never be anything else than conscious existence, and the existence of men is their actual life-process. If in all ideology men and their circumstances appear upside-down as in a *camera obscura*, this phenomenon arises just as much from their historical life-process as the inversion of objects on the retina does from their physical life-process.[2]

This one passage has probably caused more confusion, and generated more fruitless attempts at exegesis, than any other in Marx, and I do not propose to add to it here. The metaphor of the reversed image has proved very powerful – perhaps more so than it is useful. It has given rise to a literal sense of ideology as pure illusion (like an optical illusion) and to an associated notion that somehow ideology is the reverse or opposite of material reality. It is within this framework of inference that the whole vexed idea of 'false consciousness' has gained ground. To put it crudely, the train of thought goes that material conditions can specify real or true interests, for example of the working class, and that in ideology these are then mystified by simple reversal – so people see their interests as the opposite of what they really are. False consciousness is thus the mirror-image of what political consciousness should be.

Let it be said immediately that whatever the merits or demerits of the notion of 'false consciousness', they have little to do with Karl Marx. This is one reason why John Plamenatz's book on ideology should be consigned to the archives section of libraries rather than inflicted on more generations of hapless political science students. In Plamenatz are to be found apparently authoritative statements such as 'Marx often called ideology "false consciousness"'; or 'Bourgeois ideas about the state are, so Marx believed, an example of false consciousness'; or even 'Marx did not trouble to distinguish between the elements that go to make up an ideology, and therefore did not enquire whether all of them can properly be subsumed under "false consciousness".'[3]

In fact, it seems that Marx *never used* the expression 'false consciousness' at all, according to Marxologists. David McLellan, for instance, probably the most authoritative of such experts at present, writes recently that Marx never used the term 'false consciousness', that it was originated by Engels and that its *locus classicus* is Engels's letter to Franz Mehring in 1893. This, of course, was long after Marx's death and the project of separating Marx's own ideas from those of Engels's later presentation has now advanced considerably, giving us a greater awareness of the dangers of eliding the two.[4] Furthermore, the current translation of the crucial letter has now been revised to read 'the wrong kind of consciousness'.[5] These niceties of Marxist scholarship are perhaps of restricted interest, but the general point that 'false consciousness' is a post-Marx concept is surely a very significant one.

'False consciousness' encapsulates a version of Marxist theories of ideology that both supporters and critics have at times found useful as a crude shorthand. Martin Seliger, for example, in his account of 'orthodox Marxist doctrine' on ideology recognises Plamenatz's mistake (as do various commentators on this topic) but quickly argues that even if Marx did not use the term false consciousness itself, none the less it does accurately reflect his position. Seliger unerringly pounces on the camera obscura metaphor as the weakest point of Marx's thought on ideology, seeing it as the source of recurring confusion in the works of Marx and Engels in general.[6] On this point he is no doubt correct, but there are obvious arguments for looking elsewhere in Marx's writings for other, and perhaps more satisfactory, formulations on the concept of ideology. The next argument of Marx's that I want to examine, suggesting a somewhat different interpretation of ideology from the one just discussed, follows directly on from the previous passage of *The German Ideology*.

> **Marx II** In direct contrast to German philosophy which descends from heaven to earth, here we ascend from earth to heaven. ... We set out from real, active men, and on the basis of their real life-process we demonstrate the development of the ideological reflexes and echoes of this life-process. The phantoms formed in the human brain are also, necessarily, sublimates of their material life-process, which is empirically verifiable and bound to material premises. Morality, religion, metaphysics, all the rest of ideology and their corresponding forms of consciousness, thus no longer retain the semblance of independence. They have no history, no development; but men, developing their material production and their material intercourse, alter, along with this their real existence, their thinking and the products of their thinking. Life is not determined by consciousness but consciousness by life.[7]

This must be the most celebrated expression of what has come to be understood as the 'materialist' position on ideology – the belief that ideological phenomena are determined by material causes. In this passage the form of words is quite uncompromising – determination is a one-way process. Note Marx's (subsequently fateful) opposition between 'real' on the one hand and 'ideological' on the other. In the reference to religion, morality and metaphysics, Marx and Engels here set out the basic element of the view that ideology is necessarily a distorted or inadequate view of the world.

Religion is a central issue because Marx believed that the demystification of religion held the key to a more general interpretation of society. This was so central to his overall philosophy that he maintained that 'the criticism of religion is the presupposition of all criticism'.[8] A number of writers have rightly pointed to the critique of religion developed within left-Hegelian philosophy – notably by Ludwig Feuerbach – as the forerunner of the arguments developed by Marx and Engels in *The German Ideology*. Jorge Larrain, for instance, says of Marx's critique of religion that 'Here Marx anticipates one of the crucial elements of his concept of ideology, namely that religion compensates in the mind for a deficient reality; it reconstitutes in the imagination a coherent solution which goes beyond the real world in an attempt to resolve the contradictions of the real world.'[9] Larrain points out that this process of 'anticipation' involves Marx developing a theoretical position on what we would now call 'ideology', without using the term itself, and that this is also true of Marx's later work on commodity fetishism as ideology in *Capital*.[10] Leaving this aside for the moment, let us focus on the substantive point of Marx's critique of religion and other 'phantoms formed in the human brain'. Jorge Larrain has articulated, in considerable detail and with great persuasiveness, a thesis that is in general terms widely accepted among writers on Marx and ideology: that Marx's concept of ideology is one with an irreducible 'critical' core. The critique of religion can serve here as an example of the insistently critical approach that in general Marx took to the belief systems and ideational structures through which people apprehend their social worlds.

This interpretation of Marx's views has not gone unchallenged. Joe McCarney's book *The Real World of Ideology* seeks to present an alternative account of Marx's approach to ideology on this central question of whether or not it is being used as a necessarily critical category. In order to do this McCarney suggests that there has been a 'whole climate of misunderstanding that has come to envelop Marxist and non-Marxist commentators alike'.[11] The 'critical' view of ideology raises the question of what is known as the 'epistemological' definition of ideology. McCarney notes that those who see Marx's concept of ideology as necessarily critical in character presuppose that ideology is an epistemological category with a bearing on the truth or falsity of the propositions in question – that ideology is a category constituted in opposition to knowledge. Naturally the notion of false consciousness, with its direct attribution to ideology of positive error, is the strongest form of the 'epistemological' definition of ideology. (McCarney refers to the 'cognitive defect' theory of ideology.) McCarney argues that the concept of ideology as used by Marx was not an epistemological category of any kind, but a strictly descriptive term.[12] First, McCarney notes that Marx uses the term ideology, usually, with an adjective – thus the 'German' ideology or 'bourgeois' ideology – rather than as a concept on its own. In this context he puts forward the theory that one crucial mistranslation has had a significantly misleading effect. The passage in question is the notorious camera obscura one: McCarney argues that 'in all ideology', from *in der ganzen Ideologie* (literally 'in the whole ideology'), refers not to ideology in general but specifically to the German philosophy under discussion. Hence, in McCarney's view, the theoretical pretensions of the passage, and notably the optical metaphor, have been completely overstated.[13] Secondly, McCarney stresses, as have others, that false consciousness was not a notion that Marx employed.[14] Thirdly, McCarney puts forward an alternative interpretation of Marx's approach, and one that ties Marx much more closely to arguments developed later in the Marxist tradition, particularly by Lenin and Lukács.

This last point is particularly significant, because McCarney seeks to reconcile what is usually perceived as a major difference of emphasis within Marxist thought. McCarney concludes that Marx shared the view, primarily associated with Lenin, that ideology was the thought and consciousness of a particular class; hence ideology was for Marx and Engels objective, predicated upon the historical existence of social classes. McCarney defines ideology as 'thought which serves class interests':[15] this is not emphasised in terms of mystification or illusion, but in terms of the objective existence of specific historical social classes. There is a similarity between this view of ideology and that of Georg Lukács, who also saw ideologies as appertaining to classes and to be understood as progressive or reactionary according to the objective historical position of the social class to which they belonged. (Hence his analysis of the historical novel, where novels written in the period of the political ascendance of the bourgeoisie – roughly until 1848 – are construed as more progressive than those dating from the decline of the class.)[16] This relationship between Marx, Lenin and Lukács is not contingent in McCarney's view. He argues that there is thus a 'single, evolving tradition' of Marxist thought on ideology and one which 'in view of its membership, may reasonably be accorded a classic status within Marxist treatments of the subject'.[17]

McCarney's argument is directed principally at showing that the difference usually perceived between Marx's critical concept of ideology and the more descriptive, class-consciousness approaches of Lenin and Lukács is based on an error. McCarney's Marx uses a concept of ideology that has been stripped of the 'critical' and 'epistemological' overtones that traditionally differentiate Marx's use from those of many other writers in the Marxist tradition – certainly Lenin and Lukács, but also, and most significantly, Gramsci. As we shall see later, this dispute is fundamental in debates about ideology and its relentless recurrence is troubling to those who seek consistency within the Marxist tradition.

I am not myself convinced by McCarney's argument. He is right to emphasise the degree to which a 'false consciousness' position on ideology has been projected on to Marx. It is also true that many of Marx's references to ideology are merely to 'ideologues' – professional philosophers, often of idealist tendencies – that he was polemicising against. On the other hand, the overwhelming weight of evidence suggests that the general spirit of Marx's thought on this topic was critical. Although it is relatively easy to accuse writers such as Plamenatz or Seliger of lack of sympathy for their subject, it is more difficult to refute the conclusions of serious and sympathetic scholars such as Allen Wood or Bhikhu Parekh, both of whom construe Marx's concept of ideology as one with varying, but consistently 'critical', meanings.[18] And as well as the metaphors of distortion and illusion throughout Marx's treatment of the topic of ideology, the substantial arguments developed within Marx's work as a whole in this area are undeniably 'epistemological'. From the theory of alienation in the early Marx to the theory of commodity fetishism in *Capital* Marx's analysis of consciousness and ideology is grounded in the belief that mystification is susceptible to being unmasked by knowledge. Finally, it seems likely that the desire to line Marx up at the head of a 'classic' (that is, Marxist-Leninist) tradition, with an agreed position on ideology to hand down, is one that can only be realised at the expense of occluding fundamental disagreement and argument within Marxist theory.

Marx III   The ideas of the ruling class are in every epoch the ruling ideas, i.e. the class which is the ruling *material* force of society, is at the same time its ruling *intellectual* force. The class which has the means of material production at its disposal, has control at the same time over the means of mental production, so that thereby, generally speaking, the ideas of those who lack the means of mental production are subject to it. The ruling ideas are nothing more than the ideal expression of the dominant material relationships.[19]

This passage, also from *The German Ideology*, approaches ideology from a different perspective, making two separate points about the relationship of ideology to social class. Marx begins with the rather grand assertion that ruling class ideas are also ruling ideas, but when he goes on to argue why this should be so the explanation he gives is a very simple one – the ruling class control the means of ideological production. So this is a general point about the ideological power that inheres in ownership, or control, over the means by which opinion and consciousness are constructed. Taking this at face value, it is completely uncontentious, and most socialists will not need to be convinced that the level of political culture in Britain, for example, is affected by the fact that the press is owned and controlled by a small group of extremely politicised ideologues of whom Rupert Murdoch and Robert Maxwell are merely prominent examples.

There are, however, two extremely contentious dimensions of this apparently straightforward point. To say that those who lack the means of ideological production are generally speaking thereby 'subject' to the ruling class is to invoke a whole series of difficult issues around popular consciousness and popular culture. These have been raised in their most striking form by feminist work on cultural phenomena such as soap opera, royalty or romantic fiction, where the traditional notion of ideological 'subjection' endorsed by Marx in the passage does scant justice to the passionate enthusiasm of many women for the products of which they are alleged to be victims.[20] It is now widely recognised that, at the very least, we need a more sophisticated analysis of the ways in which such processes of 'subjection' work, including a consideration of participation in the construction of ideology that goes beyond the notion of collusion in what is ultimately not in one's interests. Although this problem has been most strongly raised by feminists, it is one with obvious general application, and indeed many people now argue that it strikes at a vulnerable element in the Marxist theory of ideology in general. That is, it challenges an assumption, apparently inherent in the concept, that we can specify more or less progressive levels or aspects of consciousness. This will be taken up in more detail later.

Recognition of a second problem with Marx's point might also be indirectly attributed to feminism. Dale Spender's thesis is that men control the language, control the media, control the gatekeeping institutions of publishing and criticism: they control what Marx would call the 'means of mental production', but the interests they represent are those of men rather than those of capital. The titles of Dale Spender's books – *Man Made Language, Women of Ideas – and What Men Have Done to Them* and *For the Record*, for example[21] – are indicative of the theory underlying this version of feminist critique of patriarchal culture. The theoretical position of Spender's work has been extensively criticised[22] and I do not need to dwell on this here.

Spender's extended application of Marx's point to a different ruling group – based on gender rather than class – illustrates the frailty of Marx's argument here. Is it axiomatic that the ideology of the ruling class rules, or does this occur by virtue of class control over the means of mental production? Clearly Marx's point requires considerable rethinking if it is to take cognisance not only of gender but also of racism and the associated structural inequalities of ethnicity. There is now a growing literature analysing the racist character of the British media and cultural practices[23] and the exclusion of blacks from participation, let alone control, in these areas. These anti-racist arguments also operate within the same framework of a notion of control over the means of mental production: how does this affect the argument about 'ruling class' ideas? The significance of these points lies in the challenge they pose to the assumption that Marx's theory of ideology is necessarily related to social class. It is not merely that Marx's insight can be *applied* to some other social division – such as those of gender or race – but that recognition of the importance of these other social divisions forces us to rethink what is meant by the term ruling class.

Underlying the overt meaning of the passage quoted is a far more subtle argument Marx is making about the class-generated character of ideology. He expands upon another dimension of the assertion that ruling class ideas are ruling ideas, by arguing that certain characteristic ideas of a period are not contingently but essentially connected to the relations of production of the society in question. The examples Marx gives are the aristocratic notions of honour and loyalty and the bourgeois ideas of freedom and equality.[24] Marx argues that these ideas do not just happen to coincide with modes of production to which they are neatly suited (feudalism being based on bonded labour and capitalism on formally free labour), although this is what is generally assumed. He believes such ideas to be 'the dominant material relationships grasped as ideas', hence they are part and parcel of the production relations and inseparable analytically from this material base.

This argument, too, is problematic when examined in relation to the project of developing a general theory of ideology. As we shall see later, a decisive change in Marxist theory on political ideology was made when Ernesto Laclau demonstrated that the 'class-belonging' character of political ideologies could not be taken for granted as had previously been done by many people.[25] Certainly it is now clear that there is, at the very least, a range of constructs ('patriotism' would be a well-trodden example) which it has proved possible to align with a variety of class ideologies and which therefore cannot be said to have a necessary 'class-belonging' character. The debates about whether or in what sense ideology is tied to class have been extremely significant in recent years. If we look back over the interpretations of Marx's thought on ideology we can see that on this central issue his views are problematic and a variety of readings are on offer.

Bhikhu Parekh, for example, writes that for 'Marx, an ideology is systematically biassed towards a social group, be it a class, a nation, a profession or a race. It is therefore wrong to *define* it as a body of ideas biassed towards a class.'[26] Goran Therborn, in line with a majority of interpreters of Marx on this question, refers on the other hand to 'the classical Marxist problematic centred on the material, class determination of ideologies'.[27] So we can see that in the ambiguities of Marx's own writing and in the varying interpretations within the Marxist tradition there is already the basis for considerable debate, and indeed confusion, about the relationship of ideology to social class. Yet, as we shall see later, the moment at which that link was completely broken was decisive for the viability of Marxist political theory as traditionally understood.

Marx IV [Then begins an epoch of social revolution.] With the change of the economic foundation the entire immense superstructure is more or less rapidly transformed. In considering such transformations a distinction should always be made between the material transformation of the economic conditions of production, which can be determined with the precision of natural science, and the legal, political, religious, aesthetic or philosophic – in short, ideological forms in which men become conscious of this conflict and fight it out. Just as our opinion of an individual is not based on what he thinks of himself, so can we not judge of such a period of transformation by its own consciousness; on the contrary, this consciousness must be explained rather from the contradictions of material life.[28]

By 1859 Marx had moved on from the formulations that he and Engels had drafted in the 1845–6 work *The German Ideology*. This passage is notable for the brevity with which three major theses on ideology are introduced: the famous 'base-and-superstructure' metaphor, the idea of ideological 'struggle' and the distinction between ideology and knowledge (or science). We do not need to dwell here on what has been called the 'topographical' metaphor in Marx's theory of ideology – he describes this elsewhere in the same text in the following terms: 'The sum total of these relations of production constitutes the economic structure of society, the real foundation on which rises a legal and political superstructure and to which correspond definite forms of social consciousness.'[29] Although this is a classic statement of an image of ideology that has acquired enormous force, it is worth noting that even here the formulation is ambiguous in that the relationship of 'social consciousness' to the superstructure, presented in terms of the state, is somewhat unclear. As Stuart Hall has commented in relation to a comparable passage from *The German Ideology*, there appear to be *three* rather than two levels in this embryonic base/superstructure model – first, the 'base' of material production, secondly, the level of civil society and the state, and thirdly, the area of consciousness, philosophy, religion and so on.[30] Marx's unwillingness to aggregate ideology proper with the level of civil society and the state – society as the polity – is the source of one of several ambiguities in the so-called classic determinist position on ideology. Certainly the base-and-superstructure metaphor, symbolising for many an inflexible conception of ideology as the reflection of economically given 'reality', has been subjected to considerable critical attention. This will be referred to in the more general discussion of the problem of determination in the classical debates about ideology.

A second feature of the passage under discussion is Marx's reference to men (perhaps here for once we could say people) becoming conscious and 'fighting out' class struggle at the level of ideology. This half-sentence, scarcely more than a phrase really, is the most solid evidence available for the interpretation of Marx as a Gramsci *manqué*. To elevate it to a general reading of Marx's position of ideology is to project on to Marx a more recent concern with cultural politics that, sadly, his writings as a whole do not justify.

I quote the final sentence of the passage simply to illustrate a general point about Marx's methodological position that has considerable relevance to the debate on the so-called science/ideology distinction. What clearer statement could he make to indicate that he is an epistemological realist? Marx does not accept the validity of a society's discourse about itself, he sees this as a phenomenon to be explained rather than as a source of knowledge. None the less, this, too, is less clear-cut an issue than it might be with, on the one hand, the inevitable variations of interpretation of Marx on the specific question of science and ideology, and more general disagreement about whether or to what degree the traditions of epistemological realism are incompatible with the position of, for example, Foucault.

The last two versions of 'Marx' that I want to mention are ones where recent commentators have extrapolated distinctive positions from Marx's writings. When discussing Marx's 1851–2 text, 'The

Eighteenth Brumaire', Stuart Hall emphasises the significance of the break, in the few short years between it and *The German Ideology*, in Marx's thought about ideology.

Marx V Stuart Hall writes of 'The Eighteenth Brumaire': Louis-Napoleon's regime – which appears in the form of a single despotism – in fact is seated on the back of a particular class interest: that of the 'most numerous' class in France at that moment, though one destined to decline – the small-holding peasantry. This class fraction cannot rule in its own name: it rules *through* Napoleon and through his ideas. It is this class which temporarily gives content to the expanding State – for the State is not 'suspended in mid-air': but Louis-Napoleon, revivifying spirits, names, battle cries and costumes from the past (the past of another and greater Napoleon), is the *conductor* of the power of this class to the political level. Capital settles for a 'postponement'. 'Bonapartism' is its name and form. Without examining this argument in any further detail, it should be sufficient to see from this and the related essays of the period, that the domain of the political/juridical superstructures and the forms of the State are no longer thought by Marx as in any simple reflexive or expressive sense corresponding to their base. In the development of a Marxist theory of the superstructures, this essay must occupy a *pivotal position*.[31]

Under consideration here is the specific operation of what Louis Althusser was later to call the political 'level': a section of the social formation with its own effectivity.[32] The effect of Hall's argument is to trace back to Marx himself the flourishing tradition of work in twentieth-century Marxist theory that has analysed the operations of the state in ideological terms and attempted to relate this analysis to other aspects of the social totality in a non-mechanistic way. It is to indicate, as it were, the reference point in Marx for the contributions not only of Gramsci, but of Althusser, Poulantzas and (early) Laclau, as well as to disabuse people of the assumption that Marx himself worked with an unmediated relationship between the economy and ideology. As Stuart Hall stresses, the political level – in which for the moment we can include both state and 'civil society' – provides one such important mediation in Marx's approach to the general question of determination within social relations as a whole.

Marx VI John Mepham writes of *Capital*, volume I: [Marx's distinction between phenomenal form and real relation] contains a substantial epistemological theory about the relation between thought and reality and about the origins of illusions about reality. This theory is that the origin of ideological illusions is in the phenomenal form of reality itself. ... Ideological language does not just distract attention away from real social relations, nor does it explain them away, nor even does it directly deny them. It structurally excludes them from thought.[33]

John Mepham makes an extended argument on a point recognised by several writers on Marx and the concept of ideology – that although the word ideology is largely dropped by the time Marx came to write *Capital*, it is this work that contains his most elaborate and sophisticated theoretical arguments about ideology.[34] Traditionally it has been long recognised that the theory of 'commodity fetishism' in *Capital* is a theory of ideology in capitalist society, explaining as it does the way in which relations constituted by human labour come to appear as relations between things.[35] ('Commodity fetishism' is not a description of consumerism in capitalism, as is sometimes wrongly assumed, it is an analysis of *reification*.) John Mepham notes the thesis in *Capital* linking the concepts of 'phenomenal form' and 'real relation': it is simply that the former renders the latter opaque, or invisible. Thus the form of the wage, for instance, appearing as it does to be a payment for some*thing*, masks the fact that it is really part of a contract in which what is bought is labour time rather than a product. Mepham argues that Marx's celebrated distinction between on the one hand phenomenal form or appearance, and on the other real relation or essence – a distinction on which his entire analysis of the operation of capitalism rests – has a much greater epistemological content than some notion of superficial and underlying processes. This is because, Mepham believes, the distinction is systematically invoked in relation to ideology and, specifically, where a question of *mystification* arises. Marx's analysis of the fetishism of commodities is thus only one example of a general theory that 'the origin of ideological illusions is in the phenomenal forms of reality itself'.[36]

Mepham explicitly disputes the view that Marx saw ideology as 'some sort of defective perception of clearly perceptible facts', stressing that for Marx 'it is the forms of social relations with which one is apparently directly acquainted in experience (value, wages, money, commodities, etc.) that are deceptive'.[37] It is this that is referred to in the latter part of the passage quoted, where Mepham argues that ideology operates through the systematic and mystificatory exclusion of certain perceptions from discourse. In Marx's own words: 'The characters that stamp products as commodities, and whose establishment is a necessary preliminary to the circulation of commodities, have already acquired the stability of natural, self-understood forms of social life before man seeks to decipher ... their meaning.'[38]

I have set out six different treatments of the concept of ideology to be found in Marx. They do not form a seamless web of 'the Marxist theory of ideology' and to regard Marx as having produced 'a theory' of ideology is unjustified. Some of Marx's propositions have enormous force and eloquence. The problem is that individual arguments made by Marx at different times, or extracted from his works by commentators, do not add up to a position on the issues that have become contentious in subsequent debates. There is enough in Marx to please those who like good old-fashioned economic determinism when they have to think about ideology, but there is enough, too, for those who support a more Gramscian engagement with the ideological and cultural struggle. Indeed, as is also true of Gramsci, Marx has become something of a rorschach blot, offering the raw material for a surprisingly diverse range of possible 'readings'.

Marx's propositions on ideology have become discrete sets of influences on subsequent writers and thinkers: some people opt for the 'camera obscura', others for the precursor of Gramsci, others again for commodity fetishism. All of these positions emerge, with due textual support, from the writings of Marx. In some senses, it is important to ascertain which of the varying interpretations of Marx's views on key issues is the most plausible. In another sense, it does not really matter: Marx has spawned such a range of metaphors for thinking about ideology that we each have to pick our own way through the bewildering range of images and models that have been generated. Perhaps the most significant point is that the very 'openness' or internally contradictory nature (depending on your view) of Marx's own writings has opened up a vast area of debate and dispute within the Marxist tradition. In recent years, the whole paradigm within which the debate has occurred has been extensively and tellingly criticised. Before looking at these more fundamental objections to the Marxist project, I want to try to draw out the issues that have generated the most debate within that tradition, and this will form the basis of the chapters immediately following.

As Larrain has argued,[39] perhaps the most abiding point of discussion in the Marxist tradition on ideology is the question of whether we necessarily take a 'critical' position – conceptualising ideology as illusion, mystification, distortion or apologia, for example. This 'epistemological' definition (so called because it speaks from a position of knowledge superior to that which is being categorised as ideological) is usually counterposed to writers – such as Lukács or Lenin – who have taken a more neutral view and seen ideology as the world-views of historical social classes. This issue has always been a highly politicised one within Marxism, but has now taken on a much broader and more topical political significance. In contemporary radical politics the personal voice of experienced oppression has recently acquired a new authority and the Marxist theory of ideology has some new and telling challenges to face.

Related to this is the more philosophical issue of epistemology, often discussed under the heading of the 'ideology and science' debate. Opinion varies as to how far Marx might be construed as a realist or a relativist in epistemological terms, and this is a general issue around which many local disputes have circulated. It, too, has taken on a completely new lease of life in terms of contemporary theory: Foucault's rejection of 'Truth' in favour of the operation of 'regimes of truth' is but one instance of a wholesale rethinking of epistemology. As Foucault has made crisply clear, the category of ideology itself does not emerge unscathed from such a major rethinking.

Thirdly, we can identify the question of 'determinism' as a defining characteristic of debates about ideology in the Marxist tradition, whether in the form of the 'base/superstructure' metaphor or in more recent discussions of 'articulation' or 'relative autonomy'. And here again, we see a major transformation of the question itself, and not merely the answers people have given to it, in the work of contemporary social theorists. To explain this properly we will have to go into each of these three issues in turn, starting with the question of whether ideology is necessarily a critical or pejorative term and the thorny issues that this raises.

2

Ideology: Critique or Description?

The term 'ideologue' has an inescapably critical connotation; when we speak of ideologues we imply quite deliberately that such people are more than representatives or spokespersons for certain points of view – they are skilled in the arts of persuasion and rhetoric and they may well seek to occlude uncongenial facts and mystify contradictory information. But the term ideologue is not necessarily a critical one: in the Soviet Union the various posts of party 'ideologues' were at one time respected political positions that formed an important part of political strategy. In the western capitalist democracies a government post of Minister for Ideology would be regarded with suspicion since, except in wartime when a propaganda function of government is explicitly allowed, the convention is that political beliefs and behaviour are based on rational argument about the facts rather than on overt mechanisms of persuasion. In the Soviet Union, of course, it is openly accepted that ideology is a matter for political strategy: there is no pretence of 'common sense' and no denial that political positions are always already *politicised.*

This difference in the connotations of the term 'ideologue' has its roots in two different traditions about the meaning of ideology to be found in the Marxist tradition. The 'western' view is based loosely on what I suggested in the previous chapter was Marx's position; the Soviet view based loosely on Lenin's understanding of ideology as the perspective of a particular class. Jorge Larrain, whose two recent books on ideology have rightly had considerable impact,[1] should be credited with having clarified this fundamental contradiction in Marxist thought in this area. In a summarising essay on the concept, he concludes that 'The existence of two major conceptions of ideology within the Marxist tradition is the source of many debates. Some authors of the present day believe that only one of these versions is the truly Marxist one, whereas others, unable to accept a difference between Marx and Lenin, try to reconcile both versions.'[2] Larrain centres many debates on ideology around these opposing conceptions

– the 'negative' or critical theory of ideology in Marx and the 'positive' or descriptive definition of general world-views and perspectives tied to historical social classes found in Lenin as well as in Lukács and Gramsci. There certainly is a case for seeing this as one, if not the, fundamental divide in Marxist theories of ideology. However, it could be argued that Larrain overplays this difference in his overall conception of the subject; the concept of ideology has generated several other debates of major significance, some of which have a bearing on wider debates in present-day theory.

THE 'CRITICAL' DEFINITION OF IDEOLOGY

Let us look at the debate by first considering the 'Marx' pole of the continuum. As I suggested in the previous chapter, Marx's various definitions of ideology all have a critical core. Whether he speaks of illusion and mystification, the critique of religion or the theory of commodity fetishism and other forms of reification in capitalism, Marx's uses of the idea of ideology are unquestionably based on a 'critical' conception. In Larrain's terms it is a 'negative' use in that it conceives ideology as some kind of distortion of thought. It is also an 'epistemological' usage in that Marx clearly proposes a distinction between knowledge or science on the one hand and ideology on the other: he makes claims about the inadequate knowledge status of ideology.

There is no difficulty in finding subsequent treatments of ideology in harmony with Marx's usage and I will give one or two examples of this cluster of usages. Let us take a recent one, notable for its crispness. Terry Lovell writes that 'Ideology, then, may be defined as the production and dissemination of erroneous beliefs whose inadequacies are socially motivated. This definition recognises two other categories: erroneous beliefs which are not so motivated, and valid beliefs which are, but places them both outside the category of ideology.'[3] Lovell argues that this very precise definition avoids many of the pitfalls from which a definition of ideology as either distorted knowledge or class-related ideas will suffer. Noting that Marx himself, but not all Marxist writers on the topic, follows an admirable method of argument, Lovell insists that 'To establish that a given body of ideas or theory serves class interests is always insufficient to justify the label of ideology. It is always necessary *first* to apply epistemological criteria to evaluate the work. Only when the ideas in question have had their inadequacy to their object amply demonstrated, and when the respects in which they are inadequate are also shown to touch upon class interest in a systematic way, is the critique of ideology completed.'[4] Terry Lovell's definition is a model of clarity in the 'critical' and 'epistemological' tradition of Marx's own thought. She ties her argument to a class analysis of ideology and she casts ideology exclusively at the level of conscious beliefs rather than in the wider terms of what Raymond Williams has called 'structures of feeling': both of these tend to go along with the 'critical' position, as we shall see later.

The second example of the 'Marx pole' I want to look at might be more contentious as I propose to take out of its general context Althusser's discussion of the operation of the school as an 'ideological apparatus' of the capitalist state. Louis Althusser's well-known essay contains a passage running along the following lines:

1 'The school is the dominant ideological apparatus of the state.'
2 'It takes children from every [social] class at infant-school age, and then for years . . . it drums into them . . . a certain amount of "know-how" wrapped in the ruling ideology (. . . natural history . . . literature) or simply the ruling ideology in its pure state (ethics, civic instruction, philosophy).'
3 'Somewhere around the age of sixteen, a huge mass of children are ejected [workers and peasants] . . . Another portion of scholastically adapted youth . . . goes somewhat further [technicians, clerks, lower executives] . . . A last portion reaches the summit [intellectuals, managers, police, politicians, administrators, ideologists].'
4 'Each mass ejected *en route* is practically provided with the ideology which suits the role it has to fulfil in class society'. (The exploited workers have a consciousness that is 'national' and 'a-political'; managers have 'human relations'; agents of repression can enforce obedience; ideologists can manipulate consciousness.)
5 'The mechanisms which produce this vital result [reproduction of relations between exploiters and the exploited] . . . are naturally covered up and concealed by a universally reigning ideology . . . which represents the school as a neutral environment purged of ideology.'[5]

This passage might be regarded as a text-book example of the 'critical' position on ideology. Althusser shows how certain forms of consciousness and inadequate apprehension of the world are systematically related to class interest, in this instance the need for the capitalist system to reproduce appropriate relations between its various agents. There is a clear insistence on the epistemological character of ideology (in line with Althusser's general defence of the ideology/science distinction), and a very direct attribution of specific ideological forms of consciousness to the requirements of the class system.

It is worth noting at this point two problems with Althusser's proposition. A central thrust of the argument is the explanation of the 'apolitical' consciousness of the mass of workers and peasants and, of course, this is the crucial political function of 'critical' theories of ideology. These theories must seek to explain how and why workers do not develop forms of consciousness that express their exploitation and develop possibilities for change. In Althusser's case many people have commented on the extreme position he takes up on this issue and what little room he leaves for contestation and the consciousness of resistance.[6] In dealing with workers' consciousness Althusser refers to popular common sense and most of his description is distanced by quotation marks: 'a "highly-developed" "professional", "ethical", "civic", "national" and a-political consciousness'. The only element that he is prepared to assert directly is the idea that workers have an 'a-political' consciousness. Yet there is considerable room for doubt about the empirical evidence on which Althusser's assertions might be founded. Nicholas Abercrombie, Stephen Hill and Bryan Turner, in their critical study of the widespread Marxist notion that there is a 'dominant ideology' to which the consciousness of workers is subjected, argue forcefully that 'The Dominant Ideology Thesis' is empirically false.[7] They analyse, *inter alia*, many sociological studies of the consciousness of workers in late capitalist society and conclude that far from being a-political such workers have a clearly formulated apprehension of the injustice and exploitation of the world they inhabit and one which might be summarised in the expression 'a law for the rich and another for the poor'.[8] According to Abercrombie et al., the reasons why workers accept such inequality may have more to do with the tangible economic benefits of reformism than with a notion of a 'value consensus' or 'dominant ideology' operating within the working class. They argue, on the contrary, that significant value *dissensus* exists within the working class – although the dominant class may be bound together by value consensus or 'dominant ideology'.[9] This argument clearly poses a challenge not merely to Althusser's thesis, but to many of the arguments associated with the 'critical' position and its attempt to theorize the insufficiently radical consciousness of the working class.

A second problem, more local to Althusser, is the discrepancy between the approach to ideology taken in the passage I have discussed and his approach elsewhere. For the 'other' Althusser on ideology – whose work on the role of ideological interpellation in the constitution of subjectivity will be discussed later – is hard to reconcile with this one.

THE 'CLASS CONSCIOUSNESS' DEFINITION

At the opposite, sometimes called 'positive', 'neutral' or descriptive pole of the continuum the most significant figures are Lukács and Lenin. The sharp contrast between this view and the 'critical' one can be seen in a quotation from Lenin: 'Since there can be no talk of an independent ideology being developed by the masses of the workers in the process of their movement *the only choice* is either bourgeois or socialist ideology. There is no middle course (for humanity has not created a "third" ideology, and, moreover, in a society torn by class antagonisms there can never be a non-class or above-class ideology).' In a footnote to this passage Lenin adds that workers can, of course, contribute to the development of socialist ideology – but they do so 'not as workers, but as socialist theoreticians . . . ; in other words, they take part only to the extent that they are able, more or less, to acquire the knowledge of their age and advance that knowledge'.[10] From this passage we can note that Lenin is construing ideology not so much as the world-view of a particular epoch or class but as a systematised and elaborated body of thought appropriate to such a class: he is regarding ideology as the knowledge that is produced by intellectuals and professional ideologues. Of equal importance is his insistence that no non-class ideology can exist in class society; this is so much true that the terms 'ideology' and 'class consciousness' become almost interchangeable in this tradition.

Lenin's conception of ideology is integrally linked to class struggle. Georg Lukács, in the appraisal written just after Lenin's death in 1923, stressed that Lenin was the first to see through the 'mechanistic application of Marxism' that saw proletarian class consciousness as automatically given. This error – which Lukács describes as thinking that *the proletariat could gradually evolve ideologically into the revolutionary vocation appropriate to its class*[11] – was one that Lenin tried to combat with his developing theories of party organisation and the importance of the vanguard party in raising consciousness. So Lenin's conception of ideology, although closely tied to class consciousness, does not reduce to a 'reflectionist' position on ideology where consciousness is seen as a simple mirror image of historical economic relations. Lenin's conception thus goes back to the distinction Marx made between a class 'in itself' and a class whose consciousness had been raised to the point where one can speak of a class 'for itself'. The notion of 'illusion' is quite irrelevant to this conception of ideology: consciousness is appropriate to a particular class at a specific period of history and the strengths and weaknesses of ideologies are given by this historical reality, not by the supposed relation of ideology to absolute non-historical knowledge.

It is no coincidence that it should be Lukács making this point. For underlying Lenin's understanding of ideology is the whole tradition of German thought that sees ideology and consciousness in a reflectionist mode. The Hegelian *Zeitgeist*, or spirit of the epoch, gives way to an idea of *Weltanschauung*, or general world-view, analysed by Lukács himself as appertaining to specific social classes. Lukács does not see class ideology and class consciousness as *determined* by economic relations as occurs in Marx's base-and-superstructure metaphor, he sees instead a (Hegelian) *totality* in which ideology and consciousness are analytically inseparable from these other features of a mode of production. It is this emphasis on society as a 'totality' that allows Lukács to develop some of the more striking of his literary theories: he binds together the historical organisation of production in a society with a generalised view of the world characteristic of a particular class in that society and then meshes into this the cultural and ideological expression of that class. This complex totality is all integrally connected, and it is this that leads to some of Lukács's more notorious pronouncements on culture. For example, he argues that the bourgeois realist novel could only be a progressive art-form whilst the bourgeoisie was historically a progressive class, and that modernism, as the art-form of a declining class, was a necessarily decadent style.[12] Formulations of this type are only possible if society is thought of as an 'expressive totality', and this view has proved increasingly difficult to sustain. Indeed, in the work of some contemporary theorists it is argued that society should not be thought of as a 'totality' at all, let alone one as awesomely integrated as the 'expressive' model suggests.

We can see how far Lukács's approach differs from the 'Marx pole' of the continuum by looking at a passage where he refers to

Engels's use of the term 'false consciousness' – symptomatic of the strongest 'critical' position on ideology, *pace* the likely ambiguities of translation. Lukács writes: 'as Engels emphasises in a letter to Mehring, this consciousness is false. However, the dialectical method does not allow us simply to proclaim the "falseness" of this consciousness and to persist in an inflexible confrontation of true and false. On the contrary, it requires us to investigate this "false consciousness" concretely as an aspect of the historical totality and as a stage in the historical process.'[13] Lukács here distances himself – in a paradoxically 'modern' fashion – from the problematic notion of false consciousness but not for the reasons that have in more recent times made the term so unpopular. Lukács's critique is based on his belief that all forms of consciousness can be analysed in terms of historical reality and hence the 'falseness' can be correctly attributed not to the consciousness but to the society of which such consciousness forms a part.

Lukács's *History and Class Consciousness* is the text that shows most clearly the philosophical background that Lenin was to transform in his reconceptualisation of class consciousness as a matter for party organisation and struggle. It has been much analysed, mainly because it is a text that reveals the weaknesses of the 'class consciousness' conception of ideology. Hence we can examine the arguments about it to see some of the general difficulties with the 'descriptive' approach. Perhaps the best known of these is the charge of 'historicism'. Underlying Lukács's arguments is the belief that knowledge, including historical materialism, is a product of history just as much as is class consciousness: indeed both are included in this usage of the term ideology. This, of course, constitutes a radical denial of the distinction between ideology and science, since *both* are seen as products of the totality of a society in a particular epoch. This is called historicism for the simple reason that it casts history – rather than science – as the basis of objective knowledge. It is clearly a 'charge' that can be laid against many other exponents in the roughly 'positive' or 'historical class consciousness' school of thought on ideology. It must be said, however, that it is a charge that can only be made *from* an explicit position, namely one that rests on the validity of the ideology/science distinction. Hence, although it is a widely used critical term in debates about ideology, it finds its strongest arguments only in the work of those who are themselves committed to the objective epistemological status of science. As we shall see later, the most notable crusader for the 'scientific' status of Marxism, and critic of the errors of 'historicism', is Louis Althusser.

Gareth Stedman-Jones, in a wide-ranging critique of Lukács's *History and Class Consciousness*, draws out the more general anti-scientific undertones of Lukács's stance.[14] He points to the anti-scientific tradition of German philosophy in which Lukács was immersed and the rejection of causal analysis in the German human sciences, describing *History and Class Consciousness* as 'the first major irruption of the romantic anti-scientific tradition of bourgeois thought into Marxist theory'.[15] Stedman-Jones shows how Lukács arrives at an extraordinary reversal of the usual ways of thinking about science and consciousness: science, as part of bourgeois ideology, is demoted to being merely the expression of a particular class viewpoint, whereas the consciousness of the proletariat – as the consciousness of the truly universal class – acquires an objective status.[16] This leads, as Stedman-Jones points out, to a highly relativist conception of knowledge as well as to the strange attribution of universal, objective status to the subjectivity of the working class.

Lukács, particularly in his earlier work, is a most vulnerable target for the charge of historicism. It has, however, been brought against many others who see ideology in terms of consciousness within a historical totality. Hence Lenin, Karl Korsch and sometimes Gramsci have all been regarded as 'historicist' in their orientation. None of them, however, operates with such a mechanical conception of class consciousness as does Lukács, none has the anti-scientific streak identified by Stedman-Jones in Lukács, and all pay attention (in Gramsci's case it is a major focus of his work) to ideological struggle. In this sense it is reasonable to see Lukács's *History and Class Consciousness* as the extreme 'pole' of the 'historical class consciousness' position on ideology – and one whose arguments were significantly affected by Lenin's emphasis on the role of the party in changing political consciousness. Agnes Heller has commented on the fact that Lukács's *History and Class Consciousness* 'continues to be regarded as the paradigmatic expression of his theoretical activity',[17] although it was decisively repudiated by him in later life. I am leaving in suspension the vexed issues surrounding the place of this particular book in Lukács's work as a whole, and merely using it here as an illustration of the position.

I have discussed Lukács so far principally in relation to the question of a critical, versus a descriptive, use of the term ideology. Under the heading of 'historicism' I have touched on the ideology/science distinction, which will be discussed more directly in the next chapter. We can note, though, that a number of other much debated points arise over Lukács's position – notably the question of whether

Italian political thinker Antonio Gramsci. Larrain has argued that Gramsci's work is a decisive advance for the 'positive' conception of ideology:[20] Gramsci formulates a way of looking at ideology that suffers from neither the problems attendant upon seeing ideology as illusion nor those that follow from the 'historicism' of seeing ideology as part of a mechanically related historical social totality. Larrain also points out that Gramsci's rejection of the strongly 'critical' sense of ideology in Marx occurred (as was also the case with Lukács) before the text of *The German Ideology* was available to him: so the 'positive' conception of ideology does not develop in reaction to, but in ignorance of, the strongest statement of the 'negative' model.[21]

Gramsci's work is by no means restricted to the positive/negative debate about ideology, and his distinctive contribution will be discussed under various other headings too; he is today by far the most popular theorist of ideology within the 'classical' Marxist tradition. Marx's 1859 formulation about ideology, in which he refers briefly to the idea that ideology is where men become conscious of class conflict and 'fight it out', finds a profound and elaborated exposition and development in Gramsci's work. Above all, Gramsci conceives of ideology as a matter for struggle – a struggle in which intellectuals and ideologues play a part in the long-term battles for popular support in the socialist project. It is this centring of the theory of ideology around the political salience of ideological and cultural struggle that has contributed to Gramsci's popularity among the left intelligentsia and that caused his work to be taken up afresh in recent years. Gramsci's insistence on human political agency – and it is a matter for dispute whether he ties this to *class* agency or not – differentiates his position sharply from the 'reflectionist' position on ideology and the view that society is an 'expressive totality'. His insistence on the necessity for ideological struggle as part of a broad socialist political project distances him equally from the prioritising of struggle at the point of economic production that traditionally goes hand in hand with the 'critical' view of ideology as an illusory representation of the material base. In this sense, given the power of the alternative that Gramsci puts forward in his writings, his work constitutes the most important resolution of this debate.

Gramsci's understanding of hegemony as a struggle for 'consent' leads him to propose a theory of the role of intellectuals that has generated considerable interest. Gramsci argues that 'intellectuals' play an important part in the general field in which class conflict is played out: they are not restricted to the function of individual ideologues but have a broader political significance. Most notably,

Gramsci suggested that we can distinguish between 'traditional' and 'organic' intellectuals – the former being the voices of the ruling bloc and the latter those that come to speak for progressive class forces in their struggle against hegemonic domination.[22] Intellectuals are certainly important in the 'war of position' in which classes move to better vantage points in the hegemonic contest; less so in the subsequent 'war of manoeuvre' or seizing of state power. But Gramsci, in a marked political contrast to Lenin's view, sees the winning of hegemony as something that must take place as a *precondition* to a revolutionary seizure of power.

Gramsci sees what is now generally called 'ideological struggle' as politically effective and significant in its own right: in this sense it is a theory of intellectual work that is far removed from the usual 'historicist' assumptions. Gramsci's position is quite different from the 'class consciousness' position on ideology – and his emphasis on struggle for hegemony is far removed from the 'immanentist' and 'spontaneist' tendencies usually associated with that position. On the other hand, the use of the term 'organic' to refer to the intellectuals of the working class has a Lukácsian ring to it, and this is only one example of what might be thought of as 'historicist' residues in Gramsci's arguments.[23]

The question as to whether Gramsci should be regarded as 'historicist' or not is indexical of where he is to be placed on the spectrum of critical/class consciousness definitions of ideology with which we are concerned here. In my view Gramsci does strike some kind of balance, or resolution, between the two extremes; no one could suggest he espouses the 'critical' definition and his emphasis on the struggle for hegemony brings him sharply back from the Lukácsian view of an 'expressive totality'. However, it must be said that there are substantial, indeed fundamental definitional difficulties with Gramsci's work and any thorough general statement on ideology from a Gramscian viewpoint would need to resolve them. They include: what is the relationship, or intellectual division of labour, between the concepts of ideology and hegemony? Is ideology a specifically political concept, and hegemony a broader cultural one (as suggested by Hall et al.)? How does either concept relate to an emphasis on coercion or on non-coercive aspects of consent? (for example, how do these twin concepts compare with Althusser's distinction between ideological and repressive state apparatuses?) Does Gramsci's definition of organic ideologies as 'necessary superstructures' contradict the notion of ideology as a terrain of struggle? What implications does this ambiguity have for the question of the determination of ideology? Is either ideology or hegemony explicitly tied to class analysis, or also relevant to other political conflicts and movements? Although Gramsci's insights and formulations have proved immensely fertile – particularly in the post-Leninist political discussions of the left in Western Europe – there is an urgent need to try and resolve some of the theoretical ambiguities left in the body of his writings.

SOME CURRENT PERSPECTIVES

I want to conclude this chapter by discussing briefly the extent to which this key difference in the classical tradition, on whether ideology should be thought of in a critical, 'epistemological' or in a neutral way that focuses on class consciousness, is still relevant for contemporary theorists of ideology. Within a roughly Marxisant literature, and in writing that has been influenced by the Marxist tradition, there can be no doubt that the echoes of the debate linger, necessarily, on. It is not a transcended problem, although it is given less importance in many of the newer perspectives than it had previously. To illustrate the continuing relevance of this issue I shall refer to recent work by John Thompson and Goran Therborn, as examples of positions on ideology that – though nuanced, sophisticated and 'soft' in comparison with the polar positions on the continuum – can usefully be distinguished along the critical/neutral fault line.

John Thompson's view on how ideology should be defined is clarified in the course of his detailed discussions of a wide variety of recent theorists in *Studies in the Theory of Ideology*. Thompson himself concentrates on language, as the 'principal medium' of ideology, and his approach is particularly influenced by the analysis of power and domination in writers such as Jürgen Habermas. He defines ideology in the following terms: '*to study ideology is to study the ways in which meaning (signification) serves to sustain relations of domination*'.[24] He suggests that three main processes, or modalities, can be identified in the way ideology operates. The first cited is *legitimation*, in the Weberian sense of an appeal for legitimacy on traditional, rational or charismatic grounds. A second is *dissimulation*: the 'seldom intentional' concealment of relations of domination in ways that are themselves often concealed – this is the point at which Thompson is nearest to the classical 'critical' definition (for example to the idea of a 'structural exclusion from thought' that John Mepham identifies in Marx's later approach to ideology).[25] Habermas makes a comparable point when he says that ideology serves 'to impede making the foundations of society the object of thought and reflection'.[26] A third form of ideological operation is *reification*, which for Thompson means 'representing a transitory, historical state of affairs as if it were permanent, natural, outside of time'.[27]

These modalities are not stated dogmatically, and Thompson explains that there is considerable overlap in their operation and that others may be required in particular analyses. They sketch out, however, a position on ideology that locates it firmly within an understanding of, on the one hand, a general conception of society in terms of domination and, on the other, an insistence that the crucial mechanism at work is language. In that context Thompson, whilst departing from the classical Marxist model, notably in the crucial shift from 'class' to a general theory of 'domination', has none the less taken a position on the so-called epistemological side of the issue.

Goran Therborn, by contrast, has recently argued for a definition of ideology stripped of the 'critical' dimension. He suggests that ideology 'will refer to that aspect of the human condition under which human beings live their lives as conscious actors in a world that makes sense to them to varying degrees'.[28] Therborn is principally interested in the problem of subjectivity – an issue which is completely neglected in the classical tradition but has been central to more recent debates – and he attempts to formulate a definition of ideology that will enable subjectivity to be explored as constructed both by class and by other social relations. Therborn accepts that such an approach to ideology would need to recognise the salience of unconscious psychodynamic processes and that consciousness largely functions through symbolic language codes. He concludes his definitional statement on ideology with the following remarks: 'Thus the conception of ideology employed here deliberately includes both everyday notions and "experience" and elaborate intellectual doctrines, both the "consciousness" of social actors and the institutionalised thought-systems and discourses of a given society. But to study these as ideology means to look at them from a particular perspective: not as bodies of thought or structures of discourse *per se*, but as manifestations of a particular being-in-the-world of conscious actors, of human subjects. In other words, to conceive of a text or an utterance as ideology is to focus on the way it operates in the formation and transformation of human subjectivity.'[29]

This definition might cause one to ask whether there are any drawbacks to such an all-inclusive and over-general delineation of the term ideology. All the components identified by Gramsci, from philosophical systems down to the arbitrary residues of cultural folklore, would here be included – in addition to an existentialist emphasis on social being – and this makes the approach very general. The broadness of Therborn's definition is motivated, however, by (among other considerations) a rejection of the 'false consciousness' or critical view of ideology in which class interest is given as the underlying explanation of behaviour. Therborn argues that this view, long dominant within the Marxist tradition, should be rejected in favour of the Marx of the 1859 Preface who takes the view that ideology is where 'men become conscious ... and fight out' the conflicts generated by relations of production.[30]

Therborn's work illustrates the continuing influence of the classical debate on contemporary work: though whether he is right to attach, as indeed others have also done, so much weight to this one sentence of Marx is perhaps a moot point. And, as we shall see later in considering Althusser's approach to the interpellative process of constituting subjectivity, there are difficulties in reconciling an emphasis on 'fighting out' conflicts generated by production relations with the analysis for which Therborn calls on unconscious as well as conscious dimensions of subjectivity. In practice, most existing discussions of unconscious processes have focused on dynamics quite other than class, although this is changing in some recent work in this area.[31]

Therborn is by no means concerned, as others have been, to establish the correctness of a particular reading of Marx, and in general his approach is similar to John Thompson's in the degree to which it is influenced by but independent of the Marxist tradition. His definition raises, however, some general issues about what substance and precision a theory of ideology can have if it is stripped of both the epistemological dimension and also of an organising focus on class. Gramsci, as we have seen, is the strongest candidate for having developed the 'positive' alternative approach in Marxism, and the question of whether or not his working theory operates within or beyond a class analysis remains bitterly contested in social and political theory. Therborn, in proposing a yet wider scope of reference for the concept of ideology – that includes unconscious as well as virtually all forms of conscious meaning – is making a determined bid for what is essentially a more descriptive understanding of ideology than is common. Alex Callinicos has argued that Therborn is correct in rejecting both the epistemological definition and the emphasis on consciousness and summarises Therborn's position on ideology as 'the primarily discursive practices through which human beings live their relation to reality'.[32] But it remains unclear whether Therborn's position could be engaged, as Callinicos has recommended, with a a Gramscian perspective. Callinicos calls, at the end of his discussion of ideology, for 'the confrontation of Gramsci's thought with theories of discourse' as the key to further advance,[33] but the call is easier made than accomplished.

Two key questions have emerged in considering the issue of whether ideology should be seen as necessarily weak in epistemological terms, and both of them feature centrally in contemporary theoretical debates. We can take the working definition mentioned earlier, that 'ideology is mystification that serves class interest', to illustrate this point. It is worth noting that in two crucial respects this definition, which is handed down on tablets of stone in much sociology teaching, is drawn from Marx. It has the irreducible core of an emphasis on *critique* and it binds the project of demystifying ideology to the understanding of social class. But although Marx stuck these together with a permanent theoretical superglue, attempts have been made to prise them apart. John Thompson, as we have seen, has formulated some of the basic arguments with regard to a general concept of 'domination' rather than an insistence on the unilateral role of social class, and these arguments, which raise interesting questions about both social structure and political agency, will be pursued further. In addition, there is now a ringing debate on the relationship between ideology and class that is trying to shift Marxism into a a formally 'post-Marxist' period, and this will be the focus of chapter 4.

As far as the question of 'critique' is concerned, Richard Bernstein has noted that one of the strengths of the 'epistemological' definition of ideology is that it enables us to avoid the relativism of the view that 'all "belief system" ultimately have the same epistemological status'.[34] The obvious dangers of abandoning the critical edge that ideology has traditionally carried are those of relativism, pluralism, subjectivism and a general move into philosophical pragmatism. Interestingly, these are all features that can be discerned more clearly in the politics of new social groups, where the authentic voice of personal experience has come to be very powerful, than in the conventions of the Marxist-Leninist left, which always privileged the 'correct line' above individual experience. At stake in this is a difference of view about ideology and political subjectivity, in the sense that the definition of ideology as critique and demystification is one that forces upon us a critical consideration of the ways in which we have constructed our own experience. Theories of ideology claim to offer, therefore, a reading of personal experience – a different gloss on that experience, possibly even an explanation of it.

There is often considerable tension between an experience-generated political motivation and expression (whether it be the outraged vegetarianism of youth or the moralistic ranking of oppression that characterises 'identity politics' in some versions of feminism) and an understanding of ideology as the theorisation, and critique, of the unreliable category of personal experience.

This problem has, I think, been exacerbated by the fact that Marxism, in both its theoretical development and the precepts and practices of Marxist political organisations, has tended to err on the side of over-confident rulings on what is so-called science or knowledge and what is ideology and has been guilty of a corresponding contempt for the nature of experience as subjectively lived and understood. In response, we have seen a flowering of political ventures rejecting that set of priorities. Increasingly, however, enough critiques of political relativism are emerging from the contemporary scene for us to be able to say that the tide is in some senses turning.[35] At one level this is fuelled by the rising influence of a politics based on issues, and coalitions, rather than on the cosmic truths of a major revolutionary project.

Another reason, perhaps, is that to take subjectivity seriously is by no means to defer to the tyranny of 'authenticity'. And here the most interesting subject is psychoanalysis. Traditionally, psychoanalytic theory and practice of all persuasions comes fully equipped with a very strong orientation towards explanation. A recurring theme of psychoanalysis is the idea that *work* (analytic work, dream work) is the means to greater understanding. Psychoanalysis stresses the role of unmasking, and demystification, in the process of laying bare the dynamics of repression and understanding how material is 'buried' from conscious access. Post-structuralist reworkings of psychoanalysis naturally operate with much greater caution, and tension, in this area and Lacanians express strong critiques of the essentialist bias in much psychoanalytic thought. But, even here, there is an understandable reluctance to 'let go' of explanatory objectives, be they in the clinical context or in the application of psychoanalytic ideas to cinema or literary texts. In so far as psychoanalysis is in contention with a traditional theory of ideology as an interpretation of subjectivity, the parallel is an interesting one. In any event, one might be justified in suggesting that, leaving aside more fundamental questions about the status of knowledge (with which the next chapter is concerned), the so-called 'epistemological' definition of ideology can generate useful and illuminating analyses and has a decisive edge over the perception of ideology as historical class consciousness.

3

Problems of Science and Determinism

'Ideology' and 'science'

Marx's warning to the prospective French readers of *Capital*, for whom he feared the book would prove a slow haul, has a bizarre ring for the modern reader who has discovered just how 'unscientific' much science has turned out to be. Marx writes: 'There is no royal road to science, and only those who do not dread the fatiguing climb of its steep paths have a chance of gaining its luminous summits.'[1] Here we have a kind of intellectual pilgrim's progress, in which hard work and perseverance in the manner of a nineteenth-century explorer will eventually pay off with the intrepid few arriving at 'the truth'; a somewhat moralistic approach to the pursuit of knowledge that is not uncommon in Marx. There are, however, many disagreements among philosophers of social science as to whether Marx formally held the position that a clear distinction can be drawn between ideology and science, as also there are disagreements about the epistemological claims and status of his own analyses. It is not necessary to go into detail here about these debates, although they are currently a focus of work among the new 'realist' philosophers.[2] I want instead to go back a step, to the arguments within European Marxism and particularly those made by Louis Althusser in the 1960s on science and ideology in Marx's writings, since these have posed in a sharp, and highly contentious, way some of the key problems that need to be resolved in this area. In so far as Althusser has provided us with one of the strongest, most confident (verging on bombastic, as we shall see) statements of the claim that science and ideology can be disentangled, his work is a prime subject for scrutiny.

Althusser proposed that Marx's work should be read in terms of a fundamental divergence between the 'young' Marx – a left-Hegelian humanist and historicist, best known to us now for his theses on alienation – and the 'mature' Marx whose discovery of the operations of capitalist society was both structured and scientific. Althusser does not regard the young Marx as 'Marxist': 'Of course Marx's youth did *lead* to Marxism, but only at the price of a prodigious break with his origins, a heroic struggle against the illusions he had inherited from the Germany in which he was born, and an acute attention to the realities concealed by these illusions.'[3] It is not without interest that Althusser counterposes what he insists on calling Marx's scientific 'discoveries' about capitalism to the ideological character of the Hegelianism through which Marx had to make a gruelling theoretical 'long march': Althusser in practice often used the science/ideology distinction simply to indicate the general superiority of one discourse over another. Althusser concluded that the distance between the Hegelian and scientific Marxes was so great that we can reasonably speak of a break or rupture, often referred to (following Gaston Bachelard) as an 'epistemological rupture'.

On balance, though, many subsequent readers of Marx have rejected Althusser's sharp differentiation between these 'two Marxes'. Jorge Larrain, for example, follows Rafael Echeverria in seeing three rather than two stages of development of Marx's thought. Larrain also suggests that although Marx's thought certainly evolved over time it has enough underlying coherence to rule out the idea of decisive 'breaks'.[4] It is not entirely clear how much Althusser's own reconceptualisation of the ideology/science distinction depends upon his view of Marx as at first 'ideological' and later becoming 'scientific' in his writings. In principle, one would expect Althusser's general claims about the scientific nature of Marxist analysis to be independent of this specific argument. The broader arguments will be taken up now, first looking at Althusser's theory of knowledge production and how it is supposed to differ from ideology, and then discussing briefly the implications of Althusser's position for the debate about historicism. Then we shall move on to some more general questions about epistemology raised by the ideology/science debate.

Althusser's arguments about ideology and science, put forward in 1966 in *For Marx*, generated an extraordinary degree of enthusiasm among many left intellectuals. Looking at these immensely pretentious arguments now, it is difficult to keep a straight face: like the discovery that we had been talking prose all our lives, it was revealed that sitting thinking was really nothing less than *theoretical practice*. Althusser suggested that ideology could be firmly distinguished from science, or knowledge, on the following basis. Ideology, he wrote, 'is distinguished from science in that in it the practico-social function is more important than the theoretical function (function as knowledge)'.[5] Ideology, at this point in Althusser's thinking, is 'the *lived* relation between men and their world'.[6] This relation is both real, in the sense that it describes real historical social relations and how people are positioned in them, and imaginary, in the sense that it is in ideology that conservative or revolutionary *will* is expressed. So ideology is not restricted to the conscious level, it operates as images, concepts and, above all, as *structures* that impose themselves upon us. As a general system of representations, ideology for Althusser was an 'organic' or 'indispensable' part of the social totality and he maintained – he thought controversially – that ideology would always be present even in a future communist society.[7]

Knowledge, on the other hand, was for Althusser quite different. He speaks of knowledge as a system of production, in which there are raw materials – received ideas – and a means of production – which he called a *problematic*, consisting of a set of related assumptions, methods and concepts. Althusser, in a flight of what psychoanalysts might call grandiosity, labels the raw materials *Generalities I*, the 'problematic' being used *Generalities II*, and the end result of applying II to I *Generalities III*, or 'knowledge'.[8] Althusser's notion of a 'symptomatic reading' – the careful reading of a text in such a way as to disclose the theoretical 'silences' or absences that are often a better clue to the *problematic* being used than a text's overt declarations of intent – was in many ways a useful one, particularly in its applications to literary theory in the work of Pierre Macherey.[9]

But in general Althusser's arguments have been widely and cogently criticised. Colin Sumner, for example, argues that the symptomatic reading is no more 'scientific' a technique than other forms of reading: 'it is simply the reading theorist's reflection on the differences between his grid and that of the object-text which he has comprehended and superseded'.[10] Terry Lovell, in a discussion of the weaknesses in Althusser's attempt to differentiate between ideology and science, suggests that each of the criteria he offers is inadequate to the task. His suggestions that ideology is 'obvious' and 'closed' and draws its problems from politics and practice rather than from theory, whereas science by contrast is 'counter-intuitive', 'open' and based on theoretically generated problems are, in Lovell's opinion, completely unsatisfactory.[11] Although such criteria might well help with the relatively easy job of differentiating 'science' from what Gramsci called 'common sense' or 'folklore', they are of no help in the much more difficult task of separating knowledge from elaborated ideological systems of thought or philosophy. How, for example, could it be argued that neo-classical economics, or Parsonian sociology, is 'ideological', whereas Marxist political economy is 'scientific'? Lovell points out that the most thorny problem lies in distinguishing 'theoretical ideologies' from 'scientific theories', and this Althusser has not really touched.[12] We shall return in a moment to the general epistemological issues that this raises.

Althusser, as Poulantzas pointed out,[13] put forward a theory of ideology that lifts the Marxist tradition right out of any tendencies towards historicism. The title of one of Althusser's essays – 'Marxism is not a Historicism'[14] – indicates his central preoccupation with the rejection of what he saw as the non-scientific 'problematics' of historicism and humanism. It is easy to see that the view of ideology held by Lenin, or Lukács, is one for which the notion of a science/ideology distinction is simply not relevant. For to put it as caustically as Poulantzas does, in the historicist view 'ideologies were seen as number-plates carried on the backs of class subjects'.[15] It seems unlikely, however, that Althusser's rather grandiloquent assertions about 'knowledge' have convinced many people that his alternative anti-historicist position is the solution either.

Within the traditional parameters of this debate we keep coming back to the difficulty of theorising the relationship between knowledge – particularly the science of Marxism – and the ideological weakness of the working class. Larrain has suggested that Gramsci, uniquely perhaps, thought about the relationship of knowledge and ideology as 'bi-directional'. The examples he gives certainly show that Gramsci's approach is less rigid and doctrinaire and a more suggestive guide to thinking about the question than is Althusser's. Larrain mentions three ways in which for Gramsci the science of the Marxist intelligentsia is related to the supposedly pure ideological deception of the working class: that intellectuals were created by classes rather than absolute; that science was developed from activity rather than absolute; that proletarian ideology can be a mixture of (ideological) common sense and (scientific) philosophy of praxis.[16]

These sorts of considerations lead many writers on the subject to the view that a strict division between ideology and science is difficult to defend, certainly to specify in practice. It is, however, a long way from a position of reservation on this issue to one of complete relativism about the status of knowledge or science. Yet this is the other side of the coin in the debates on science and ideology. For if at one extreme we have Althusser with a rigidly scientistic position, at the other we have the position that since all knowledge is necessarily social, we cannot speak of objective or scientific knowledge at all. It is to this question that we should now turn.

Jacques Rancière, a former colleague of Althusser, has decisively rejected the Althusserian approach to ideology and science. One point that he makes is fundamental. This is that Althusser's ideology/science distinction construes as separate two phenomena which are in fact integrally connected: 'Scientific theories are transmitted through a system of discourses, traditions and institutions which constitute the very existence of bourgeois ideology. ... The dominant ideology is not the shadowy Other of the pure light of Science, it is the very space in which scientific knowledges are inscribed, and in which they are articulated as elements of a social formation's knowledge. It is in the forms of the dominant ideology that a scientific theory becomes an object of knowledge.'[17] Rancière's specific point is designed to show that Althusser fails in terms of a class analysis, since he does not understand the class character of scientific knowledge. More generally, the position from which Rancière is here taking issue with Althusser is one of philosophical 'conventionalism'. This leads into a set of related issues about science and epistemology. Is Marxism committed to a 'realist' epistemology or is this conventionalism equally compatible with Marxism? Does Marxism insist on the class character of all knowledge or does it allow forms of knowledge independent of the class affiliations of which Rancière speaks? The case of natural science is the one usually referred to here: Timpanaro has argued that Marxism has exaggerated the class contextualisation of natural scientific knowledge, leaving too little room for an objective engagement with the substantive debates within natural scientific fields of enquiry.[18] What implications do these debates have for different definitions of ideology within Marxist theory?

Terry Lovell has taken a strong stand against 'conventionalism' – a term used to describe anti-empiricist arguments that insist on the theory-impregnated character of all languages of observation – on the general grounds that such positions inevitably lead to relativism and the abandonment of all claims to objective knowledge. Lovell writes that 'The limit position which all conventionalisms more or less approach is one in which the world is in effect constructed in and by theory. Given that there is no rational procedure for choosing between theories, relativism is the inevitable result. Epistemological relativism does not necessarily entail a denial that there is a real material world. But if our only access to it is via a succession of theories which describe it in mutually exclusive terms, then the concept of an independent reality ceases to have any force or function.'[19] Lovell, in common with many others, argues that Marxism tends towards the opposite of conventionalism – realism – in its epistemological position, and certainly there is little doubt that Marx himself believed in the possibility of objective knowledge. The case of Althusser, however, is more in contention. Terry Lovell suggests that Althusser fails to specify adequately the basis on which relativism might be avoided, but her imputation to him of an explicitly conventionalist position is more difficult to demonstrate other than in terms of contradictory or changing elements in his approach. As she points out, Althusser tried to solve (or duck) the realist/conventionalist problem by proposing a 'real-concrete' world that existed independently of the 'concrete-in-thought', but by which it could be apprehended. This formulation is clearly not satisfactory and, as Ted Benton has noted, does *not* resolve the problem anyway.[20] But to regard Althusser as systematically conventionalist goes against the general drift of many of his arguments – specifically on the ideology/science distinction. It is not hard, for instance, to find passages in Althusser that are so explicitly anti-conventionalist as the following: 'Marx never fell into the idealist illusion of believing that the knowledge of an object might ultimately replace the object or dissipate its existence.'[21]

That many of Althusser's followers have taken up full-blown conventionalist, or relativist, positions could, however, not be doubted. Terry Lovell sees this as a direct line of inheritance from Althusser; Ted Benton, in my view more plausibly, sees it as a lopsided resolution of the realist/conventionalist 'dilemma' or tension in Althusser's thought. Whatever the reason, it is indisputably the case that the most notable British Althusserians, for example Paul Hirst, developed from there to a position of extreme conventionalism. *Marx's Capital and Capitalism Today*, the text in which the new post-Althusserian 'discourse theory' was elaborated in Britain, has since been subjected to considerable criticism – and perhaps not surprisingly, given the sweeping nature of its theoretical project.[22] Central to this debate was the rejection by these authors of all 'epistemological theories': any theories based on a division between on the one hand a realm of objects and on the other a realm of knowledge about them. They proposed instead that objects and knowledge should be considered as constructed in discourse and that no assumptions could be justified about which discourses might reflect 'reality'.[23] This radical rejection of epistemology has been criticised on a number of grounds. Terry Lovell insists that the adequacy of discourses can be referred to external reality for corroboration and we are not dependent on the internal consistency of discourses as the only criterion by which to judge them.[24] More generally, both John Thompson and Jorge Larrain have pointed to the fundamental problem with the argument that epistemology must be rejected: that it is *itself* an epistemological proposition that proposes to 'know better' what the relation between objects and knowledge really is. Thompson points out that 'Hindess and Hirst, despite their presumptuous dismissal of "epistemology", proffer no shortage of claims to know.'[25] Larrain notes that Hindess and Hirst are effectively saying 'their discourse is to be preferred because it properly effects the correlation between discourse and object' and he comments that they are 'up to their necks' in the epistemological enterprise.[26] These disagreements serve to show the difficulty of maintaining the grounds either for the confident assertion of an ideology/science distinction, or for adopting a position that rejects epistemology outright. As we shall see, in discussing discourse theory and particularly the work of Michel Foucault, these problems have led many people to 'bracket off' or hold in suspension the vexed question of whether there is any reasonable basis for defending 'knowledge', 'truth' or 'science' as against ideology or a more neutral concept of discourse. In a very famous passage in an interview, Foucault has summarised his objections to the term ideology as follows: 'The notion of ideology appears to me to be difficult to make use of, for three reasons. The first is that, like it or not, it always stands in virtual opposition to something else which is supposed to count as truth. Now I believe that the problem does not consist in drawing the line between that in a discourse which falls under the category of scientificity or truth, and that which comes under some other category, but in seeing historically how effects of truth are produced within discourses which in themselves are neither true nor false.'[27]

Thus, in one sweeping conceptualisation of what Foucault elsewhere calls 'regimes of truth' the entire ideology/knowledge issue is cleared away. For some, though by no means all, this is a solution to the vexed old chestnut of the science/ideology debate. Yet even for them, as we shall have cause to see in a variety of ways in this book, the banishment of epistemology is harder to effect in practice than at the level of theoretical pronouncement. To let go of epistemological ambition is a more difficult project than many people concede and knowledge claims, or truth claims, slide back in to much Foucauldian and post-structuralist work just as easily as epistemological claims have slid back in to even those theoretical discourses that sought to reject them. Alex Callinicos, for example, writing of Derrida's 'textualism', points out that this has its own 'meta-narrative': a hidden agenda of evaluation that contradicts the overt Derridian intention of registering discursive difference.[28] So it proves difficult in practice to operate *without* the kinds of judgments that a theory of science, or knowledge, attempts to justify. To say this is not, however, to say anything very satisfactory – but we will return later to some newer, and in some ways helpful, formulations on the issue of knowledge, discourse and our apprehension of the social world.

The problem of determinism

> When we leave the terrain of "determinations", we desert, not just this or that stage in Marx's thought, but his whole problematic.[29]

Stuart Hall here rightly identifies the definitional status of the notion of *determination* in the classical Marxist tradition of work on ideology. Modern work on, and beyond, the theory of ideology has taken up a variety of positions highly critical of this determinist aspect of Marx's position. Before looking at these arguments, however, it is as well to remind ourselves of the intellectual background against which Marx developed his ideas in this area. As is well known, Marx worked through, over a number of years, the characteristic viewpoint of the German philosophical tradition, particularly the work of Hegel. Marxist materialism was explicitly developed as an alternative to the philosophical idealism of the Hegelian school.

Some aspects of this theoretical revolution should be emphasised in relation to ideology. First, Marx insists that materialism is a methodology that enables us to explain the forms taken by consciousness and culture with reference to economic relations. He believed in travelling, as he puts it in *The German Ideology*, 'from earth to heaven' and not the other way round. The Hegelian tradition, of course, goes 'from heaven to earth' in Marx's view: it proposes that the characteristic ideas of a given epoch (as in the much popularised idea of a *Zeitgeist*) imbue all the social relations of that society with their distinctive meaning. Many of Marx's most famous statements – 'being determines consciousness' would be a good example – spring from a rejection of Hegelianism as idealist in its attribution of determining historical power to the realm of ideas. In the process of insisting that ideas and consciousness must be explained from else-where – that is, that their motive force is ultimately economic – Marx by definition makes a separation between what for convenience we could call the material and the ideal. This separation in itself is a further significant break with Hegelianism, for it disrupts the notion of 'totality' that is central to a Hegelian reading of society and it proposes a completely new meaning to the theory of 'reflection' within that totality.

Instead of seeing society as a *whole*, whose constituent elements are essentially and integrally part and parcel of each other, Marx's view of society – whilst still a totality – has a far greater division of elements and labour within it. Throughout the development of his thought Marx increasingly rejected the assumption that society is an 'expressive totality' whose essence permeates every cell like a sociolo-gical DNA code. Thus the theory of 'reflection' found in Marxist materialism is not at all the same as the Hegelian view that all appearances reflect the underlying ideational essence of the society; it is specifically a theory that seeks to understand the relationship between two areas, the material and the ideal, that are analytically constituted as separate.

It can be said that Marx's famous metaphor of the 'base and superstructure' makes a crucial break with the Hegelian tradition. Whatever difficulties have later been seen in this topographical image – and indeed they are daunting – it must be understood initially as representing Marx's attempt to break away from the conceptual rigidity of the notion of totality. An interesting angle of light is cast on the history of these ideas by considering Franz Jakubowski's attempt, in the 1930s, to retrieve Marx for a 'totality' position along broadly Lukácsian lines. Jakubowski makes the point that the base/superstructure metaphor has a merely heuristic or methodological value, but his argument as a whole reveals the classic preoccupations of those who have seen society as an 'expressive totality'. He wrote:

'Superstructure' in the writings of Marx and Engels is a very broad and indeterminate concept. It embraces the whole of social life apart from its 'real base', the direct relations of production. The economy is assigned a special place in the totality of social relations, the founda-tion of which is the production of immediate subsistence. This does not mean that economic relations are to be strictly separated from the rest, nor that they can be, even in a purely conceptual sense. The unity of social life is so strong that the only possible distinction is a methodological one, for the purpose of throwing light on any particu-lar one of the fundamental relationships. It is a complete mistake to think that Marx's differentiation between base and superstructure was an absolute distinction between two different, unoverlapping spheres. All we can do is make a very general *paraphrase* of the concept of 'superstructure'. It cannot be determined *concretely*, and it certainly does not mean that a comprehensive tabulation of all social relationships is possible.[30]

Jakubowski's reading of the metaphor is interesting because it is so different from the perception that we would find in any more recent exposition. He wanted to pull Marx back into a more Hegelian, more totalising, model while almost all modern critics speak from virtually the opposite position. In fact, even Jakubowski himself is hard put to maintain consistently his argument that the metaphor is merely methodological and has no 'concrete' referents and he mentions, for example, that the 'legal superstructure stands even closer than the political superstructure to the economic base'.[31] It would be nearer the truth to say that the extraordinary influence and resonance of Marx's metaphor – rightly or (more likely) wrongly – lies in the fact that so many people have found it a seductive one for imaging ontological reality and for substantive classification of society's varying forms.

In recent years the base/superstructure metaphor, as an emblem of Marx's determinist position on ideology, has been criticised from a quite different point of view from the Hegelian tradition that Marx was rejecting. Since Marx's death the Marxist tradition has tended, particularly during the years of the Second International, to simplify the metaphor into one of straightforward 'reflection' of economic relations of production in a superstructure conceived of as purely reactive. Thus the major twentieth-century form of the determinist argument was economic reductionism. A one-way model, which sees the economics of production simplistically as the domino at the beginning of a line of political, cultural, legal and intellectual pieces that will inevitably fall down when that first one is pushed, has been attributed to 'Marxism' in general. And certainly there was, and remains, enough crude determinism within Marxism to make this caricature to some extent a self-inflicted one.

Yet objections to economic determinism have been made, and forcibly, for a long period of time within the Marxist tradition. Karl Korsch concluded his essay *Marxism and Philosophy* with a plea for intellectual struggle based on a thesis of what would later have been called the 'relative autonomy' of ideology. Referring to the ideologies of art, religion and philosophy in bourgeois society, he makes a perceptive critical point about the reflection theory of ideology: 'If it seems that there are no objects which these representations can reflect, correctly or incorrectly, this is because economic, political or legal representations do not have particular objects which exist independently either.' Ideological forms, says Korsch, 'must be criticised in theory and overthrown in practice, together with the economic, legal and political structures of society and at the same time as them'.[32] These arguments are, of course, familiar to us through the work of Gramsci, but it is worth emphasising that the critique of determinist thought is not a new one.

It is, however, with the rise of 'Althusserianism' in Europe that the widespread rethinking of these issues is historically associated. In *For Marx* (1966) Althusser had disputed the formulation made by Engels that the economy was determining 'in the last instance' and had put forward an alternative concept of 'overdetermined contradictions' that allowed him to attach weight to patterns of determination that did not run from the economic to the ideological in a monolithic manner. The flavour of the text can be taken from the much quoted passage where Althusser asserts that the superstructures 'are never seen to step respectfully aside when their work is done or, when the Time comes, as his pure phenomena, to scatter before His Majesty the Economy as he strides along the royal road of the Dialectic. From the first moment to the last, the lonely hour of the "last instance" never comes.'[33]

Within this framework Althusser developed concepts of 'structures in dominance', and of 'relative autonomy', and elaborated the notion of 'articulation': these ideas were to have a tremendous effect on Marxist theory, sociology and cultural, literary and film studies in France, Britain and many other European countries (though, noticeably, not in the United States, where the Frankfurt School had long been more popular than writers from the mainstream of the Marxist tradition).

It might be right to suggest that on the issue of determination, as in other areas, Althusser's recasting of Marx pushed Marxism further than it can logically go. Certainly, his work has provoked responses, and criticisms, which have taken their authors beyond Marxism and these will be discussed in part II of the book. Paul Hirst, for example, has made very clear why the Althusserian formulation of 'relative autonomy' is the end of the line for the old paradigm of 'totality'-based theorising such as Marxism. Responding to the 'charge' that he and the other authors of *Marx's Capital and Capitalism Today* were seeing 'the political level' (Althusserian terminology) as wholly autonomous, Hirst asks, 'autonomy from what?' He argues that the social topography approach, in which society ('social formation') is conceived of as having 'instances' which are definite sectors of the totality and governed by their place in the whole, is fundamentally misguided and absurd. Hirst continues with a critique of general theories of historical causality, such as Marxism's account of the development of successive modes of production, and concludes that 'these patterns are an incubus whose parasitic grip has long enslaved and enfeebled Marxism as a political theory'.[34]

It certainly is plausible to argue that 'the' Marxist theory of ideology has not withstood the assault of time very well. As I have tried to explain, the concept of ideology was never consistently elaborated by Marx at the outset, though some may regard this as the proverbial 'hobgoblin of small minds' and draw attention to the inspiring nature of the insights Marx did set down. In any event, we have inherited a range of different interpretations with which to begin. In so far, however, as a working consensus emerged around a definition of mystification tied to class interest, the concept of ideology has been fraught with difficulties. As we have seen, the epistemological issues underlying the distinction between ideology and knowledge are far from resolved, and the issue of determination and social totality more contentious than ever. The classical dispute discussed in chapter 2, between ideology as a critical term and as a concept for thinking about historical class consciousness, has tended to be resolved in the direction of the critical definition. But, as we shall soon see, the attempt to disentangle political ideology from its 'class-belonging' nature has in practice driven another nail into the coffin of a Marxist theory of ideology.

Debates around the concept of ideology are best understood by considering the legacy of Marxism in this area. Ideology is, as mentioned earlier, an indigenously Marxist concept, if one that has now taken hold in a much broader frame of theoretical and cultural reference. And it is equally arguable that it was only within Marxism that a powerful theory of ideology, as opposed to a descriptive account of values or culture, was worked on. Developments in social theory that take us as surely into 'post-Marxism' as they do into post-structuralism and post-modernism have provided us with cogent criticisms of some of the fundamental assumptions of the Marxist framework. In the next section of the book I shall be looking at some of the arguments that provide the cusp of this process of critique, and principally focusing on modern readings of Gramsci and Althusser as major turning-points.

I have entitled part II 'collapse' of the Marxist model as I believe this is a case where we see a theoretical paradigm being challenged, ever more powerfully, from within its own terms of reference and then, of course, this meshes in with developments outside. In terms of a theory of ideology, we have a situation where accumulating difficulties with the concept itself come to coalesce with the competing, and increasing, attractions of a newly elaborated theory of discourse. This will be the subject matter of part III.

Part II

Collapse of the Marxist Model

4

Ideology, Politics, Hegemony:
From Gramsci to Laclau and Mouffe

Gramsci is something of a paradox in radical political thought. On the one hand, his work is much admired as the most sympathetic treatment, within the classical Marxist tradition, of cultural and ideological politics. He has become the adopted theorist of, for example, the Eurocommunist strategy in Italy, Spain and other countries and, in Britain, the inspiration for many of those who wish to realign Labour politics in a new and realistic mode. His approach to ideology, his theory of hegemony, his account of the role of intellectuals, his insistence on the importance of tactics and persuasion and his detailed attention to questions of culture, and the politics of everyday culture, have all been taken up enthusiastically by a generation sick of the moralising rules and precepts of both the Marxist-Leninist and Labourist lefts.

Yet, in theoretical terms, Gramsci's work has posed many unresolved questions in the area of a theory of ideology – partly because (like Marx, perhaps) his brilliant insights often stand alone or in some tension with each other. It is not clear, to take an example I shall discuss in more detail, exactly how his approach to ideology ties in with the now celebrated definition and use of the idea of hegemony. More generally, Gramsci's thought has taken on an iconic significance for the contemporary left, both intellectual and cultural, but it is also Gramsci – at least the Gramsci read by Ernesto Laclau and Chantal Mouffe – who stands at the crucial breaking-point of Marxism as a viable political theory. This latter argument, which hangs on the central status of the concept of class in Marxist theory and politics, will occupy much of this chapter. As we shall see, a very important feature of that debate is the question of whether particular ideologies necessarily pertain to different social classes, or whether this imputation of the 'class-belonging' nature of political ideology is a mistake.

IDEOLOGY AND HEGEMONY IN GRAMSCI

Gramsci, as is no doubt known to all readers, wrote most of what has come down to us as the body of his writings in the extraordinarily coercive circumstances of an Italian fascist prison. The conditions under which he wrote, including his progressively poor health, obviously have a bearing on the nature of the texts we have, and a further important consideration is the fact that his works incorporate many strategies and detours related to the prison censor. These bald facts explain, to some extent anyway, the relatively fragmentary and 'open' nature of these crucial writings.

If we look first at one passage from the *Prison Notebooks* where Gramsci addresses directly the concept of ideology in the Marxist tradition, we find the following points made. Gramsci refers to the 'negative value judgement' that has (erroneously) become attached to the meaning of ideology in Marxist philosophy; here we should take note of Larrain's point that, first and foremost, Gramsci must be identified as taking a 'positive' rather than 'critical' stance on ideology. Gramsci suggests – though not quite in these words – that the weak understanding of ideology in Marxist thought can be blamed on those who have seen ideology as merely determined by an economic base and therefore ' "pure" appearance, useless, rubbish etc.': in this regard he lines himself up with Korsch's critique of 'vulgar-Marxism'. Gramsci then stresses that 'historically organic ideologies' – those that are 'necessary' – have a psychological validity and they 'create the terrain on which men move, acquire consciousness of their position, struggle etc.': it is this attention to 'psychological validity' that has made Gramsci in some senses unique in the Marxist tradition.

In the same brief, but highly condensed, set of theses Gramsci suggests that 'organic' ideologies can be distinguished from the polemics of individual ideologues, and he distinguishes between ideology as the 'necessary superstructure of a particular structure' and ideology in the sense of these 'arbitrary elucubrations' of individuals. Gramsci refers to Marx's view that 'a popular conviction often has the same energy as a material force' and concludes the passage with the following formal statement: 'The analysis of these propositions tends, I think, to reinforce the conception of *historical bloc* in which precisely material forces are the content and ideologies the form, though this distinction between form and content has purely didactic value, since the material forces would be inconceivable historically without form and the ideologies would be individual fancies without the material forces.'[1]

A difficulty in considering these linked theses is that even such a short passage contains some complex, but distinct, shifts of position. The last sentence would be enough on its own to mark Gramsci out as a clear 'historicist', but this is tricky to assess when it falls at the end of a paragraph in which the now classically 'Gramscian' idea that ideology is a 'terrain of struggle' has been suggested – a view that sits rather ill with the historicist tendency to think in terms of 'expressive totalities'. Another problem is that frequently Gramsci is not explicit about whether something is or is not to be thought of as an 'organic ideology', hence his discussions of cultural and intellectual struggle are often somewhat ambiguous. (This is not a criticism, but it certainly has a bearing on the fact that Gramsci's work has become such a rich field for different interpretations.) These ambiguities surround even fairly basic questions. It is often assumed, for example, that Gramsci's general discussions of cultural and intellectual phenomena are couched under the rubric of ideology, but this is not exactly or necessarily the case. It is not clear whether Gramsci's illuminating classification of different levels of 'making sense of the world' – from philosophy to folklore – should be thought of as a treatment of ideology or not. Gramsci distinguishes, in another famous passage from the *Prison Notebooks*, between philosophy, religion, common sense and folklore as conceptions of the world with varying (decreasing) degrees of systematicity and coherence. Philosophy involves intellectual order, which religion and common sense do not, 'because they cannot be reduced to unity and coherence even within an individual consciousness, let alone collective consciousness'. Gramsci goes on to say that 'Every philosophical current leaves behind a sedimentation of "common sense": this is the document of its historical effectiveness. . . . "Common sense" is the folklore of philosophy, and is always half-way between folklore properly speaking and the philosophy, science and economics of the specialists. Common sense creates the folklore of the future.'[2]

Thus we have a hierarchy of forms, in which philosophies – systematic bodies of thought which can be espoused coherently – take their place above religion, which is subject to philosophical criticism. 'Common sense' will take many forms, but is a fragmented body of precepts; 'folklore' he describes as 'rigid' popular formulas. Gramsci points out that there may be considerable conflict between these levels, noting that there may be contradictions between the philosophy one espouses at a systematic (rational) level and one's conduct as determined by 'common sense'. Hence we arrive at Gramsci's notion of 'contradictory consciousness' and of a distinction between intellectual choice and 'real activity'.[3] Gramsci himself, as is now increasingly appreciated in Britain from the new translations of his cultural writings,[4] devoted considerable attention to popular culture and ideology, ranging over topics as diverse as architecture, popular songs, serial fiction, detective fiction, opera, journalism and so on.

Yet it remains somewhat unclear how far Gramsci is thinking of these various phenomena as ideology. Gramsci discusses these forms under the heading of philosophy, but most people have tended to assume that they are ideological forms. A rather impressionistic use of the concept of ideology can occur with impunity in Gramsci's approach largely because he has taken the explanatory weight from the shoulders of ideology. This he can do as in turn he deploys another concept to carry the theoretical burden that in other writers is taken by the concept of ideology. Thus in order to see how Gramsci's treatment of ideology meshes in with the tradition, we have to take it in conjunction with its companion term – hegemony. Although the Italian word *egemonia* was often seen as synonymous with Gramsci's contribution, its roots, as Perry Anderson and others have emphasised, lay in debates over the proletariat's need for 'hegemony' (persuasive influence) over the peasantry in the pre-revolutionary period in Russia.[5]

The concept of 'hegemony' is the organising focus of Gramsci's thought on politics and ideology and his distinctive usage has rendered it the hallmark of the Gramscian approach in general. Hegemony is best understood as *the organisation of consent* – the processes through which subordinated forms of consciousness are constructed without recourse to violence or coercion. The ruling bloc, according to Gramsci, operates not only in the political sphere but throughout the whole of society. Gramsci emphasised the 'lower' – less systematic – levels of consciousness and apprehension of the world, and in particular he was interested in the ways in which 'popular' knowledge and culture developed in such a way as to secure the participation of the masses in the project of the ruling bloc.

At this point it is worth remarking a significant difference of interpretation about hegemony. It is not clear whether Gramsci uses hegemony strictly to refer to the non-coercive (ideological?) aspects of the organisation of consent, or whether he uses it to explore the relationship between coercive and non-coercive forms of securing consent. Stuart Hall et al. suggest that Gramsci's fundamental question – how can the state rule without coercion? – is one that causes him to draw attention to non-coercive aspects of class rule. But, they argue, this is because of his underlying interest in the *relationship between* the state and 'civil society': it is not the product of a detached interest in the 'superstructures' or in 'culture' in the abstract.[6] Perry Anderson gives this question a somewhat different inflection; he notes that Gramsci's use of hegemony is inconsistent, since sometimes he uses it to mean consent rather than coercion, at other times it seems to mean a synthesis of the two. Anderson's explanation – based on his view that state power is the 'linchpin' of bourgeois hegemony – is to say that Gramsci 'slipped' towards focus on consent partly as a result of the difficulties of getting the coercion-related arguments past the prison censor.[7]

Leaving this on one side for a moment, we can say that Gramsci's emphasis was on hegemony in relation to a political and cultural strategy for socialism, and this was also where his greatest interest lay. His concepts of 'war of position' and 'war of manoeuvre' form the heart of a conceptualisation of strategy that involves classes moving, on the analogy of trench warfare, to better vantage points and 'positions': hence the 'war of position' is the battle for winning political hegemony, the securing of consent, the struggle for the 'hearts and minds' of the people and not merely their transitory obedience or electoral support. 'War of manoeuvre', by contrast, comes at a later stage: it is the seizing of state power, but (in direct opposition to the Leninist tradition of political thought) cannot take place except in a situation where hegemony has already been secured.

This model of socialist strategy had built into it a theory of the political function of intellectuals. Gramsci did not see these as expressive of particular classes, or as locked into specific and socially defined roles; he saw intellectuals as important actors on the field where class conflict is 'played out' at the ideological level. In particular, he saw the hegemonic process – from the left, that is – as one that would involve detaching 'traditional' intellectuals from their base in the ruling bloc and developing what he called 'organic' intellectuals of the working class.

Gramsci's view of these processes is one that folds a theory of ideology, construed mainly as the varying forms of popular and systematic knowledge discussed earlier, into a more general political and cultural project that he theorises in terms of the broader concept of hegemony. His interest in the relation between the state and civil society leads directly to his work on what has been called the socially 'cementing' functions of ideology and the ways in which consent is secured at a non-violent level.

Having said this, however, it is useful to consider what solutions Gramsci offers to some of the 'classic disputes' about ideology discussed in previous chapters. Two of these can be despatched fairly rapidly, and in both instances Jorge Larrain's interpretation of Gramsci seems to me the most helpful: we have dealt in chapter 2 with Gramsci as what Larrain regards as the highest expression of the 'positive' conception of ideology in the Marxist tradition, and in chapter 3 with Gramsci's constructively 'bi-directional' approach to the relationship between knowledge or science and ideology.[8] The third issue to be taken up previously is that of determinism, and here it is that Gramsci has come into his own as the exponent, *par excellence*, of a non-deterministic theory of ideology. Chantal Mouffe, writing back in 1979 about a thinker whose work she was later to become more critical of, declared approvingly that 'a radically anti-economistic problematic of ideology is operating in the practical state in Gramsci's conception of hegemony'.[9]

Stuart Hall's article on 'base and superstructure' has, definitively, laid out the terms of the debate on determinism within the Marxist theory of ideology. Hall reads Gramsci as delivering a 'polemic against a reductionist account of the superstructure', and he argues that Gramsci has shown us how capitalism is not just a system of production, but a whole form of social life. The superstructures, in Hall's reading of Gramsci, are vital in that they draw culture and civil society into increasing conformity with the needs of capital. They *enlarge* capitalism's sway, creating new types of individual and civilisation, working through the various institutions of civil society such as the family, law, education, cultural institutions, church and political parties. This is not a matter of economic interest alone, for Gramsci opposes economic reductionism and conceptualises hegemony as political, cultural and social authority. Yet, concludes Stuart Hall, in Gramsci's view 'the superstructures *do* all this for capital'.[10]

There is, however, an issue that was never entirely articulated *within* the classical Marxist tradition but on which some aspects of Gramsci's ideas have recently been brought to bear with striking consequences: this is the question of whether or not ideologies should be described as 'class belonging'. As we shall see, the exploration of this issue has brought about a major challenge to Marxism, which Ernesto Laclau and Chantal Mouffe argue has now been superseded. It is an issue that was never raised within the Marxist tradition because it was taken for granted that – whatever your theory of ideology – it would be organised around social class as the essential and formative category of an analysis of capitalism. Hence it would not really matter if you saw ideologies as expressions of the consciousness of particular social classes (the most common, if 'historicist', variant of the positive approach), or if you saw ideology as mystification serving class interest. It would in either case, and with other definitions too, be axiomatic that in an analysis of capitalism the role and function of ideology was construed in terms of social class. It is precisely this that has now been problematised at a very fundamental level, with consequences that are of obvious interest to feminists and others who have been questioning the status of class analysis with reference to the competing theoretical and political claims that arise from other salient social divisions.

CLASS AND NON-CLASS POLITICAL IDEOLOGIES

Let us begin by looking at the formulations of Ernesto Laclau's *Politics and Ideology in Marxist Theory* (1977), noting at the outset that the argument made in that book has proved far more acceptable to most Marxists than those of his later works, and particularly *Hegemony and Socialist Strategy* (1985), co-authored with Chantal Mouffe.[11] Laclau's earlier text was concerned with the problem of 'reductionism' in Marxist political theory, and in particular he was critical of those who had tended to see political ideology exclusively, as, almost by definition, class ideology.

To 'reduce', philosophically speaking, is to explain a phenomenon that appears in term A by invoking (or reducing it to) something else – term B. Within Marxism, the problem of reductionism has been acute, for a classic explanatory strategy has been to say that a particular phenomenon (often an awkward one such as working class conservatism, racism or homophobia) is *really* caused by, or functional to, the overriding dynamic of class and class conflict. Marxism has no monopoly on this style of thought: psychoanalysis, for example, has an even more pronounced tendency towards explanatory reductionism. But within Marxist theory the issue has in recent years been a much debated one, particularly in response to the question of gender and race as competing explanatory factors in thinking about the generation of social inequality.[12] In any case, Laclau was interested in the ways in which Marxists had ignored aspects of political ideology that did not fit into an analysis in which political ideology was explained by, or reduced to, the effects of social class interests.

A key figure in this debate was Nicos Poulantzas, whose attempt to demarcate 'the specificity of the political' in Marxist theory met in general terms with Laclau's approbation. By way of background, we could refer back to Stuart Hall's reading of Marx's 'Eighteenth Brumaire', discussed in chapter 1, as a comparable model of the project of establishing the political 'level' as a relatively autonomous element in the social formation. According to Laclau, however, the enormous contribution made by Poulantzas was vitiated by 'the general assumption that dominates his whole analysis: the reduction of every contradiction to a class contradiction, and the assignment of a class belonging to every ideological element'.[13]

Laclau proposed a different, and entirely original, approach. He argued that Althusser's theory of the interpellation (hailing) process through which ideological subjects were constructed could be applied to the analysis of political ideology. This would enable us to see that non-class ideological elements operated, for example, in the integration of popular-democratic themes into fascist ideological configurations and that these processes might, historically, be either independent of class or articulated with class but were in no circumstances *reducible* to class ideologies. He suggested that fascist ideology could be understood, in particular historical instances which he described, as the articulation of 'popular-democratic' elements in political discourse rather than (as had been common in Marxist political analysis) the natural political discourse of extreme conservative groups. By 'popular-democratic' Laclau means that the ideology addressed, and therefore constituted, its subjects as 'the people' rather than as 'the working class'. Laclau justifiably claimed that his rethinking of fascism gave 'a perfect demonstration of the non-class character of popular interpellations'.[14]

Interestingly, then, Laclau was at pains in *Politics and Ideology in Marxist Theory* not to depart too radically from the received wisdom of Marxism. At one point he explicitly rehearses the doxa 'We do not intend to cast doubt on the priority of production relations in the ultimate determination of historical processes':[15] a formulation that he would now reject entirely. Even more interesting, perhaps, is the formulation he arrived at to express the relationship between the non-class ideological elements that he had so illuminatingly uncovered and the traditional ground of class struggle. In a passage that reveals the extent to which, in that period, he had not as yet emancipated himself from the logic of Marxism's theoretical closure, he veers himself towards a perverse form of reductionism: '*The popular-democratic interpellation not only has no precise class content, but is the domain of ideological class struggle par excellence*. Every class struggles at the ideological level *simultaneously* as class and as the people, or rather, tries to give coherence to its ideological discourse by present-ing its class objectives as the consummation of popular objectives.'[16] This is interesting precisely because it takes away what with the other hand Laclau had just given us: instead of allowing us to savour the full independence of the non-class elements of political ideol-ogy that he so eloquently explained, we are enjoined here to restore 'class objectives' as the striven for, if hidden, agenda of popular-democratic appearances. We shall return to these ambivalences in discussing Laclau's later work.

Meanwhile, it must be emphasised that – although highly conten-tious – Laclau's book had a terrific impact on work in the field of political ideology. Colin Mercer's study on Italian fascism would be one example. Mercer discusses the fascinating material, brought to light by Maria Macciocchi among others, about Mussolini's operatic events where women swapped their gold wedding rings (in the interests of the production of armaments) for iron bands symbolising their marriage to *Il Duce*. Mercer theorises this and many other instances as a 'sexualisation' of the social sphere and an 'aestheticisa-tion' of politics, seeing these as strategies that enabled popular-democratic discourses to circulate freely within fascist political ideology. This he regards as a 'testament to Gramsci's assertion that in regimes of this nature, the terrains of the *people* and of *culture* are of key strategic importance and are foregrounded' and he concludes by quoting Gramsci's words that in these circumstances 'political questions are disguised as cultural ones'.[17]

Nothing could make more clear the thorny question that continues to dog the issue of political ideology and 'class belonging'. Mercer's quotation from Gramsci, the darling of the anti-reductionist school, reveals to us a Gramsci who certainly takes ideology, culture and populism seriously, but ultimately as a cover for 'political' (for which in practice read class) politics. Here lies the basis for much of the continuing disagreement over the interpretation of Gramsci.

Stuart Hall's work on 'Thatcherism' as a political ideology is perhaps one of the most well-known attempts to use Laclau's in-sights in the context of a Gramscian interpretation of contemporary British politics.[18] One of the most accessible routes into this style of thinking might be to consider the theme of patriotism – decisively 'captured' by Mrs Thatcher at the outbreak of the Falklands War as a Conservative party-political identification, which it had not previously been. The success of this has been striking, to the extent that the idea of a 'patriotic socialism' has become somewhat anomalous in Britain. We have for so long now heard the insistence on an identity between the government and the nation that, as Margaret Drabble recently remarked, we are actually surprised to encounter the old parliamentary expression 'Her Majesty's Loyal Opposition'.

Stuart Hall has analysed 'Thatcherism' as a political ideology which 'combines the resonant themes of organic Toryism – nation, family, duty, authority, standards, traditionalism – with the aggressive themes of a revived neo-liberalism – self-interest, competitive individualism, anti-statism'.[19] In his successive writings in this area Hall has elaborated these arguments, originally developed in advance of the election of the Thatcher government and addressed, historically, to the consequences for the left of the collapsing 'post-war consensus' of British politics. In the earlier statements of his analysis, Hall concentrated on explaining how Thatcherism was not to be seen as some error of judgement on the part of the masses, who had fallen for a political right wing that did not represent their true interests, but should be seen in terms of ideological developments that had spoken to real conditions, experiences and contradictions in the lives of the people and then recast them in new terms. The term 'authoritarian populism' was developed to try and explore these ideas.

Thatcherism was 'hegemonic' in its intention (if not successful as such) in that its project was to restructure the whole texture of social life, to alter the entire formation of subjectivity and political identity, rather than simply to push through some economic policies. In Gramscian mode Stuart Hall summarised this political intention: 'Thatcherite politics are "hegemonic" in their conception and project: the *aim* is to struggle on several fronts at once, not on the economic-corporate one alone; and this is based on the knowledge that, in order really to dominate and restructure a social formation, political, moral and intellectual leadership must be coupled to economic dominance. The Thatcherites know they must "win" in civil society as well as in the state.'[20]

Stuart Hall is noteworthy for having devoted considerable attention to the inflection of Thatcherite themes, both 'organic Tory' and the aggressive neo-liberal strands of the ideology, in political constructions of gender, family and sexuality and with regard to racism and the politics of ethnicity. So, if his analysis was frequently directed, as I believe it was, to an audience of 'the left' (particularly those that clung to the hope that one morning they would wake up and find that it was all a bad dream and the working class had come to its senses) it nevertheless addressed 'the left' as a group that is in significant ways internally differentiated and divided by gender and race. That Stuart Hall's interpretation of Thatcherism occasioned so much criticism from the left is, to my mind, symptomatic of the political weight carried by the theory of ideology. Bob Jessop and others, in a lengthy critical discussion of Hall's work, argued that one of his main errors was 'ideologism' or a tendency to neglect the 'structural underpinnings' of Thatcherism in his concentration on ideological processes and his analysis of patently ideological institutions such as the media.[21] This is the classic charge of idealism and, as we shall see, it surfaces a great deal in contemporary debates about ideology. Hall's reply, that he found it 'galling' to be accused of ideologism simply for tactically drawing attention to important and specifically ideological aspects of Thatcherism, is an apt one.[22] As I have suggested elsewhere, for classical Marxists *any* serious consideration of ideology is, in practice, nearly always too serious.

POST-MARXISM

It might seem a long way from debates about whether or not all elements of a political ideology should be designated as class-bound to the position described by this subheading. Yet this is the end point of Ernesto Laclau's trajectory (so far) and it marks the very interesting point at which critical arguments made within Marxism have coincided with some important 'post-structuralist' ideas in such a way as to challenge the viability of Marxism as a systematic theory. It seems to me that we can speak of a 'paradigm shift' here, however loosely such expressions are often used, since the philosophical project of post-structuralist thought, whilst scarcely winning over all comers, brought about a rethinking of Marxist certainties that verges on a major transformation. 'Ideology' is a key element of this, indeed in my view it is a central focus of the debates, precisely because of the epistemological and political weight that theories of ideology have carried within Marxism.

In considering such a shift it is worth noting a prophetic point made by Laclau in his earlier book, where he suggests, following Althusser, that theoretical problems are never, strictly speaking, 'solved': they are 'superseded'. This is because if they can be solved within the terms of the existing theory, they are not 'theoretical'

problems as such, but rather empirical or local difficulties of applying the theoretical framework in that particular case. By definition,
says Laclau, if there is a genuine theoretical problem '(i.e. one
involving an inconsistency in the logical structure of the theory)'
then the only way forward is to accept that 'it cannot be resolved
within the systems of postulates of the theory', which would mean
that the theoretical system would then go into internal contradiction
or conflict. From this, suggests Laclau, the 'only way forward is to
deny the system of axioms on which the theory is based: that is, to
move from one theoretical system to another'. And, as he correctly
points out, the originating problem is 'dissolved' in the new system
rather than 'solved' within the terms of the old.[23]

There is little point in reading Laclau and Mouffe's *Hegemony and
Socialist Strategy* if you refuse to countenance the starting-point
that Marxism is one among several general theories that are not now
viable: they state categorically in the introduction that 'Just as the
era of normative epistemologies has come to an end, so too has the
era of universal discourses.' The arguments that Laclau and Mouffe
bring to bear on Marxism are central themes of post-structuralist
thought and they form part and parcel of that more general theoretical perspective. At times, their arguments are specifically indebted to
those of Derrida (particularly), or Lacan. Laclau and Mouffe have
themselves constructed, in the field of Marxism and political theory,
theses that are complementary to, but distinct from, arguments that
others have developed elsewhere – be this in literary criticism,
psychoanalysis or economics, for example. It is important to note the
depth of the theoretical critique of Marxism that Laclau and Mouffe
are posing. They now believe that *theories such as* Marxism are not
viable on general grounds, and it is inappropriate in my view for
Marxists to respond to their arguments, as some have, with excoria-
tion of them personally as lapsed, ex- or anti-Marxists.[24]

For Laclau and Mouffe, Marxism is founded on a political 'imaginary': it is a conception of socialism that rests on the assumption
that the interests of social classes are pre-given, the axiom that the
working class is both ontologically and politically privileged in its
'centrality', and the illusion that politics will become pointless after
a revolution has founded a new, and homogeneous, social order.
In one sentence describing this 'Jacobin imaginary' before its final
stages of dissolution, Laclau and Mouffe condense some central
themes of post-structuralist thought: 'Peopled with "universal" subjects and conceptually built around History in the singular, it has
postulated "society" as an intelligible structure that could be intellec-

tually mastered on the basis of certain class positions and reconstituted, as a rational, transparent order, through a founding act of a political character.'[25] It is worth noting here the allusions to post-structuralist critiques of 'foundationalism' in the epistemology of social and political theory, the critique of the (Cartesian) model of the unified subject, the critique of history as a monolithic and uni-linear process, the glancing blow at phallocracy in the reference to mastery and so on. It is also worth noting that 'the imaginary' (as opposed to the more everyday use of 'imaginary' as an adjective) is, of course, a Lacanian concept and one that will trail particular resonances for some readers.[26]

Laclau and Mouffe insist that they are not obliterating Marxism without trace (an impossible project, of course, for good Derridians), but are in some senses working through it: they are post-*Marxist* as well as *post*-Marxist. This, as we shall see, has led to some critics of their book saying that Laclau and Mouffe are themselves not really free from the residues of totalising and essentialist thought that they have acquired on their long tramp through Marxism. (One might ask: if you want to end up with a theory of the rainbow coalition, why pick Kautsky as the place to start?)

The substantive arguments of *Hegemony and Socialist Strategy* pivot on Laclau and Mouffe's reading of Gramsci, and here, as they say 'everything depends on how ideology is conceived'.[27] Their account of Gramsci's theory of ideology and hegemony stresses, initially anyway, his break with the critical conception of ideology, in favour of a positive (which they call 'material') perspective and his rejection of the deterministic base/superstructure model of ideology. They insist, too, that for Gramsci 'the ideological elements articulated by a hegemonic class do not have a necessary class belonging'.[28]

Gramsci is a pivotal figure for Laclau and Mouffe because he represents the furthest point that can be reached within Marxism and the intrinsic limitations of the theoretical problematic. For even the 'articulatory' role of the working class is, in their reading of Gramsci, assigned to it on the basis of economic location and thus has a necessary rather than their preferred contingent character. Gramsci's view is therefore, in the last analysis, an 'essentialist' one. It is essentialist with regard to the privileged position of the working class, and with regard to 'the last redoubt of essentialism: the economy'.

Their own conclusions, bracingly headed 'Facing the Consequences', are to deny that the economy is self regulated and subject to endogenous laws, to deny that social agents are constituted,

ultimately, in a class core, and to deny that class position is necessarily linked to 'interests'. The propositions of the new theory can be
reduced to two, at its most simple. They are (1) a general philosophical position on 'the impossibility of society', explicated in the
chapter entitled 'Beyond the Positivity of the Social', and (2) a
theorisation of the issue of agency in radical democratic politics, in
an epoch where class essentialism has given way to the pluralist
demands of the 'new social movements' – feminism, anti-racism,
lesbian and gay rights, ecology, peace etc.

THE IMPOSSIBILITY OF SOCIETY

'The Impossibility of Society' is the title of an article published by
Ernesto Laclau in 1983, prefiguring the more detailed argument on
this theme to appear in *Hegemony and Socialist Strategy*.[29] Laclau and
Mouffe are making a Derridian point here: not that there is no such
'thing' as society but – as they put it, echoing Derrida's famous *Il n'y
a pas de hors-texte* – ' "Society" is not a valid object of discourse.'[30]
What do they mean by this? This is a decisive step in their
argument and it might be helpful to quote the passage at greater
length, since it contains a number of key allusions and some characteristic 'moves'. They write: 'The incomplete character of every
totality necessarily leads us to abandon, as a terrain of analysis, the
premise of *"society"* as a sutured and self-defined totality. "Society"
is not a valid object of discourse. There is no single underlying
principle fixing – and hence constituting – the whole field of
differences.'[31] The first and most obvious point to extract from this
is the rejection of a model of society as a totality. Marxists have, it is
true, differed as to how far they thought of societies as integrated
totalities, but certainly they have tended to see them at least as
bounded entities. In recent years, however, this notion of a social
'totality' has come under renewed scrutiny and reflection. In sociology, too, there has been a drift towards what we might call
anti-totality models, with the rise of more micro-sociological and
phenomenological approaches. Another aspect of this would be the
reconsideration now under way of models of social entities that were,
effectively, based on individual nation-states: as if 'the sociology of
Britain' or 'of India' were a viable project in an increasingly global
social environment. Anthony Giddens has provided incisive critiques
of the naïve assumptions underlying some conceptions of 'societies'
and indeed the slogan 'Think globally, act locally' has recently been

held up to sociologists as a better model for the discipline than some of the previous ones.[32]

The general criticisms of 'totality' models of society have been encountered in an earlier chapter (the end of chapter 3), where I considered Paul Hirst's crisp rejection of the framework of 'relative autonomy' with all its determinist baggage and absured images based on social topography. Hirst has subsequently set out in an extraordinarily clear way the differences between his position and the totality model, as follows: 'He [Althusser] conceives social relations as *totalities*, as a whole governed by a single determinative principle. This whole must be consistent with itself and must subject all agents and relationships within its purview to its effects. I, on the other hand, consider social relations as aggregates of institutions, forms of organisations, practices and agents which do not answer to any single causal principle or logic of consistency, which can and do differ in form and which are not at all essential to one another.'[33] Hirst is in agreement here with Laclau and Mouffe on two issues, which are key entry-points into their argument as a whole: that 'society' (in so far as any of them would be willing to use the word occasionally for the sake of convenience) should be thought of in terms of aggregates rather than totalities and, secondly, that the relationships between the various elements of those aggregations should be thought of in terms of contingency rather than the logic of causality and determinism.

Laclau and Mouffe do not rest at a critique of the idea of social 'totality', but move into a more fundamental – philosophical rather than sociological – set of arguments about the 'impossibility' of society. Before going into these, it might be useful to summarise the schema of interlinked concepts that they propose for the analysis of social relations. They define four terms – *articulation, discourse, moment, element* – of which the second, 'discourse', has generated the most controversy. *Articulation* is defined as 'any practice establishing a relation among elements such that their identity is modified as a result of the articulatory practice', *discourse* is 'the structured totality resulting from the articulatory practice', *moments* are 'differential positions, in so far as they appear articulated within a discourse' and an *element* is 'any difference that is not discursively articulated'.[34] The most important point to note about these definitions is that the very extended definition of 'discourse' by Laclau and Mouffe does not, as has been immediately concluded by several materialists, represent a vertiginous leap into idealism. The concept of discourse in their hands is a materialist one that enables them to rethink the analysis of social and historical phenomena in a different framework. Their concept of discourse has been developed in a mode of explicit criticism of the assumptions traditionally governing discussion of the 'material/ideal' split in Marxist theory and thus cannot (or at least should not) be assimilated automatically to one position within a polarity that they have explicitly rejected. It has something in common with Foucault's use of 'discourse', but there are important differences too. As I shall clarify later, whatever the problems associated with their concept of discourse, Laclau and Mouffe, in their general epistemological orientation, do not occupy the 'idealist' and 'relativist' boxes into which their critics have tried to push them.

Departing, for the moment, from the contentious definition of 'discourse' in *Hegemony and Socialist Strategy*, I want to consider the related set of propositions put forward in the book as to the 'impossibility' of society and represented, in the passage under discussion, by the sentence 'There is no single underlying principle fixing – and hence constituting – the whole field of differences.' What does it mean for them to say that 'absolute fixity' of meaning (and absolute non-fixity) is not possible? A complication with their argument is that, as well as carrying its own considerable weight, it deploys concepts drawn from other theorists whose import to Laclau and Mouffe's argument will be differentially understood by readers. I propose to look at two key concepts of this type, as a way in to Laclau and Mouffe's argument: *suture* and *difference*.

Suture is a term whose current theoretical use is drawn from Lacanian psychoanalysis and has been developed, as Laclau and Mouffe describe (p. 88, n. 1), in semiotic film theory. Conventionally, in English, meaning 'stitch', the term suture is rendered by the *Oxford English Dictionary* as 'the joining of the lips of a wound' and this original surgical meaning is given a neat and modern gloss in Landry and Maclean's remark that 'a "suture" marks the absence of a former identity, as when cut flesh heals but leaves a scar marking difference'.[35] Laclau and Mouffe present us with a body politic whose skin is permanently split open, necessitating ceaseless duty in the emergency room for the surgeons of hegemony whose fate it is to try and close, temporarily and with difficulty, the gaps. (This patient never makes it to the recovery ward.) Their reference to Stephen Heath's account of suture stresses a 'double movement', between on the one hand a Lacanian 'I' whose hallmark is division and lack, and on the other hand the simultaneous possibility of coherence or 'filling-in' of that lack. Their application of the concept of suture to the field of politics carries with it an idea that Derrida's work on deconstruction has made influential: the traces of the old cannot be destroyed but remain as sedimentary deposits, even, and indeed especially, where the new is trying hardest to exclude the old. (Deconstruction being the method of uncovering these buried traces.) Thus Laclau and Mouffe say, 'Hegemonic practices are suturing in so far as their field of operation is determined by the openness of the social, by the ultimately unfixed character of every signifier. This original lack is precisely what the hegemonic practices try to fill in.' They conclude that the closure implied in the idea of a totally sutured society is impossible.[36]

The 'ultimate fixity of meaning' is, explain Laclau and Mouffe, a proposition that has been challenged by a powerful strand of philosophical thought 'from Heidegger to Wittgenstein' and, most importantly perhaps for our purposes, by the post-structuralist philosopher Jacques Derrida. This is not the moment to attempt a summary of his views, but one might usefully refer here to Derrida's over-arching insistence on meaning as positional rather than absolute. Derrida has elaborated a theory of language as the infinite 'play of signifiers' and of linguistic meaning as constructed through relations of difference within a chain.

Difference has come to stand, in a broad range of modern social theory, as the exemplar of this approach to language and as the mark of a rejection of absolute meaning or, as Laclau and Mouffe put it here, of 'ultimate fixity' of meaning. At this point in their argument they quote Derrida's generalisation of the concept of discourse, in *Writing and Difference*, as an approach that is 'coincident with that of our text'. Derrida writes: 'This was the moment [he gives as temporal examples the works of Nietzsche, Freud and Heidegger] when language invaded the universal problematic, the moment when, in the absence of a centre or origin, everything became discourse – provided we can agree on this word – that is to say, a system in which the central signified, the original or transcendental signified, is never absolutely present outside a system of differences. The absence of the transcendental signified extends the domain and the play of signification infinitely.'[37] Hence, for Laclau and Mouffe, a discourse is 'constituted as an attempt to dominate the field of discursivity, to arrest the flow of differences, to construct a centre' and they describe the 'privileged discursive points of this partial fixation' as *nodal points*, with reference to Lacan's *points de capiton* (privileged signifiers that fix meaning in a chain).[38]

As far as the impossibility of society is concerned, we can see in Laclau and Mouffe's perspective a very close and powerful fusing of

Lacan and Derrida. The images and metaphors cut across the divisions of psychoanalytic, philosophical and political fields and the guiding principle is the analysis of a tension between the always already (indeed essentially) split and decentred, be it the Lacanian psyche or signification in Derrida, and the 'suturing' hegemonic project of coherence. Thus Laclau and Mouffe conclude that 'If the social does not manage to fix itself in the intelligible and instituted forms of a *society*, the social only exists, however, as an effort to construct that impossible object.'[39] 'Society' is the impossible object of the operations of the social, just as, we might say, the 'Jacobin imaginary' figured as an empty and illusory prospect for the operations of the political.

THE UNSATISFACTORY TERM 'NEW SOCIAL MOVEMENTS'

If in their constitution of 'society' as an impossibility Laclau and Mouffe draw on the ideas of other post-structuralist thinkers such as Derrida and Lacan it will be conceded even by their sternest critics that in their analysis of the 'new social movements' they have delivered an original and highly influential development in political thought. An obvious explanation of the enormous current interest in their work is that it speaks to a problem – the weight to be attached to social class as opposed to other salient divisions such as gender, ethnicity or age, for example – that has exercised a major hold on both academic analyses and on practical political activity across the traditional right/left spectrum.

On the academic front, we have seen a variety of debates around this topic, largely (not surprisingly) in Marxisant treatments of sociology, politics and economics. Partly these debates concern the massive re-theorisation required to apply Marx's own concepts and descriptors to societies whose class structures and relationships have changed radically in the ensuing century – here one could point schematically to the debates around the work on class of Erik Olin Wright and Carchedi, around the questions that continue to arise from the writings of Poulantzas on politics and class and from the revolution in 'rethinking Marxism' spearheaded by the economists Steve Resnick and Rick Wolff, and indeed one could also mention the major developments known under the umbrella heading of 'rational choice theory' as it continues to sweep across the field of what we might still, rather loosely, call Marxism. In all of these debates, there has been a potential for engagement with the actualities of *non-class* divisions, but (to express the situation tactfully) this has remained in many instances a potential rather than a nettle to be grasped.

Partly, too, academic debates around class have taken place in a conscious dialogue with the work of feminists and the writings of those who have sought to rethink class in relation to the major concern of national identity and nationalist politics, as well as in relation to the issues of ethnicity and racism. It is perhaps worth stressing how rich and varied the challenge to 'class primacy' has become in social science: whole schools of thought now exist devoted to the ways in which housing, for example, or life cycle effects, cut across cherished assumptions about the determining effects of social class. So it seems very clear that a radical new theorisation of politics, in which the iconic factor of class is dramatically shifted from its privileged position, would be of great interest to many people. (Why Laclau and Mouffe's book has been take up so extensively in literary critical theory is a more complex question, which I will not take up here.)

In terms of practical politics, there can be no doubt that *Hegemony and Socialist Strategy* addresses a problem of tremendous pertinence and significance. This is, perhaps, most obviously true of the beleaguered left, which has had, in a variety of contexts, to rethink not only its images of class themselves but the role it should occupy in 'left' politics more generally, where it is in competition with the claims of environmentalism, gay rights, feminism, anti-racism and so on. As we no doubt all know, dispute on this question has concerned the left very deeply in recent years. The 'coalition politics' to emerge from some of these political interactions, of which perhaps the most notable example in recent years has been the Jesse Jackson campaign for the US presidency in 1988, are exactly what the book addresses at a theoretical level. Given, however, that it has been the right and centre (certainly in Britain and the USA) that have articulated some of these new connections and meanings, we should not suppose at all that the phenomenon is restricted to the politics of the left.

Laclau and Mouffe, presumably sensitive to the predicted charge that they are moving rightwards, suggest that their iconoclasm about social class paves the way for a new political radicalism. 'The rejection of privileged points of rupture and the confluence of struggles into a unified political space, and the acceptance, on the contrary, of the plurality and indeterminacy of the social, seem to us the two fundamental bases from which a new political imaginary can be constructed, radically libertarian and infinitely more ambitious in its objectives than the classic left.'[40]

At the most elementary level the term 'new social movements' is unsatisfactory, to Laclau and Mouffe among others, in that it encodes its own historic marginality. These are, precisely, 'new' movements in that they are *not class* movements, and this reference back to class will remain there as long as we use that style of nomination. What is being referred to is the phenomenon, which Laclau and Mouffe try to locate historically in the web of post-1945 changes in labour process, state and cultural diffusion, of new antagonisms being articulated, in a novel way, in relation to increasingly numerous social relations. In practice, the term groups together struggles as diverse as 'urban, ecological, anti-authoritarian, anti-institutional, feminist, anti-racist, ethnic, regional or that of sexual minorities'.[41] Laclau and Mouffe see in these struggles the articulation of antagonisms in a wide range of sites beyond the traditional workplace in which class conflict has been situated by Marxism, and they point, for example, to consumption, services and habitat as terrains for these new conflicts.

As well as extending such antagonisms far beyond the limits conventionally operating in Marxist analyses, they suggest that the bureaucratisation of post-war (western, industrial capitalist) society has given rise to new forms of regulation of social relations. They thus recast the arguments of Foucault and Donzelot by seeing as 'consequences' of post-war bureaucratisation the process of 'the imposition of multiple forms of vigilance and regulation in social relations which had previously been conceived as forming part of the private domain'.[42] Acknowledging the familiar political ambiguities surrounding political resistance in a 'welfare state' context, Laclau and Mouffe see, amongst the various factors in play in such struggles, a newly articulated broad sphere of social 'rights'. Categories such as 'justice' and 'equality' have been, in a sense, lifted from their liberal context and articulated within a democratic political discourse. Laclau and Mouffe conclude here that commodification and bureaucratisation, and the reformulation of a liberal-democratic political ideology, form the context in which we should understand the expansion of social conflict and the constitution of new political subjects, which in turn they describe as 'a moment of deepening of the democratic revolution'.[43]

They add, however, that a third aspect of the new 'hegemonic formation of the post-war period' plays an important role: the expansion of mass communication and the retreat of traditional cultural identities. Laclau and Mouffe see, in the ambiguities of a cultural massification that interpellates subjects as theoretically equal consumers as well as providing some elements with subversive potential, a general homogenisation of social life. They point, in a very interesting passage, to the fact that resistance to this has tended to take the form of a 'proliferation of particularisms' and the 'valorisation of "differences"', especially those geared to the creation of new cultural identities. In these demands for autonomy, so often slighted by the left for their apparent individualism, Laclau and Mouffe see a reformulation of the demand for 'liberty' – one of the central themes of the democratic imaginary.[44]

In considering Laclau and Mouffe's argument in general one might want to draw attention to a key emphasis on what they describe as 'the logic of equivalence'. This can be explained as follows: the French revolution was an important moment in the development of a democratic imaginary in that it ushered out a hierarchical social order ('ruled by a theological-political logic in which the social order had its foundation in divine will') where political discourse could only be the repetition and reproduction of inequality. (A striking instance of this is the notorious English hymn verse 'The rich man in his castle, The poor man at his gate, God made them, high or lowly, And ordered their estate.') Here let me quote a crucial sentence from Laclau and Mouffe: 'This break with the *ancien régime*, symbolised by the Declaration of the Rights of Man, would provide the discursive conditions which made it possible to propose the different forms of inequality as illegitimate and anti-natural, and thus make them equivalent as forms of oppression.'[45] Thus the 'logic of equivalence' is born: we have moved from a social order in which subjects are differentially, but fatefully, positioned, to a social order in which the democratic project can articulate itself in a political discourse which takes those differential positionings as an object of struggle. So the democratic revolution brings about a logic of equivalence, a logic of the comparison of subjects that are, essentially, construed as equals, through its new discourse of 'rights', 'liberty' and 'equality'.

There are ambiguities at the heart of Laclau and Mouffe's use of the idea of 'equivalence'. For one thing, it is not clear how the 'anti-natural' element of the democratic imaginary could ever operate without lapsing into the humanism and essentialism that they consistently deplore. Secondly, there is a more confusing ambiguity as to whether 'equivalence' is being construed as similar to 'equality', which is at times implied, or whether Laclau and Mouffe's logic of equivalence is more appropriately captured with reference to the chemical use of equivalence to denote the proportional weights of substances equal in their chemical value. This would emphasise a notion of equal value, but introducing the tension between equality and – precisely – *difference* is difficult to square with the 'one man one vote' (*sic*) logic of democratic equality.

There is, however, no ambiguity on one central point of the logic of equivalence and this is the secondary place that class occupies with regard to the prior category of the democratic imaginary. Laclau and Mouffe write that socialist demands are not only 'a moment internal to the democratic revolution' but are 'only intelligible on the basis of the equivalential logic which the latter establishes'.[46] They write earlier of Marx that he had sought to rethink social division on a new principle – that of class – but that this was undermined from the start by 'a radical insufficiency, arising from the fact that class opposition is incapable of dividing the totality of the social body into two antagonistic camps' and they comment that Marx's sociological predictions (about capitalist society becoming increasingly polarised) were an effort to project a future simplification on a social world that in Marx's own time did not fit a crude class-reduced model.[47] Thus, in general, we have an account of Marxism's preoccupation with class as an articulation of political demands whose preconditions lay in the democratic revolution of the century before. Hence Laclau and Mouffe see no need for subsequent antagonisms and the 'new' social movements articulating the demands of those oppressed by them, to cede place to class on the basis that social class is a founding principle. It is only, in their analysis, one of numerous contradictions that may be articulated within the parameters of democratic political discourse.

POST-MARXISM, DISCOURSE AND IDEOLOGY

Several major considerations present themselves in thinking about the issues raised by *Hegemony and Socialist Strategy*. I have two reasons for taking its critique of Marxism very seriously, and both of them relate to longstanding difficulties with the arguments of Marxism: the first is the question of social class, in a political environment where it is increasingly obvious to everyone except the dogmatists of the far right and far left that social inequalities and political differences simply cannot plausibly be subsumed under or reduced to the question of class. Hence any attempt to advocate new ways of thinking about these different political struggles should be welcomed and considered.

Secondly, Laclau and Mouffe's argument addresses, although not in a predictable way (as I shall explain) the vexed question of how to theorise the concept of ideology. I say this is vexed, but its vexatiousness has a particular history and will be of more salience to some than to others. Within, roughly, 'socialist' versions of feminism there has been an attempt to use the concept of ideology to theorise the oppression of women in capitalist society but this has remained problematic since that theory is itself (as I have tried to show in chapters 1 to 3) embedded in an analysis that not only argues/assumes the primacy of class but also normally construes ideology in a determinist model such as the metaphor of 'base and superstructure'. The ensuing problem was raised by the arguments of an earlier book of mine in which, according to Johanna Brenner and Maria Ramas, 'ideology is Barrett's *deus ex machina*, her means of escape from the vexing dilemma of the Marxist-reductionist/dual systems idealist impasse of socialist-feminist thought'. What, they and other critics wanted to know, was the material basis – in a capitalist society – of this ideology that oppressed women?[48] Laclau and Mouffe, in rejecting the 'class-essentialist' logic of Marxism, in providing so many arguments against the automatic privileging of class in Marxist analysis, have, albeit very contentiously, struck at the heart of this problem.

In part this is a crisis of 'class politics' and, as Richard Wright has noted in a review of the divergent responses of Barry Hindess and Ellen Wood, it has produced polar reactions: a pragmatic approach to class that has been shorn of the theoretical pretension of the Marxist model, and a reaffirmation of classical class politics.[49] The reason the polarity has developed is because the position of arguing in detail for the complexities and specificities of gender in relation to class, against the ceaseless rehearsal of so-called received truths about class, is an unenviable one and the 'centre' of the debate has, increasingly, been evacuated. It is not without interest that the theoretical models attempting to reconcile conflicts between the claims of class and gender, as these emerge in social science anyway, have proved unequal to the task of dealing with the 'newer' (to some) questions of ethnicity and racism. As I have suggested elsewhere, it is as if existing theories of social structure, already taxed by attempting to think about the interrelations of class and gender, have been quite unable to integrate a third axis of systematic inequality into their conceptual maps. And it is easy to point, by contrast, to the veritable explosion of work that does combine these three interests (the 'holy trinity' of class, race and gender) in disciplines and genres where these structural/morphological constraints do not hold back the exploration of new issues.[50]

It might be relevant to add, here, that the general orientation of Laclau's earlier work rejecting the 'class-belonging' dimension of political ideology has proved a useful framework for thinking about political discourse in a nuanced manner. I have previously mentioned the influence of that work on the exploration, by Colin Mercer and Stuart Hall among others, of nationalism (the Gramscian 'national-popular'), patriotism and Thatcherism, for example. The idea of 'political discourse', as a concept that can accommodate a variety of groups, demands and interests as they are articulated, opens the way for an analysis of gender that was by definition marginalised in the 'reflection of class' school of thought about political ideology. We have certainly seen, drawing loosely on the ideas of 'early Laclau', several analyses of contemporary political discourse as gendered: they consider the ways in which, for example, feminism and anti-feminism, constructions of 'family' and sexuality, or articulations and denials of women's reproductive rights, figure in the discourses.[51]

It remains to be seen, however, how far *Hegemony and Socialist Strategy* really does carry through its iconoclastic project of the complete dismantling of class privilege. To say this is not to make a cheap point of the order of 'caught you using the word society' but to address a more serious issue that surfaces in relation to the majority of post-structuralist work. This is the intrusion, or return in disguise, of elements (often of the kind that post-modernists refer to as 'meta-narratives') which have been explicitly rejected elsewhere in the texts in question. We shall see numerous examples of this phenomenon in the course of part III of this book, and indeed the question is aptly raised by the character in a David Lodge novel who asks 'whether Derrida's critique of metaphysics lets idealism in by the back door'.

As far as Laclau and Mouffe are concerned, we revert here to the question of their post-Marxism. Let me take as an example the section of their argument where they set out the hegemonic transformation of the post-war social order, in which they locate the emergence of new social antagonisms and their articulation in new social movements.[52] Far from subscribing to a logic of 'contingency', the sequence of their propositions, and the model of causality expounded in them, are entirely characteristic of the traditional patterns of Marxist thought. If we take the sequence of the argument first, it is astonishing that – in their historical reconstruction of the new hegemonic social formation – they automatically move first to the 'economic point of view' which, drawing on the work of Michel Aglietta, they analyse in terms of that most orthodox of Marxist concepts, commodification. Then we have a brief registration of environmental and urban issues, though, interestingly, the argument here does not operate by means of any concept equivalent to commodification. Next (and by contrast we find the concept of bureaucratisation mobilised) Laclau and Mouffe move, in fact, to the state, and then on to political articulation and the reformulation of liberal-democratic ideology. The classical Marxist mind-set – economy, then state, then ideology, then 'culture' – is then fully completed in the addition of the 'important aspect' of mass communication and its new cultural forms. So, whatever their theoretical protestations about the economy as 'the last redoubt of essentialism' it is undoubtedly true that in one of the rare places where a substantive social/historical account is offered in the book it exactly reproduces, in its own ordering, that economistic and determinist logic.

As does the content of the argument, too, at this point. The thesis about capitalist development in this period is concerned with the expansion of capitalist relations into previously non-capitalist areas but it rests on an extraordinary construction of capitalism as being about 'commodification' but not necessarily about labour/capital contradictions. They write: 'Today it is not only as sellers of labour-power that the individual is subordinated to capital, but also through his or her incorporation into a multitude of other social relations: culture, free time, illness, education, sex and even death. There is practically no domain of individual or collective life which escapes capitalist relations.[53] The entire discussion of this phenomenon is interesting in that it is uncritically couched within a Marxist reading of this historical process that has long been challenged, on the one hand by the Foucault/Donzelot position on the historical emergence of 'the social' and on the other by feminist insistence on the *non*-capitalist power relations at play in the world of the 'private domain'.[54] So, although Laclau and Mouffe gesture in the direction of feminism by noting the subordination of women in traditional community networks, they adopt a highly 'functionalist' and 'reductionist' and classically orthodox 'Marxist' formulation about the welfare state and the reproduction of labour power and one which has been explicitly criticised by feminists. And what is interesting about their constitution of 'capitalism' is that it remains an elemental and undefined agent in the argument – yet an agent whose existence they have in general terms challenged.

If all this is to say that Laclau and Mouffe are 'still too Marxist' – a position taken in Landry and Maclean's reading of the text[55] – it is a far cry from the usual tenor of responses to the book. Most of these have taken the form of a polemical engagement with the apostasy, from a Marxist point of view, of Laclau and Mouffe's arguments. Ellen Wood, to take one of her criticisms at random, accuses them of 'not only a breathtaking misreading of Marx, but also a very substantial failure of reasoning'.[56] Many of these debates are concerned, which I am not, with a doxological restatement of the primacy of class to Marxist theory and practice, but some issues are worth recapitulating briefly. One of these is the question of materialism, and the issue of whether Laclau and Mouffe's rejection of the discursive/non-discursive distinction necessarily makes them 'idealist'. I have suggested earlier that it does not, and that their use of the category discourse is defensible in relation to what people like to call 'the real world': the elementary point to make is that discourse *is* 'real'. In their reply to a critique by Norman Geras, Laclau and Mouffe explain with some examples the sense in which they use the term 'discourse', which is defined in the book as the structured totality resulting from articulatory practice. First of all, but it is a source of some misunderstanding, they include within the category of discourse both linguistic and non-linguistic phenomena – discourse is not a text or speech or similar. The term is principally concerned with *meaning*, and they give the example (which Geras finds 'patronising' but others have found useful) of football. 'If I kick a spherical object in the street or if I kick a ball in a football match, the *physical* fact is the same, but its *meaning* is different. The object is a football only to the extent that it establishes a system of relations with other objects, and these relations are not given by the mere referential materiality of the objects but are, rather, socially constructed.'[57] The example is helpful in that it answers those who think that their use of the term discourse is in some way a threat to ontological reality: they do not dispute referential materiality ('the discursive character of an object does not, by any means, imply putting its *existence* into question') but insist that the meaning of physical objects must be understood by apprehension of their place in a system (or discourse) of socially constructed rules. What applies to footballs, we could add, applies to tanks, police horses, jails, fighter bombers and any other material appurtenances of the suppression of the working class. Laclau and Mouffe are not 'collapsing' or 'dissolving' everything into discourse: they are insisting that we cannot apprehend or think of the non-discursive other than in contextualising discursive categories, be they scientific, political or whatever.

Related to this is the question of relativism. It is sometimes assumed that Laclau and Mouffe must be taking up a position of epistemological relativism, but nothing could be further from the case. As may readily be noted, although 'truth' is always theoretically contextual in their frame of reference, there is no shortage of truth claims in their own theoretical discourse. One interesting example here is to look at their treatment of the question of ideology, for so long a stumbling block in terms of the assignation of real interests, correct consciousness and so on. Laclau and Mouffe's attachment to epistemological security is such that they even take on, within the terms of their own model, the old conundrum about whether people can be said to be 'oppressed' if they themselves do not think they are. This is the subject of a fascinating distinction that they draw between 'subordination' and 'oppression': the former simply marks a set of differential positions between social agents, whereas the latter requires a point *exterior* to the discourse from which – for 'oppression' to exist – the discourse of subordination can be interrupted. And just for those who still see relativism as indexically linked to privileging the discursive, let me quote their definition of 'relations of domination': 'those relations ... which are considered as illegitimate from the perspective, or in the judgement, of a social agent external to them.'[58] Far from being 'relativist' these confident formulations, spoken naturally from the position of the judging external agent rather than that of the judgees, err on the side of being hard to justify in epistemological terms.

So it is perhaps not surprising to find Laclau and Mouffe offering us a defence of the 'critical', 'epistemological' view of ideology, but of course a fundamentally reformulated one. There are points in the argument of *Hegemony and Socialist Strategy* where one can say that for Laclau and Mouffe something is 'essentially' of such and such a character, and this is an important recognition. A key point of interaction between epistemology and the general concerns I have indicated about ideology can be found in the conclusion of Laclau's article 'The Impossibility of Society'. Here Laclau clarifies the solid epistemological foundation of their 'anti-essentialism'. 'We cannot do without the concept of misrecognition, precisely because the very assertion that the "identity and homogeneity of social agents is an illusion" cannot be formulated without introducing the category of misrecognition.' Hence Laclau concludes that both the category of ideology and that of misrecognition can be retained, but by inverting their traditional content: he suggests that 'the ideological would not consist of the misrecognition of a positive essence [an illusion as to real class interests, for example], but exactly the opposite: it would consist of the non-recognition of the precarious character of any positivity, of the impossibility of any ultimate suture.'[59] The substantive thesis put forward here – that ideology is a vain attempt to impose closure on a social world whose essential characteristic is the infinite play of differences and the impossibility of any ultimate fixing of meaning – is thus couched in a framework in which the traditional distinction within Marxism between knowledge and ideological 'misrecognition' is (paradoxically to some) retained.

In general, perhaps it would be a good thing for Marxists to look at the world, even if only for an experimental (but it would have to be open-minded) period, through the glasses of Laclau and Mouffe. It certainly is a different place, and despite all the refined and detailed arguments about their theses one is left with a sense that these people have woken up one morning and, simply, seen 'society' differently. This is a possible interpretation of Paul Hirst's differentiation between himself and Althusser: 'He conceives social relations ... I, on the other hand, consider social relations ....' What makes the passage interesting is the assertion, cool and reflective with only a hint of the *ex cathedra*, of a simple difference of view. Much argued over in the past, but now a difference of vision rather than opinion.

Perhaps one could draw an analogy with the normal curve on which IQ testing rests. Leave aside for the moment the morass of detailed problems about whether IQ tests are culture-bound, or racist, and consider the more fundamental question of whether intelligence occurs through the population on the basis of a 'normal distribution' with regression to the mean. Strictly speaking, this cannot and could not be proved, but people continue to 'measure IQ' on a basis that only makes sense if this assumption is true. Some of Laclau and Mouffe's arguments can be responded to at the level of whether they are substantively accurate (if you like, the level of whether IQ testing is, within its own terms, objective) but some of their arguments are characteristically 'post-structuralist' in that they lift us out of the frame of reference in which we began (of denying, or querying, the proposition about the normal curve and hence delegitimating the whole exercise). The most interesting example of this type of argument is the treatment, in *Hegemony and Socialist Strategy*, of the issue of 'positivity' and 'negativity' in a social context and it is to here that I want to round off this discussion.

It is curiously disturbing to encounter the word 'positive' as a negative term, but this is indeed how it figures in Laclau and Mouffe's text. What does it mean to advocate a movement 'beyond the positivity of the social'? I have tried to explicate earlier what is meant by this in the context of the impossibility of 'society', and of the proposition that the social is always an attempt at suture rather than a complete closure. In more general terms, however, Laclau and Mouffe are in harmony with a strand of modern philosophy that might go under the headings of a celebration of negativity, a certain nihilism, a delight in destruction/deconstruction, an emphasis on meaninglessness. All these currents can be found, as is mentioned in the book, in modern European philosophy from Sartre's existentialism to the more 'negative' side of the phenomenological tradition, in Heidegger, Nietzsche and parts of Wittgenstein. In this sense, as will be discussed in more detail in chapter 6, contemporary post-structuralism has a long history in twentieth-century European philosophy and this is the context in which we need to read Laclau and Mouffe. What is unique to them is the project of a rigorous re-engagement or rereading of the Marxist tradition of political thought through the lens of these ideas.

At the heart of their project is a recognition that Marxism delivers some elements of this 'negative' world-view, but is, in contrast, by and large what Timpanaro has called 'triumphalist' in its orientation. Marxism was born of a confident moment, indeed an imperialist one, and it speaks that 'Victorian' sense of conquest of the natural world in Marx's founding ideas about human nature and human labour.[60] As Laclau puts it, 'it would be absurd to deny that this dimension of mastery/transparency/rationalism is present in Marxism'. Rather disarmingly, Laclau, in summarising the 'negative' dimension of Marxism that he finds inspiring (negativity, struggle, antagonism, opacity, ideology, the gap between the real and the sensual), comments that for this reading to be possible one has to ignore at least half of Marx's work.[61] It is for this reason that *Hegemony and Socialist Strategy* is '*post*-Marxist'. Laclau, in the slightly later article from which I am now quoting, sees the negative dimension as the founding one: 'it [the moment of negativity] shone for just a brief moment in theoretical discourse, only to dissolve an instant later into the full positivity which reabsorbed it – positivity of history and society as totalisations of their partial processes, the positivity of the subject –

the social classes – as agents of history'.[62] Laclau's tone is elegiac
here, and indeed he goes on to cite Stalin as the end point of the
affirmation of positivity in Marxism.

There can be no doubt that the critique of 'positivity' and the
critique of essentialist thought, which are applied by Laclau and
Mouffe to Marxism, are aspects of a broader challenge to a wide
variety of thought. The article to which I have just referred is, in
fact, a consideration by Laclau of points of comparison between this
'reading' of Marxism (now 'post-Marxism') and psychoanalysis.
Here, to anticipate some themes that we can take up later, Laclau
offers some links between the Laclau/Mouffe conception of hegemony (dislocation, the attempt at suture) and a Lacanian notion of
'lack' and he recommends a possible confluence of post-Marxism and
psychoanalysis 'around the logic of the signifier as a logic of unevenness and dislocation'.[63] What Laclau does not mention at this point,
however, is that this reading of psychoanalysis requires us to ignore
not just half but almost all of 'psychoanalysis' and take up a strictly
Lacanian interpretation. For about 90 per cent of psychoanalysis is
burdened with a leaden weight of essentialism and it is, in fact, only
the Lacanian reworking of the theory that has stripped it of these
positivities. Hence it could be more appropriate to be discussing a
confluence of 'post-psychoanalysis' with post-Marxism.

At this point we might turn to Charles Jencks's useful comment on
'the paradoxical dualism' that the hybrid term 'post-modernism'
entails: it is, he writes, at one and the same time the continuation of
modernism and its transcendence.[64] So it is with Laclau and Mouffe,
whose work remains in some respects locked inside a Marxist
framework and in others breaks out into an altogether different
philosophical frame of reference. And if you conclude that the 'axioms' of Marxism, particularly with regard to the relationships between class, ideology and political discourse, are not self-evidently
true in the contemporary world, then their challenge to Marxism's
class essentialism will represent a considerable cracking, indeed collapse of the Marxist model.

5

Subjectivity, Humanism, Psychoanalysis: Beyond Althusser's Lacan

Any assessment of the long-term significance of the work of Louis Althusser has to contend with a complex set of considerations. In the first place, although we can easily see a collapse of Althusserianism from a position of erstwhile influence (with two commentaries using the expression 'rise and fall' in their titles), the dates of these events are unclear. The reason for this is that the influence of Althusser's work, and particularly its popularity in radical thought in Britain and France, as well as in other European countries, can readily be seen persisting well into the 1970s. As a *system* of thought, however, and in terms of the internal coherence and power of the arguments intrinsic to the theory, its demise had occurred much earlier. Vincent Descombes, in his account of *Modern French Philosophy*, announces that in '1969 Althusser did away with Althusserianism' in the sense that he restored the primacy of the political over the theoretical at that point, and then goes on to declare that subsequently the 'Althusserian undertaking' was brought 'to an official close'.[1]

Descombes is here using 'official' to indicate Althusser's own theoretical project as a political writer, but Gareth Stedman-Jones has taken a much wider view and suggested that '1968 already represented the end of Althusserianism'.[2] Against this conclusion one might point to the stream of 'Althusserian' texts of the 1970s, of which Terry Eagleton's *Criticism and Ideology* (1976) could be taken as an example.[3] In addition, and much more importantly, many of Althusser's concepts have continued to be used from that period to this – albeit in more modest contexts than they occur in the original 'grand theory'. Nevertheless, the use up until the present time of ideas such as 'articulation', 'interpellation', or 'over determination' in social, political and cultural theory reveals the extent to which the legacy of Althusserianism is still an influential one. In this sense, one would have to draw a distinction between the intellectual coherence of Althusser's own work as a theoretical system and the more eclectic, but highly persistent, uses to which some of his ideas have been put. In his case more than others, scholars have tended to concentrate on the *production* of knowledge, stressing the historical political context in which Althusser's texts were first written, and indeed one sometimes feels that it is impossible to pick up anything written about Althusser without having first to negotiate the question of the French Communist Party's ambivalence about Stalinism. We might, perhaps, find it useful to attend more seriously to the patterns of *consumption* of these ideas and the ways in which Althusser's writings have been used in subsequent work.

One immediate aspect of the consumption of Althusser's ideas is that their impact on the two sides of the Atlantic has been dramatically different. In the United States the phenomenon of 'Althusserianism' was virtually unknown, for reasons that obviously relate to the relatively weak Marxist tradition there in comparison with continental Europe. (Radical thinking being more widely associated with, for example, the Frankfurt School and critical theory.) Perhaps the most significant consequence of this difference is the likelihood that a full-scale challenge to humanism arose in the United States with the subsequent influence of Foucault, and Derrida, whereas the European tradition of critical social thought had digested this challenge in its absorption of Althusser's critique of Marxism as a form of humanism. In any event, the effect of Althusserianism on the European Marxist tradition would be hard to overestimate. Taking simply the case of journals, one can point not only to the undiluted pure Althusserian water of *Theoretical Practice* (a project of some of Althusser's earliest British disciples) but to the massive influence of Althusser's work, ideas and vocabulary on British journals as relatively diverse as *New Left Review, Economy and Society, Screen* and the *Working Papers* of the Birmingham Centre for Contemporary Cultural Studies. Thus when the end of this reign of ideas eventually came, it was a fall from a high point indeed, and made the more painful by the fact that Althusser's personal reputation eventually sank dramatically into criminal insanity.[4]

Hence, from a European point of view, the project of locating Althusser and Althusserianism in the history of Marxism is both difficult and necessary. As I shall argue later, it is a particularly important task in relation to the theory of ideology. Like Gramsci's, Althusser's thought represents a point at which a new weight was given to ideology and a complete recasting of Marxism occurred as the framework for that new theorisation. In Althusser's case the theory of ideology that he put forward was a more fundamental break with anything recognisable as classical Marxism than is the case with Gramsci. In that sense it was Althusser's own ideas, and the internally inconsistent character of his corpus of works, rather than the interpretations of subsequent readers, that clarified the degree of strain the Marxist model was under. Yet, just as I argued in the previous chapter that one can track a coherent 'route' from Gramsci to post-Marxism, so we shall follow an even clearer route from the dilemmas and contradictions of Althusser's work to an equally post-Marxist position. For Althusser is another limit position, from which Marxism has to recover or move away, rather than a 'stage' through which Marxism has passed. In so far as Althusser's work is misguided, it is a cul-de-sac from which steps must be retraced; in so far as it is insightful, it points us in directions beyond Marxism. This is because the issues that Althusser took on – or at least those of most concern to the theorisation of ideology – are impossible to square with Marxism without doing violence to its general character. To summarise the issues: (1) one cannot say that Marxism 'is' anti-humanist when all the evidence points to the salience of humanism in Marx's own thought and when attempts to develop anti-humanist Marxism have proved virtually impossible, and (2) Althusser's substantive contribution to the theorisation of subjectivity – his development of the concept of 'interpellation' – attempts the impossible task of integrating Marx and Lacan, but without even appearing to comprehend the enormity of the gulf to be thus bridged. These two central issues will be addressed in some detail in what follows.

Before doing so, let us consider first the question of how, at the most general level, Althusser conceived of ideology. There is considerable consistency between the approach he takes to this question in works such as *For Marx* and in the later and now canonical essay, 'Ideology and Ideological State Apparatuses':[5] *ideology is a system of representations through which people live their relationship to the historical world*. Each aspect of this definition is unpacked by Althusser. He regards ideology as a system in that it has its own 'logic and rigour', and by using the term 'representations' he leaves open the possibility of discussing 'images, myths, ideas or concepts, depending on the case'. Ideology is, he believes, an organic part of every society, and is essential to the historical life of societies. The emphasis Althusser places on 'living' one's relationship to the world is a crucial one, for he argues that ideologies do not operate principally through conscious beliefs but are best thought of as 'structures' that impose on people. 'They are perceived-accepted-suffered cultural objects and they act functionally on men via a process that escapes them.'[6]

If this last sentence sounds conventionally 'Marxist' in its echoes of cognitive deficiency, it is also an approach strangely in tune with Raymond Williams's more humanistic idea of historically varied 'structures of feeling'. Where Althusser moves on to a much more precise, and original, definition of ideology is the point at which he introduces a distinction (drawn from Lacan) between the 'real' and the 'imaginary' aspects of people's relationship to history. Ideology, he suggests, is a complex relation between relations: for in ideology people express not only the relation between them and their condition of existence (a 'real' relation) but also *the way they live* that relation (an 'imaginary' relation). This is a crucial point for understanding his general concept of ideology. He concludes that 'In ideology the real relation is inevitably invested in the imaginary relation, a relation that *expresses a will* (conservative, conformist, reformist or revolutionary), a hope or a nostalgia, rather than describing reality.' Althusser considers this relation of the real and the imaginary (which he regards as an instance of 'overdetermination' or causal reciprocity) to have an important consequence for thinking about ideology. Because it involves the will, and operates at deeper levels than those of surface consciousness, ideology cannot be used, politically, in a purely instrumental way. On a note of warning he writes: '[those] who would use an ideology purely as a means of action, as a tool, find that they have been caught by it, implicated by it, just when they are using it and believe themselves to be absolute masters of it'.[7]

We have noted earlier that Althusser is one of the most confident, nay bombastic, defenders of a clear distinction between ideology and science. Among the several difficulties of maintaining such a distinction is one mentioned by Terry Lovell – that of distinguishing between 'theoretical ideologies' and 'scientific theories'. Naturally this is a much more taxing problem than distinguishing between scientific theories and *ad hoc* pieces of common sense or prejudice, for we may readily concede that 'theoretical ideologies' often have 'scientific' elements to them, and vice versa. Although Lovell sees this as a problem that Althusser simply cannot address, one might suggest that in his substantive analyses and writings he does often attempt such a differentiation.

HUMANISM AS IDEOLOGY, SOCIALISM AS SCIENCE

One such case, which I propose to take up here as a way of thinking through his approach, is the claim Althusser makes that ('for Marx') humanism is only an ideology, whereas socialism is a scientific concept. Both sides of this claim seem to me to be completely untenable, and consideration of the issues involved may lead to some clarification of the implications of Althusser's general arguments about ideology as a 'relation between relations'. We shall need also to look at the question of Althusser's own relation to the elaborated theories, principally of Marx but also of Lacan, on which he worked.

Althusser's writings have, historically, been extremely powerful in establishing the proposition that Marx was not only *not* the humanist that many had previously thought him to be, but was positively anti-humanist. Sloughing off his idealist past as a thinker influenced by Kant, Fichte, Hegel and Feuerbach, Marx discovered – in a momentous break with his past which Althusser dates at 1845 – a new system of social analysis which is founded upon what Althusser describes as 'theoretical anti-humanism'. Even allowing for the fact that Althusser is here writing specifically about the question of humanism, it is rather surprising that his description of the new theoretical system compresses a totally comprehensive rereading of Marx into one sentence whilst expanding the question of humanism to form two out of the three 'indissociable elements' of the new system. I quote:

> In 1845 Marx broke radically with every theory that based history and politics on an essence of man. This unique rupture contained three indissociable elements:
>
> 1 The formation of a theory of history and politics based on radically new concepts: the concepts of social formation, productive forces, relations of production, superstructure, ideologies, determination in the last instance by the economy, specific determination of other levels, etc.
> 2 A radical critique of the *theoretical* pretensions of every philosophical humanism.
> 3 The definition of humanism as an ideology.

Althusser continues this passage by saying that 'This rupture with every *philosophical* anthropology or humanism is no secondary detail; it is Marx's scientific discovery.'[8]

It is no exaggeration to say that Althusser's recasting of Marx stands or falls on the issue of humanism. For Althusser believed that the early humanistic Marx, who made certain assumptions about human nature in order to develop his theses about alienation, for example, gave way to a Marx whose entire system was predicated upon the error of this view. Althusser insisted that the development of Marx's thought had implications for virtually every area of theory and analysis. This is because a belief in *human nature* implies both a universal *essence* of man and that this essence is present in each *individual*. Althusser refers to this as a combination of 'empiricism', in that concrete subjects are held to exist, and 'idealism', in that it attributes the essence of humanity to each of them. (In more modern terminology, it is essentialist as regards the supposedly 'human' attributes shared by all individuals, and also it presupposes a pre-social individual self.)

Althusser argues that in rejecting this humanist set of assumptions, or 'problematic', Marx was able to cut a swath through the working principles of much (western) social and political thought. Economics, for example, is based on the presumption of an individual whose needs and faculties are known to us, and this is likewise true of history and ethics. It is, however, in philosophy itself that the Althusser/Marx critique of the 'transcendental subject' was to hit the hardest: for it challenged the basis on which philosophers had established the ground rules of both knowledge (epistemology) and existence (ontology). Althusser delivers a list of the fallen heads, which includes Hobbes, Rousseau, Locke, Descartes and Kant. In more recent debates the emphasis has been put on both the Kantian 'transcendental subject' and the oft referred to 'Cartesian subject' (from Descartes's celebrated argument that *cogito ergo sum*: I think therefore I am) as representing this humanist and essentialist tradition of philosophical thought.

Althusser maintained that Marx was able to banish these unsatisfactory inferences drawn from so-called 'human nature' because he had formulated a complete systemic alternative to the previous paradigm. The details of this need not concern us here, although one should record that Althusser's attempt to present the 'authentic' Marx as an anti-humanist sociologist of the articulated levels of practice of a social formation called forth bitter objections from those who saw Marx as more of a historian and political resister than sage.[9] What is of central concern, however, is the argument Althusser then makes (again 'for Marx' in the double sense of being on Marx's behalf as well as in tribute to Marx) that it was this new conceptualisation of the place of ideology in a social formation that enables Marx confidently to ascribe humanism to that category. Thus humanism may have no theoretical status as science, or knowledge – it is simply wrong – but we can examine its 'practical function as an ideology'.[10]

Althusser's position on the intrinsically 'ideological' character of humanism is obviously bound up with his insistent claims that he is able to formulate a clear distinction between science and ideology. In one sense one could demolish his argument with reference to the failures of the general epistemological claims that he makes. Paradoxically, however, although few modern thinkers now accept Althusser's broader distinction as a basis for a critical position on humanism, the one piece of his system that has widespread cogency still is the critique of humanism and the subject referred to earlier. It is, therefore, of some interest to consider the case of 'humanism' a little further, in its own terms, rather than as a means to return to the ideology/science question.

Althusser's essay 'Marxism and Humanism' begins by taking up a critical position with regard to 'socialist humanism'. Fairly early on he asserts the position he will attempt to argue. 'But precisely in the couple "humanism-socialism" there is a striking theoretical unevenness: in the framework of the Marxist conception, the concept "socialism" is indeed a scientific concept, but the concept "humanism" is no more than an *ideological* one', and he warns that failure to separate the two will result in confusion and error.[11] Before embarking on humanism we would do well to pause a moment and consider the claim that socialism is a scientific concept. Certainly Marx and Engels passionately wanted to prove that socialism would emerge from the contradictions of capitalism, and indeed they argued militantly against 'ethical' and 'utopian' versions of socialism which appeared to 'reduce' the project to one of political goodwill. Yet it is precisely the 'scientific' dimension of socialism that has stood least well the test of time, in the sense that the predictions about capitalist society made by Marx have not exactly come true and nor was Marx right in his predictions about which situations would be most conducive to socialist revolution. Where Marx has been proved most clearly right, and where some might want to make a claim for the 'scientificity' of his concepts, would be in aspects of his explanatory model of the underlying dynamic of capitalist accumulation. One could, for example, make a good case for saying that in concrete (historical) instances one can see evidence for 'laws' such as the tendency of the rate of profit to fall or for a specific relationship between technological change and the extraction of relative surplus value. On these sorts of questions one might readily concede that

Marx gave a brilliant, and according to one's lights, maybe even 'scientific', account of the organisation of capitalism. But to argue that the concept of 'socialism' in Marxism is a scientific one is an uphill struggle indeed. From the vantage point of the early 1990s, where the collapse of communism in Eastern Europe has rendered the ambivalences of western Marxist intellectuals towards the chequered history of the Soviet Union politically irrelevant, Althusser's argument looks particularly stretched. To grope for the security of a scientific label for 'socialism' may have been an act of intellectual desperation in the early 1960s: now it seems just downright implausible. This is because Althusser's search for the validation of science is an attempt to avoid the crucial issue of political *will*.

It is significant that Althusser's own analysis of ideology turns on this point. Ideological relations, to return to his definition, are those that are invested in the imaginary, that 'express a will' – they concern a hope or a nostalgia, rather than describing reality.[12] Who would now dispute that the project of socialism in the political world of today was one that is invested with hope rather than a datum of science? In this context one can see the overwhelming political superiority of Gramsci to Althusser. Gramsci's famous dictum 'pessimism of the intellect, optimism of the will' injected human motivation and agency into the political project, while Althusser locked them up with the errors of ideology.

Of humanism itself, we can point firstly to a distinction that Althusser draws between the *theoretical* bankruptcy of humanism and the *historical* existence of human ideology: knowledge of the ideology in its practical social function is, he says, simultaneously knowledge of the conditions of its necessity. So he dissociates Marx from the (idealist) tendency to believe that ideology could be 'dissipated' simply by knowledge of it and indeed he suggests that humanist revisions of Marxism might have enough political efficacy to 'weigh down on real history'.[13] (Note again, the curious use of 'real'.) Althusser's confusing insistence that a strategy could be built from both a *theoretical anti-humanism* and a recognition of the historical necessity of humanist ideology has left open considerable room for interpretation. Paul Ricoeur has observed that 'it is very difficult to comprehend that there may be something abolished theoretically but still existent in such a way that we must rely on it in order to act'; this follows directly from his view that in so far as Marxism is a *politics* rather than (only) a *science* it must itself be ideological in Althusser's sense. Ricoeur writes: 'if politics is itself based on the assertion that human beings have certain rights, then Marxism must take something from the ideological sphere in order to accomplish something practically.'[14]

It is, in fact, on the issue of political agency that Althusser's grand systemic model has been most widely challenged, and which perhaps more than other considerations prompted his subsequent 'essays in self criticism'. As we shall see later in this chapter, his response was to reaffirm the political importance of class struggle, and although this answered those critics who felt that the system was weighted towards 'structure' at the expense of class agency, it does not offer any comfort to those interested in political agency on other than a class basis. In short, the question of political agency in struggles that are not class struggles was, at this critical juncture for Marxist thought, completely bypassed. The sorry Althusserian legacy to feminist, anti-racist or ecological politics is, simply, an implacable and doctrinal 'anti-humanism'.

One central form this anti-humanism takes is in the 'critique of the subject'. There is a problem here of overstatement and over-simplification, that can be traced directly to Althusser's own account of humanism. One does not need, having seen the errors of an overly universalistic and essentialist view of human nature, to say that there is 'thus' nothing recognisable or distinct about humans – this should be a matter for further investigation. Even those two doughty critics of humanism Paul Hirst and Penny Woolley point out: 'An *unlimited* range of human attributes and abilities is as mistaken a notion as that of a fixed and preconstituted "human nature". . . . human attributes depend on definite socially constructed techniques, practices, ac-quired competencies, and patterns of association which exclude others of the kind by their very existence.'[15]

Recent discussion of humanism, and the closely related question of how to theorise 'the subject', has tended to oversimplify the issue and to leap from a critique of the transcendental subject to dogmatic anti-humanist conclusions that are neither justified nor, eventually, useful. We may well agree with Althusser that the idea of human nature is highly contentious, though many will not agree with his view that Marx was the architect of its downfall. Many, on the contrary, have argued that Marx himself was one of the most elo-quent writers on the theme of the abilities of 'man' to transform nature, of the imaginative capacities that are distinctively human, and so on. Timpanaro, more critical of this than some others, has argued that 'triumphalism' is a problem in Marx and we may readily see that it springs from the time and place from which Marx was inevitably speaking: the heartlands of colonialism.[16] But the question of whether Marx was himself 'anti-humanist' is a secondary one here; the success of 'Althusserianism' was precisely the popularity of Althusser's ideas rather than Marx's and it is Althusser's anti-humanism and its influence that we should examine.

One introductory point to be made is that we must try to disentangle in a more measured way the issue of flaws, weaknesses and biases in the way certain ideas have been used historically from the question of their future use. For Althusser to say that Marx saw that the use of the term 'human nature' had been universalising and essentialist is one thing; to conclude that Marx was therefore theoretically anti-humanist is quite another. Yet this completely fallacious argument of Althusser, which amounts to a very powerful sleight of hand, is reproduced everywhere. We see that the phrase 'human nature' has been a problematic one and so out go both its constituent elements – at a tremendous cost. The cost is that we neither have a basis for engaging with the discourse of the 'humanistic' side nor do we have any common ground to discuss the arguments of biologists and other scientists. In practice, anti-humanism has involved not only a dogmatic refusal to engage with these arguments, but also a thoroughgoing refusal to speak boldly of anything that might be contaminated by the humanist tradition – be it morality, sexuality, pleasure, art or faith. This is far too high a price to pay for our critique.

Let us imagine the celebrated 'Cartesian subject'. He is made in the image of his inventor. He is white, a European; he is highly educated, he thinks and is sensitive, he can probably even think in Latin and Greek; he lived a bit too soon to be a bourgeois, but he has class confidence; he has a general confidence in his existence and power; he is not a woman, not black, not a migrant, not marginal; he is heterosexual and a father. (This fellow only emerged from a struggle with existential doubt, but we will ignore that as it spoils the picture.) It is entirely clear to us that this model of the subject is centred, and unified, around a nexus of social and biographical characteristics that represent power. We fully understand that in so far as this definition of the 'subject' takes that power, it is denied to others. We know from Frantz Fanon that the material subjections of colonialism involve the stunted subjectivities of an 'interior colonialisation' of the mind and a blurring of political direction. We know from Simone de Beauvoir that the full subjecthood of man is constituted at the expense of the definition of woman as 'other' and that this model of subject and other is a powerful one in our culture.[17]

Yet to conclude that the category of the subject is 'therefore' to be rejected is as ridiculous as it is impossible. Perhaps we might even take a leaf from Derrida's book and consider the ways in which the 'unified bourgeois subject' contains and reveals its own recognition of the exclusionary practices from which it can never securely escape, the anxieties that are never fully vanquished. There is more ambiguity and uncertainty in this 'centred subject' than is sometimes allowed. Furthermore, without ascribing to the view that political agency has to be driven by a completely reliable and uncomplicated internal motor (for it may well be irrational and/or unconscious in its motivation), we need to be aware that a too cavalier 'critique of the subject' *tout court* can remove the basis for thinking about social action and political agency. Hence we can and must insist that the white, male, bourgeois subject in western culture has quite wrongly been universalised, and taken as typical; at the same time we should not concede the ground of 'the subject' in the abstract or more general sense.

Here it may be helpful to note that discussions in this area employ a multitude of distinct terms that are not always clarified. We have 'the subject', 'subjectivity', 'the individual', 'the individual subject', 'the speaking/desiring subject', 'decentred subjectivity', 'subject position', 'the self' and so on. Although many of these will come into play later in this book, it might be useful to set out a few markers at this point. Roughly speaking, we can say that *the subject* is used in modern debates (particularly in Marxist and post-structuralist contexts) to refer to the model of cognitive security and confident agency that I have just been discussing. It is complicated by two factors: (1) the one I have mentioned that 'the subject' as a generality is often conflated with the historically specific 'subject' articulated in western philosophical thought and its cultural correlates, and (2) there is an ambiguity running through the use of this term around the issue of 'the subject' as a powerful agent (the subject as opposed to the object or other) and the meaning of subject as in subjection. This internal play of meaning is often significant in current uses of the term. *Subjectivity* is, on the face of it, a more descriptive term, seeking to allow us to speak of the private sense that individuals make of their experience and how this varies from content to context. The term subjectivity is to some extent popular because it includes both conscious aspects of private experience – reflection upon experiences, memories etc. – but also the unconscious and its effects; it can also encompass the vast unspoken territory of emotionality and affect. It is thus a conveniently broad term, allowing one to situate oneself at a distance from the narrow rigidities of 'consciousness' as used in classical Marxist theory and yet to speak of questions of affect and private experience that are often illegitimate in antihumanist discourse.

The individual is a more sociological term and although widely used in these debates some of its connotations are a little awkward. As Raymond Williams points out, the history of the term is complex, but modern usage reflects the developing emphasis on personal existence that came to replace feudalism's accent on a person's social place and function.[18] In capitalism there is a new stress on the individual, whether it be as the basis for labour, as direct interlocutor with God where previously the church had mediated, as consumer and protagonist of that most personal of literary forms, the novel. As well as carrying this meaning of attaching weight to personal existence, the term 'individual' has tended to create an unfortunate dichotomy between 'the individual' on the one hand and 'society' on the other. Although most sociologists would recognise this as an error, it is an indication of the persistence of ideas of a non-social, or pre-social, self. It is, in fact, largely for this reason that many try to avoid use of the word – it leads to an essentialist way of thinking about things. Hence Althusser, for example, will refer to 'concrete individuals', 'individual men and women' or 'real men' etc., but would not use the term 'the individual' with its connotations of, precisely, a universal and pre-social subject. *The individual subject* is a very unsatisfactory hybrid and is best avoided.

Two variations drawn from the work of the French psychoanalytic thinker Jacques Lacan are those of *the speaking desiring subject* and *decentred subjectivity*. They derive, however, from different periods and interpretations of his writings. The idea of a speaking subject, one who is fully inserted into the cultural, 'symbolic' order and can 'speak' its desire in the context of that plenitude, arises in conjunction with an account of the signification of 'lack' at the heart of a patriarchal culture. The idea of 'decentred' subjectivity is a subsequent interpretation, clearly geared to the critique of the 'unified' subject that we have been discussing. As we shall see later, it involves a recognition of the failures of patriarchal psychic socialisation and, to some extent anyway, a celebration of them. The term *subject position* has emerged from the Derridian stable as a means of registering an interest in the 'point of enunciation' of a particular discourse. It gestures towards the mundane data of individual biography, without conceding too much weight towards that level of interpretation: it allows us to ask what investment a speaker/writer may have in the subject in hand. As for Foucault, he has single-handedly rehabilitated the notion of *the self* albeit, as with his account of 'the body', in a manner that contradicts any assumptions of authenticity and existential integrity associated with the term.

If there has been a tendency to conflate the critique of the falsely universalised subject with that of 'the subject' in any form, this is certainly also true of 'humanism', which has both a generic and a historically specific existence. The confusion of the two has been extremely damaging. My favourite example comes from the index of Terry Eagleton's *Literary Theory*, which simply refers you to 'liberal humanism' under the entry for humanism. This is far from being a reference to a sort of tolerant humanism; it is a code word for the 'impotent' and reactionary values of the bourgeois literary canon builders of the eighteenth to twentieth centuries, whose demolition is the task of Marxist criticism.[19] In general, one might say that it has been in the cultural field, in literary, film and art criticism, that the 'anti-humanist' position has taken the greatest practical hold, to the extent that in some circles *it is assumed that* 'humanist' is a derogatory term. This is historically a great injustice, in that it ignores the immensely progressive role that humanism – as an 'ideology' – has played. In particular, one can point to the honourable tradition of humanism as a secularising force and, indeed, to its enormously important role to that end even in terms of contemporary politics. One does not have to look for long to find a humanist element in arguments against religious fundamentalism (and indeed some may find the notion of 'freedom of expression', so central to the defence of Salman Rushdie, a little too tainted by its social history for comfort). Religious fundamentalism, however, takes many forms, and we might less contentiously look to the massive revival of Christian fundamentalism in the USA – including the attempt to outlaw the teaching of evolution in schools, and the campaign to make abortion less available, for example – as an instance where we can reach for humanism as an infinitely preferable ideological and political position.

Ethnocentrism is another aspect of an intolerant rejection of humanism. How does one apply an anti-humanist position to South African politics, where the strongest card the black majority has to play, in the politico-moral arena, is an argument based on 'human rights' and 'equality' and other equally liberal humanist ideas? Antihumanism, politically speaking, may be an appropriate position to take in the context of a particular western society where 'bourgeois' democratic freedoms are historically assured, but it would be a dangerous matter to export it to the vast area of the globe where rule is secured by other means. And, as Francis Mulhern rightly says, 'our common humanity is less a heritage than a goal, and ... will be defined, in its "essential diversity", by all or by none'.[20]

Humanism as an ideology can, of course, be separated from ideas about 'human nature' which may perhaps be treated more calmly and empirically. Althusser proposed that Marx rejected a concept of 'human nature' out of hand, but Geras has offered a definitive refutation of this 'legend' and makes a convincing case that Marx continued to deploy a concept of human nature throughout his work.[21] What, in Geras's terms, 'the old Man' thought is not the main issue now. Paul Hirst and Penny Woolley have made a strong argument to the effect that attributes we may regard as human are constructs of times and places rather than essential characteristics of people. Stephen Horigan has brilliantly exposed the consequences for social thought of the conventional (but metaphysical) distinction between nature and culture, and the correlative separation of humans and animals in the social sciences.[22] Horigan's conclusion is also instructive: that we cannot move straight from a rejection of crude biologistic arguments about 'nature' to a crude sociologistic argument from 'culture' because to do so is to operate within the unhelpful framework of an assumed opposition between nature and culture. (Nowhere has this been more obvious than in the excessive sociologising of gender, now rightly challenged within feminist theory.)

Presumably we could remain open-minded as to whether evidence might come forward on the existence or otherwise of significant differences between humans and other animals. It is not necessarily a doctrinal sticking-point, although by and large there seems to be more weight on the side of those who see a continuum rather than a distinct break between the categories. In any event, the political implications are somewhat unclear and we need to interrogate the use to which such conclusions have been directed. It is interesting that the new ecological consciousness has tended to come hand in hand with the discrediting of claims about the superiority of the human. If humans have more resources and capacities than other animals, this far from legitimates the exploitation of other species, rather it behoves humans to take a greater responsibility for the well-being of the planet as a whole. These are, effectively, new political conclusions drawn from a new way of thinking about politics on a global scale. The older ways of posing these issues are, perhaps, irrelevant to them. Certainly one can suggest that Althusser's 'theoretical antihumanism', and the wholesale elimination of all the empirical debates around the issue of what a concept of 'human nature' might imply, are not helpful for this task.

Earlier in this chapter I suggested that Althusser's theoretical model might stand or fall on the question of humanism. It seems to me that Althusser did not show that Marx had a critique of 'human nature' and even less did he prove his contentious assertion that Marx's founding theoretical principle was an anti-humanist one. Considering the matter in terms of Althusser's own views (rather than the reading of Marx that he presents), I have noted a number of points concerning the difficulties that arise on taking up an unqualified anti-humanist position. I think one can argue, and I shall attempt to do so in other contexts later in the book, that a simplistic and overstated anti-humanism – whether Althusser's or the comparable variants of the thesis put forward by other writers – has been a problem that has permeated recent debates in social theory. A second major issue to which I drew attention in the preceding discussion was the problem of political agency in Althusser's system. The key point here is the way in which Althusser describes ideology in terms of an investment of will. Given that Althusser argues for a clear distinction between ideology on the one hand and knowledge on the other, the implication is to locate politics in the essentially unstable framework of the ideological.

My discussion so far has been drawn principally from the collection of Althusser's earlier essays (*For Marx*) published in the mid 1960s, and particularly focused around the issue of humanism. It is a moot point whether the framework of the Althusserian system from that period has survived – 'structures in dominance', 'articulation' 'overdetermination', 'determination in the last instance', 'social formation' and so on – either intact or at all. There are those, such as E. P. Thompson, Simon Clarke and Terry Lovell, who have argued all along that the Althusserian system was simply wrong. There are erstwhile Althusserians, such as Paul Hirst or Barry Hindess, who have arrived at a point of complete difference of opinion with the system. There are the historians of ideas (taking up the role of intellectual tombstone masons), of whom one might mention Stedman-Jones, Benton and Descombes, who have suggested that by the end of the 1960s the Althusserian project was intrinsically over. But there are also those who have sought to retain some productive aspects of the Althusserian 'problematic' and vocabulary. Of these, perhaps the most interesting are Etienne Balibar and Stuart Hall, who have adapted and used some earlier Althusserian ideas in their subsequent thinking about a much deeper and broader range of issues than Althusser himself dealt with, notably questions of nationalism, migration, race and ethnicity.[23]

ALTHUSSER'S MARX, ALTHUSSER'S LACAN

If the Althusserian engine was running out of steam at the end of the sixties it received a massive new burst of energy with the publication of what was to become known ubiquitously in English as 'the ISAs essay': 'Ideology and Ideological State Apparatuses'. The essay is divided into two parts, and the division is, I shall argue, not merely one of convenience; it reflects the profoundly divided and contradictory nature of the argument Althusser was attempting to make. In the first part of the essay Althusser advanced an idea that was to bring about a revolution in Marxist thought: the thesis that we had to understand 'reproduction', and in particular the way a social formation must reproduce itself over time, and not restrict ourselves to an analysis of production. Since classical Marxism had concentrated almost exclusively on production, in both its sociological analysis and its workplace-based political practice, Althusser's argument hit a raw nerve and exposed the obsessional 'economism' and 'productivism' that had defined European Marxism from the Second International onwards. Althusser (as ever) sought textual authority from Marx, citing an 1868 letter to Kugelmann as proof that Marx understood – but subsequent Marxists had neglected – the importance of understanding the need for a society to reproduce its conditions of production as well as simply to carry on producing.

In practice, Althusser came up with a surprisingly 'sociological' account of reproduction, focusing on the division of labour (as in the example given in an earlier chapter of the functions of the school system) and the role of the family in reproducing labour power and the 'relations of production', rather loosely defined.[24] Pursuing Gramsci's distinction between the state and 'civil society', Althusser drew a distinction between the repressive apparatuses of the state (army, police etc.) and the state's ideological apparatuses which, in his model, resembled the institutions of Gramsci's civil society: political parties, the church, education, family, media, trade unions and so on.

In the second part of the essay, which begins with the subheading 'On Ideology', Althusser elaborates the theory of ideology put forward in earlier works (ideology as the lived relationship of individuals to their historical conditions of existence) through an exposition, in a Lacanian context, of the idea of 'interpellation'. As we shall see in a moment, his argument on the question of subjectivity is best read in conjunction with the companion essay 'Freud and Lacan'. In general, in the first part of the essay we are invited to see ideology as an aspect of the reproduction of class relations in capitalism and in this second part we are invited to understand subjectivity through Freud's 'science of the unconscious'. Althusser's failure to reconcile these two perspectives, in what was to become an extraordinarily influential essay, has contributed in no small measure to a continuing divide between two traditions of work on ideology: those who see ideology as functional to the reproduction of capitalism and those who see ideology as a key to the understanding of subjectivity as an important question in its own right.

I want to take the 'social reproduction' thesis first, as it can be dealt with more briefly in the context of this book. Within Marxism generally, perhaps the most typical (non-Althusserian) response was to regard the argument as unduly functionalist – in stressing the smooth reproduction of the ideological relations of the social formation Althusser had left no room for resistance, contestation and struggle. Hence those who felt that their tireless activities, in such organisations as schools or trades unions, were politically worthwhile took exception to Althusser's account of their role as – more or less – that of cogs in the capitalist machine. Richard Johnson, criticising Althusser on this point, suggests that the term 'reproduction' is conceptualised very differently by Gramsci as 'a hard and constantly-resisted labour, a political and ideological work for capitalism and for the dominant classes, on very obstinate materials indeed'.[25]

One place where the social reproduction model was taken up enthusiastically was, paradoxically it might seem now, in feminism. In the 1970s many socialist and Marxist feminists used the theory of social reproduction, and particularly Althusser's reference to the 'school/family couple', as a means of integrating a discussion of gender and the sexual division of labour with a Marxist account of capitalism. It seemed at that point as if Marxism was, finally, going to move into a consideration of the home as well as the workplace, reproduction as well as production, the private as well as the public and so on; very detailed debates about the analysis of both wage and domestic labour in capitalist economies flourished at that time.[26]

As I have suggested elsewhere, however, the project of using an Althusserian concept of reproduction to 'explain' the position of women in capitalism is a vexed and ill-fated one.[27] In the first place, although there is an obvious link between biological reproduction and the provision of the next generation of workers (that is, the reproduction of labour power in Marxist terms), there is no necessary link between this procreative process and the division of labour or the division of the population into the class relations characteristic of capitalist production. As we know, class position is *in practice* heavily affected by birth (a sociologist's best advice to someone wanting to get rich is still 'find yourself some rich parents') but it is nevertheless *theoretically* independent of biological reproduction. Class is a purely social category, whereas the division of labour in biological reproduction has to be theorised in terms that reflect the biological component of the process as well as its social place and interpretation. So it is not clear that an interest in how capitalist societies reproduce themselves is, at any level other than the most obvious one of the biological reproduction of the population from one generation to the next, going to tell us much about how we should analyse kinship patterns, the economic organisation of households or prevailing ideologies of family and sexual mores in a given mode of production. In short, a theoretical link between biological and social reproduction is simply not made in Althusser's essay.

Looking back on the essay now, one might even ask why it had been thought that the 'social reproduction' thesis did or might imply a loosening up of an exclusive focus on social class. Perhaps the most dramatic rebuttal of this interpretation can be found in the postscript that Althusser added (written in 1970), where he excludes from his definition of what is 'social' everything except for class. Althusser literally wrote, and here I quote: '*social* (= class)'. Nothing could be clearer than this telegraphic formulation, which occurs in a passage where he is trying to demonstrate that 'the point of view of reproduction' is an abstract one, and its practical effects (its 'realisation') have to be understood in the context of production and circulation.[28] His central concern in the postscript is to redress the balance of his arguments, in response to the criticisms I mentioned earlier, so that they can be construed as having more purchase on struggle and resistance. He is keen to emphasise this factor of class struggle, as opposed to a more mechanistic approach, but in the very process of doing so he rules out a looser, less class-reductionist, interpretation of the theses on reproduction. In emphasising that the theses are about class *struggle*, he at the same time limits the reproduction argument to *class* struggle and clarifies once and for all that we are not speaking of a more general analysis of, say, the social relations of capitalism. One sentence will stand in for the many in this postscript that one could quote to demonstrate Althusser's insistence that no social division other than class is of any consequence in capitalism: 'In fact, the State and its Apparatuses only have meaning from the point of view of the class struggle, as an apparatus of class struggle ensuring class oppression and guaranteeing the conditions of exploitation and its reproduction.'[29]

I make these points not for general interest (although the misreading of the reproduction thesis in an earlier period of interpretation is interesting) but simply to show the backdrop against which we are going to have to set the second part of the essay, which deals with ideology and subjectivity. Before moving on to part II, we might note that the postscript appears in the text not as an addendum to part I, but at the end of the essay – after the discussion of subjectivity which is cast in terms of psychoanalysis. It is as if Althusser 'forgot' part II as soon as he had written it. Althusser remained locked in a conventionally class-based Marxism, which we might illustrate by looking at his footnote on 'the family'. He begins auspiciously: 'The family obviously has other "functions" than that of an ISA.' Certainly, if one is even vaguely attuned to a psychoanalytic perspective, the family's 'functions' as an arena for psychic drama and conflict, libidinal cathexes, and processes of sexed identification – among others – leap to mind rather starkly. But Althusser is thinking of something else entirely. He continues: 'It intervenes in the reproduction of labour power. In different modes of production it is the unit of production and/or the unit of consumption.'[30] Scarcely a meeting of the Marxist and psychoanalytic minds! This is simply an illustration of the extent to which, although he used some Lacanian ideas in thinking about ideology and 'the subject', Althusser remained completely unaffected by them in going about his usual theoretical business as a Marxist.

Althusser's one-sidedness is complemented by its double: Freud and Lacan do not write about class, and certainly do not organise their theories around class. They have little comment to make on any class component in subjectivity and even less on class in relation to the unconscious – which *is* the central category of their theories. This is not a 'problem' for psychoanalysis; but it certainly poses a problem for those who want to arrive at a theory that uses aspects of both Marxism and psychoanalysis. Marxism's tendency has been to think of subjectivity in the narrow terms of 'class consciousness' – not only emphasising *consciousness* rather than attaching any weight to the *un*conscious, but also understanding conscious thought and experience principally in terms of the effects of social class. Psychoanalysis, on the other hand, emphasises the unconscious as the key to understanding subjectivity, and has traditionally (though this is now more debated) cast the contents of the unconscious principally in terms of sexual difference. The 'reconciliation' of these two models is, obviously, not an easy task.

Althusser begins the second part of his essay with a parallel between himself and Freud. His approach to ideology is not only *like* Freud's to the unconscious, it is 'not unrelated' to it. The obliqueness of the reference is symptomatic of both Althusser's deference to Freud and the tendency he has to proceed by way of comparison and homology rather than in terms of the content of the argument. In fact, for him to use such a passive formulation as to say that his argument and Freud's are 'not unrelated' is extremely revealing: he cannot state the connection but he wants to claim it – using the work 'justified' twice in as many sentences – and this is an illustration of the fundamental problem with the whole thesis, as we shall see.

Althusser's first thesis is one that recapitulates the argument we have encountered before several times, and therefore we will pass over it rapidly: ideology represents the imaginary relationship of individuals to their real conditions of existence. It is worth noting, however, that Althusser does tie these conditions of existence – in the proverbial 'last instance' – to relations of production. Significantly, he prefaces this point with a statement of what would normally be the obvious, reflecting his recognition that he is about to stray a little: 'To speak in a Marxist language ...'. His formulation emerges as the conclusion that 'all ideology represents ... above all the (imaginary) relationship of individuals to the relations of production and the relations that derive from them.'[31]

Althusser's second thesis at this point – that ideology always exists in material apparatuses, and their practices and thus *its* existence is material is a more nuanced proposition than the crude 'ideology is material' slogan that emerged from early readings of the essay. He suggests that materiality has a variety of 'modalities', which are left on one side, but that we should attend to the practice and rituals of apparatuses such as schools, churches and so on.

The central thesis of this part of the essay is as follows: *Ideology Interpellates Individuals as Subjects.* Under this heading Althusser explains how he sees 'the subject' as the constitutive category of all ideology: the action of ideology is to enable/ensure the subject's recognition of itself as a subject and it is a process that works through securing the obvious. In one sense, ideology works by making the subject recognise itself in a certain specific way, and simultaneously to construe that specificity as the obvious or natural one for itself. A function of ideology is thus *recognition*, which one can think of as a circuit of recognitions – by the self and others – that both construct the subject and are predicated upon what Althusser describes as '*always already* subjects'. This is an important point to untangle, for Althusser is using a careful counterpoint here, and one might say it is merely an heuristic device for him to say that the process of recognition constitutes the subject – since he also wants to say that the process of recognition is not possible without an already constituted subject. At the least, we are speaking of an ongoing constitution and reconstitution, with no apparent finite point of origin since, as Althusser points out, the subject is positioned as such even before birth.

Althusser focused his account of the ideological constitution of the subject on the idea of 'interpellation', which is introduced in the deceptively simple terms of 'hailing' someone in the street. In the moment of acknowledging a shout of 'hey, you there!', of turning round to respond to the call, of confirmation that 'it really is he' who was hailed, the subject is both positioned in ideology and confirmed in his own recognition of himself. It is difficult to resist pointing out here the gendered aspect of Althusser's example. 'Experience shows that the practical telecommunications of hailings is such that they hardly ever miss their man: verbal call or whistle, the one hailed always recognises that it is really him who is being hailed.'[32] Many women might say that their experience of being hailed (especially by whistling!) on the street more often has the opposite effect of denying their individual identity and interpellating them in unnervingly generic terms.

Althusser uses the interpellation thesis to move towards a way of thinking about the construction of subjects that is indebted to some key ideas of the psychoanalyst Jacques Lacan. Echoing Lacan's celebrated theory of the 'mirror phase' as a crucial moment in the construction of the child's subjectivity, Althusser argues that the structure of ideology is a 'speculary' one, since there are processes of mirroring involved. The first aspect of this is the way in which individual subjects are constructed in the image of, or as reflections of, the dominant ideological Subject which, in Althusser's example of Christian religious ideology, is God. Subjects are formed, then, in a relationship of subjection to the Other, the Subject, and this relation is a speculary (mirroring) one. The whole ideological process is doubly specular, according to Althusser, since this mirror image is necessary for subjects to recognise each other and themselves *as* subjects. Finally, Althusser concludes with a characteristic mixture of a quintessentially Lacanian point – that ideology is *misrecognition* (*méconnaissance*) – but one that he casts in terms of what has to be misrecognised or ignored 'in the last resort' for the relations of production to be reproduced. Whether or not it makes sense to try and combine the insights of Lacanianism with a functionalist version of the Marxist reproduction thesis is a point I shall return to later in this chapter.

Before doing so it might be useful to discuss briefly some key points differentiating Lacan's thought from Althusser's. I have already suggested that the central Althusserian concept in this discussion is interpellation, which is not a Lacanian concept. However, Althusser's exegesis of the speculary nature of the (ideological) construction of the subject, his deployment of the subject/Subject or subject/Other distinction, and his reference to misrecognition, are all points which render his analysis one that is closely drawn from Lacan. One elementary difficulty, though, is that Althusser does not reproduce Lacan's theories in a precise way, and indeed uses many of Lacan's concepts very differently. An obvious example of this is the term 'imaginary', which can (like Laclau and Mouffe's expression 'the Jacobin imaginary') trail Lacanian resonances in Althusser but is fundamentally a different concept.

For Lacan the imaginary is one of the three orders of imaginary, symbolic and real. The 'imaginary order' includes images and fantasies, both conscious and unconscious; it is a key register of the ego and its identifications, evolving from the mirror stage but continuing in adult relationships; it particularly includes material from pre-verbal experience. The 'symbolic order', on the other hand, is the domain of symbolisation and language, and it is through the social and cultural processes of this symbolic order that the subject can represent desire and thus be constituted. The 'real' is defined as that which exists outside symbolisation, and outside the analytic experience which is necessarily contained by the limits of speech: it is that which is formally outside the subject. These three orders are all in play in Lacan's writings, although the definitions shift constantly.[33] As far as Althusser is concerned, 'imaginary' might be reduced to 'lived': it is the domain of emotion, affect, will and experience. His usage is not the everyday meaning of a fiction or mental construct ('not real'), but neither is it consistent with Lacan's distinction between imaginary, symbolic and real. Comparable issues arise if we compare Lacan and Althusser's use of the term 'real'.

A second major point of difference between Lacan's theories and Althusser's use (or misuse) of them concerns the issue of recognition and misrecognition. For although Althusser speaks of misrecognition, his entire approach is cast in terms of the process of recognition as the means by which the subject is constituted to itself and to others. His use of the vocabulary of specularity – of the process of mirroring – occurs in this context. Yet Lacan's account of the 'mirror phase' could not stress more unequivocally that the founding moment is one *mis*recognition – the whole point of his argument is to say that the infant falls for its image in the mirror because it offers a *false* representation of a whole body *Gestalt* and thus transcends the infant's own knowledge of physical dependence and psychic frustration. The pleasures of the image in the mirror, for the infant, are thus pleasures of a sense of self that is founded on a misrecognition of itself. Lacan describes the 'jubilant assumption of his specular image by the child at the *infans* stage, still sunk in his motor incapacity and nursling dependence.'[34] So there is an important gulf between the way in which Lacan developed the theory of the mirror stage – as speaking to the 'alienating destination' of the *I* as well as its mental permanence – and Althusser's use of these ideas simply as metaphors in the context of a theory that emphasises recognition rather than misrecognition.

As Althusser made clear at the end of the essay 'Freud and Lacan', he appreciated this emphasis in Lacan's account of the ego; yet it is a moot point as to how well he translated the essential instability of the Lacanian 'I' into his account of the ideological interpellation of individuals as appropriate subjects in regard to systems of production. The issue at stake is not whether Althusser properly 'understood' Lacan's focus on misrecognition, but whether he (or anyone else, indeed) could integrate such an argument into an account whose backdrop was the Marxist theory of reproduction of the relations of production. At the end of 'Freud and Lacan' Althusser's summary of Freud's discoveries – which is in effect a summary of Freud as read through the eyes of Lacan – places a significant emphasis on misrecognition in the formation of the ego: 'Freud has discovered for us that the real subject, the individual in his unique essence, has not the form of an ego, centred on the "ego", on "consciouseness" or on "existence" – . . . – that the human subject is de-centred, constituted by a structure which has no "centre" either, except in the imaginary misrecognition of the "ego", i.e. in the ideological formations in which it "recognises" itself'.[35]

This passage is qualitatively closer to Lacan than anything Althusser said in the course of the ISAs essay. The reason for the disparity is that the framework of a theory of social reproduction (particularly in the functionalist form in which Althusser had already argued the thesis) pressures one towards an account of the psychic construction of the subject that fits in with these 'requirements'. Thus, for example, Althusser spoke of subjects recognising themselves in social categories: 'It really is me, I am here, a worker, a boss or a soldier!'[36] These social categories may fit in with the Marxist framework that Althussser was operating within in the essay, but they do not correspond at any meaningful level with the content of Lacan's arguments about the ego and its identifications.

There are a number of further points that one could make to suggest that Althusser's borrowings from Lacan are highly selective. One rather light-hearted *ad hominem* example would be the issue of 'human nature'. Lacan is in general terms an anti-humanist but he suggests that the discovery of the mirror phase in human infants sprang directly from the comparison between their behavior and that of chimpanzees who appear not to recognise themselves in a comparable way. Benvenuto and Kennedy draw the obvious conclusion from Lacan's remarks: 'It might be that the chimpanzee does not recognise what he sees as his own image, unlike the child, and that this is what distinguishes the human as a subject from the animal who merely remains fascinated by reflections.'[37] It is not necessary here to go into the details of Lacan's caveats and qualifications as to what might be meant by 'nature' and so on – the irony lies in Althusser making use of a theory whose origins, according to Lacan himself, emerged from positivist human/primate comparative psychology. Irony might also figure in any Lacanian response to Althusser's view that psychoanalytic theory was 'a science' rather than speculation.[38]

More seriously, perhaps, we should address the question as to whether the theoretical paradigm within which Althusser was working is in any sense compatible with the Lacanian model as a theoretical system. Althusser himself was aware of this problem, at least at the time of writing his essay on Freud and Lacan, but many of those who felt that he had successfully brought off an introduction of psychoanalytic thought to Marxism were less deterred by the difficulty. With the advantage of hindsight the gulf between Althusser and Lacan appears now as completely unbridgeable. As an illustration of this we could take the comment Althusser made in the letter published with the English translation of his article 'Freud and Lacan'. As is often the case, the informal, contextualising style of the letter is extremely clarifying. In particular, it shows that Althusser's project is what we might now regard as an intellectually colonialist ideology is necessarily a 'class-belonging' concept, and the issue of 'humanism'. Both of these will be pursued in later chapters.

SOME 'CLASSICAL' MEDIATIONS

A number of writers in the classical tradition have proposed ways of looking at ideology that fall into neither of the two categorical extremes discussed above. Although the resolution of this problem has proved a central theme for many Marxist theorists, I propose to look – mainly just to illustrate the possibilities – at only one or two. In 1923, the same year as Lukács's *History and Class Consciousness*, Karl Korsch wrote an essay in which he dealt with the question of ideology in such a way as to carve out a position equally distanced from the two poles of the critical/descriptive debate. Korsch flatly rejects what he calls the 'vulgar-Marxism' of the Second International. He describes the 'ideology as illusion' position, with an admitted element of caricature, in the following terms: 'for vulgar-Maxism there are *three degrees of reality*: (1) the economy, which in the last instance is the only objective and totally non-ideological reality (2) Law and the State, which are already somewhat less real because clad in ideology, and (3) pure ideology which is objectless and totally unreal'.[18]

Korsch himself insists that ideologies must be grasped as 'real' and engaged with from a historical materialist theoretical position and in revolutionary struggle. He quotes approvingly the Marx of the 1985 Preface (Marx IV in chapter 1 of this book), for whom, Korsch says, under specific conditions certain mental representations can be thought of as ideological. He argues that Marx and Engels did not fall into the error of seeing either political consciousness or political philosophies as mere ideology, and in general seeks to distance Marx from the extremes of the 'critical' viewpoint. On the other hand, Korsch attacks with vigour the mechanistic 'reflection' model, suggesting that the approach that regards consciousness as an abstract reflection of material development is wholly dualistic and even 'metaphysical' rather than materialist or Marxist. Korsch proposes instead that intellectual life be understood 'in union' with consciousness as a 'real yet also ideal (or "ideological") component of the historical process in general'.[19] As such, it is a field of struggle rather than illusion that can be ignored or the inevitable manifestation of historically given class consciousness.

Korsch's resolution – if such it be – of the two varying conceptions of ideology leads us to the major contribution to these debates of the one: he wanted to harness Lacanian psychoanalysis to the project of Marxism, even to the point of renaming (although he does not say why) the founding concept of psychoanalysis. He writes: 'the suggestions at the end of the article are correct and deserve a much extended treatment, that is, the discussion of the forms of *familial ideology*, and of the crucial role they play in initiating the functioning of the instance that Freud called 'the unconscious', but which should be re-christened as soon as a better term is found.

'This mention of the forms of familial ideology (the ideology of paternity-maternity-conjugality-infancy and their interactions) is crucial, for it implies the following conclusion – that Lacan could not express, given his theoretical formation – that is, that *no theory of psycho-analysis can be produced without basing it on historical materialism* (on which the theory of the formations of familial ideology depends, in the last instance).'[39]

The passage is interesting for showing how Althusser wanted to make use of Lacanian psychoanalysis where possible within the terms of his own theory, rather than to square up to its claims in their own terms. We are now, certainly, more aware of the difficulties of attempting to do this. Althusser may have thought that Lacan 'could not' express the view that the psychic should be theorised as reducible to the social, because of his 'theoretical formation' – as if childhood measles had left him with poor eyesight; the truth of the matter is quite otherwise. Lacan himself had little hesitation in offering psychoanalytic interpretations or explanations of social behaviour and there can be no doubt that Althusser, clutching his grandiose project of historical materialism, would fall under Lacan's knowing observation that 'we place no trust in altruistic feeling, we who lay bare the aggressivity that underlies the activity of the philanthropist, the idealist, the pedagogue, and even the reformer.'[40]

The problems left in the wake of the 'Althusserian revolution' in terms of a Marxist theory of ideology seem to me to be twofold: one concerns the general way in which 'the subject' is theorised, and the other concerns the specific implications of working within a psychoanalytic framework. A number of commentators have drawn attention to the question of what general theory of agency Althusser is using in his thesis of interpellation, and indeed this has been a topic of considerable dispute. As I suggested earlier, many critics have found Althusser's account to be one that strips 'the subject' of powers of agency in its unduly mechanistic approach to the process whereby individuals are constituted as 'subjects' in a social formation.

Paul Hirst, however, has argued that Althusser was insufficiently critical of the legacy of the subject that he had inherited and suggests that he made too many presuppositions about the capacities of the nascent subject. Althusser's theory only works if, according to Hirst, we 'fill the child's cradle with anthropological assumptions'. Hirst observes that in Althusser's model the subject-to-be is, on an a priori basis and without justification, credited with certain cognitive abilities, for these are necessary for the process of recognition to operate in the speculary structure. At the root of the problem is Althusser's invocation of an 'individual' who is pre-ideological and indeed must be pre-ideological if Althusser's most fundamental thesis (that ideology is the process by which individuals are constituted as subjects) is correct. As Hirst writes: 'the "individual", who is prior to ideology and whose pre-ideological attributes of subjectivity are necessary to its becoming a subject, cannot be erased in Althusser's text'.[41] Hirst's critique draws attention to what Althusser illegitimately presumes about the 'individual', just as sociology, for instance, has often wrongly presumed the existence of individuals with certain attributes who are then socialised into social 'roles'.

It is tempting to add at this point that Althusser has given us the worst of all possible worlds in presenting a model of the subject which manages (going back to Ricoeur's point) to strip out or weaken adult powers of political agency at the same time as retaining (in Hirst's view) metaphysical and essentialist assumptions about the pre-social capacities of the individual child. Although Althusser had correctly identified a major lacuna in Marxist thinking about ideology, namely the unsatisfactory theorisation of the subject, it is hard to argue that the formulation he offered can take it significantly forward.

In rounding off this discussion of Althusser's use of Lacan, I want to take up some issues relating specifically to the implications of the fact that Lacan was a psychoanalyst rather than a social theorist. The name of Lacan is frequently cited, along with those of Derrida, Lyotard or Foucault, as an intellectual pillar of 'post-structuralist' thought and indeed his work shares some basic themes of post-structuralism, as I shall discuss in part III of the book. Yet there are dangers in assimilating his writings to this definition, and forgetting that Lacan was also a clinician and teacher whose project was to 'return to Freud'. Too heavy a post-structuralist reading of Lacan can have the effect (as I suggested in relation to the version of psychoanalysis invoked by Ernesto Laclau) of detaching Lacan from the psychoanalytic tradition so dramatically as to render his work a kind of 'post-psychoanalysis', in the sense of being both a continuation and a transcendence of psychoanalysis. In terms of psychoanalytic theory Lacan is obviously the most distant from those who operate with essentialist categories or simplistic notions of psychic cause or origin. The characteristic emphasis on mental representation in Lacanian thought has made Lacanianism the branch of psychoanalysis that is nearest to a project of cultural enquiry, and least able to defend intellectually a clear boundary between clinical and non-clinical use of the theory and ideas. Nevertheless, it would be a big mistake to detach Lacan too sharply from the historical institution of psychoanalysis – in which he had a very considerable influence[42] – and float him off as a theorist of culture and psyche.

One aspect of this has a direct bearing on Althusser. As I have suggested elsewhere, there has been recently a significant change in interpretations of Lacan as well as a significant change in the perception of whether some kind of compatibility exists between psychoanalysis and a (Marxist) theory of ideology.[43] Jacqueline Rose has argued that a concern with issues such as sexuality, and a tendency to locate (as Althusser had) psychoanalytic theory within a theory of ideology, had the effect of 'displacing' the concept of the unconscious from its rightful place at the centre of the debate.[44] Certainly one can say that there has been an increasing tendency in recent debate to offer a psychoanalytic approach as an alternative, rather than complement, to social argument and explanation. This is perhaps particularly true in Britain, where the fear of 'sociologism' infecting psychoanalysis is great, and less true in the USA, where a more pluralist and eclectic approach has tended to prevail on these matters.

Arising from the question of whether a focus on the unconscious is compatible with a more sociological approach – such as a theory of ideology – is the issue of how the contents of the unconscious are to be theorised. Of particular interest is the question of whether psychoanalytic method can be used to consider questions that have a new political resonance in social and political theory (racism, or heterosexism, or changing cultural definitions of masculinity would be good examples). Often this will involve regarding psychoanalysis as a method, rather than an accurate account of the contents of the unconscious predicated upon certain known principles, and opinion varies widely on how flexibly the system should be treated. Whilst there are obviously major differences between the various schools of psychoanalytic thought as to what these principles are (Freud and the psychic consequences of anatomical difference, Klein and the move from paranoid-schizoid to depressive positions etc.), neverthe-less none of the classic founding thinkers of psychoanalysis focuses on these newer themes I have mentioned. How much licence can be taken with their ideas, and at what point are substantive arguments about the contents of the unconscious being reduced to metaphors allowing us to consider quite other materials?

In this context there is a further debate around the issue of sexual difference. Modern readers of Althusser's writings will see im-mediately a degree of simple sexism in the way he writes, not to mention a surprisingly conventional gendered and familist vocabul-ary of, for example, theory as male. In Lacan's case, the issue of phallocentrism is a much debated one. Feminists in Britain, notably Juliet Mitchell and Jacqueline Rose, have argued strongly for a feminist interpretation of Lacan, although they have yet to respond to David Macey's eloquent critique of Lacan on precisely the charge of phallocentrism.[45] In the USA, there can be no doubt that feminist appropriations of psychoanalysis are much less seduced by the charms of the so-called 'patriarchal' tradition of Freud and Lacan, where sexual difference figures as an organising principle. There, much greater attention has been paid to variants of psychoanalytic thought where mothering as opposed to the Oedipal role of the father, or where the psychic formation of daughters rather than sons, are major concerns.[46] These issues will be taken up again in chapter 7.

It is useful to consider the historical significance of what I have called 'Althusser's Lacan'. There is, initially, the question of whether Althusser managed to deliver a plausible account of the constitution of subjectivity, combining a Marxist with a Lacanian perspective. In my view, he did not: the ISAs essay is hopelessly contradictory between its two halves and no serious resolution of the problem of how to square the 'reproduction thesis' with a Lacan-ian analysis is offered. In the essay itself, one might suggest that Althusser's use of Lacan was a very diluted one, principally because he took up certain ideas metaphorically – as in his very loose use of the vobaculary of specularity – rather than taking on board the substantive content of Lacan's arguments.

Nevertheless, Althusser's *attempt* to juxtapose these two bodies of theory was, I think, enormously important and contributed to some highly influential trends in areas such as film and cultural studies, literary theory and criticism, as well as in Marxisant branches of social science. Yet it is easy to see that there was a bifurcation in those areas of research that reflected the very split that separates the two halves of Althusser's essay. On the one hand there are those who saw the theory of the ideological state apparatuses as a means to bring back into the materialist fold some awkward areas, such as 'culture' or 'family' for example, that threatened to subvert Marxist certainties. For them, the ISAs essay provided a welcome justification for extending the scope of an economically reductionist analysis into hitherto unreachable areas of social life. For others, on the contrary, the second part of the ISAs essay seemed to be encouraging them to take up issues of subjectivity and identity – of the structures of interpellation of individuals as subjects – as important in their own right. For this category of interpretation of the essay, it was precisely Althusser's invitation to move away from a reductionist position that was attractive. Althusser's 'rise and fall' is an interesting and salutary one to study, partly no doubt because the circumstances of his 'disappearance' from the intellectual scene have contributed to the sense one has that the 'legacy' of Althusser has not been rationally assessed in the depth that it might otherwise have been.

I want to suggest that Althusser's theories, specifically with regard to ideology and subjectivity, represented a point of no return within Marxism. There is a parallel between the case of Gramsci, and Laclau and Mouffe's post-Gramscian trajectory towards 'post-Marxism' discussed in the previous chapter, and the case of Althusser. For Althusser's negotiation of some elements of 'post-structuralism' (in particular his anti-humanism and use of some aspects of Lacan's work) raised issues analogous to those raised by Laclau and Mouffe in their supersession of Gramsci. In both instances we can see that an attempt to surmount *from within* the tensions and weaknesses of the Marxist theory of ideology has shown the non-viability of the original paradigm.

Althusser had inherited a Marxist theory of ideology with certain characteristic weaknesses.

First, it tended to see ideology in terms of conscious belief systems, whereas a theory was needed that would loosen this 'rationalist' basis. It was necessary to consider subjectivity more generally, including unconscious as well as conscious processes, and to analyse personal experience and perceptions as well as cultural and symbolic systems. It was also desirable to extend the analysis of ideology into the operation of institutions and practices – such as schools or the media, for example. Althusser's influence on both these trends in Marxism was immense.

Secondly, the dominant view in Marxism had been to operate with a theory of ideology as illusion, or distortion. Although in theory Althusser mobilised a crude distinction between ideology and science, his own substantive theses on ideology are considerably more sophisticated, in that they attempt to explore ideology as a 'lived' or historical relation to conditions of existence.

Thirdly, Marxism had tended to tie the analysis of ideology to social class, and on this Althusser is yet more contradictory. As I have suggested above, in even introducing the ideas of Lacan he made a fundamental break with the 'class-belonging' assumptions about ideology in Marxism, but in so far as he sought continually to recuperate a class-reductionist model and to turn Lacanianism to a historical materialist purpose, he undermined his own radical break.

In general terms, I would argue that Althusser's theses on ideology and subjectivity expose the impossibility of going back to the earlier, classical model within Marxism. But they leave unsolved a number of fundamental problems, suggesting the conclusion that a different way out of the impasse is essential. In part III of the book, I shall consider the attempts that have been made to circumvent the 'classical' Marxist approaches to ideology – a task for which the term 'discourse' has proved a key instrument.

SUBJECTIVITY

I want to turn now to subjectivity in general, as it seems to me that although there has been considerable (and sometimes, it must be said, confusing) attention paid to 'the subject' in debates around ideology, there is much more that might be said with regard to how we understand different aspects of the question of subjectivity. This, in some ways, is a massive lacuna in Marxism, and one which not only has had its effects in terms of a crude understanding of political agency and consciousness but has stood in the way of a broader consideration of experience, identity, sexuality, affect and so on. As will readily be noted, the 'new social movements' have all attached much more importance to issues to do with subjectivity, and the politics of personal life and the self, and this only serves to highlight the particular refusal of Marxism to deal with these questions.

Much of what I have to say here will concern psychoanalysis, which I think has raised the most interesting questions – and the most difficult debates – about subjectivity. But before doing this I want to mention one important line of thought that may help to situate the consideration of subjectivity in a historical context. First, there is the recent interest in, and a fascinating web of ideas woven around, Marcel Mauss's 1938 lecture entitled 'A Category of the Human Mind: The Notion of Person; the Notion of Self'. Mauss traces the history of the notion of person back to the Latin (or Etruscan) for an actor's mask, suggesting that (from the Greek) the notion of 'person' carried the meaning of the individual, stripped of his mask, while at the same time retaining the sense of the artificial. As Foucault was later to elaborate in *The Care of the Self*, Mauss also suggested that this 'person' became increasingly moralised and given a metaphysical basis as Greek culture gave way to Christianity. Thus evolved the modern self, consciousness, the Cartesian subject, the self of reason and morality, which Mauss regarded as a 'great posses- sion to defend'. It is irritating that Mauss, now cited so enthusiasti- cally for having shown the historical and cultural specificity of the modern 'self', should have been so embarrassingly 'modernist' in his defence of the now reviled autonomous subject: 'Each of us has our "self" (moi), an echo of the Declaration of the Rights of Man ....'[47]

Interest in the Mauss lecture includes the use of it in Paul Hirst and Penny Woolley's *Social Relations and Human Attributes* and a seminar series published as *The Category of the Person*. It speaks to a more general awareness that we need to understand further the consequences of western individualism in relation to 'our' thinking about subjectivity. Niklas Luhmann, for example, has taken the extreme position of rejecting (in print at least) even a residual notion of a fragmented or decomposed self, arguing that 'there is no dual or even pluralistic self, no "I" distinct from "me", no personal identity distinct from social identity. These conceptions are late nineteenth century inventions, without sufficient foundations in the facts of consciousness.'[48] In a much less anti-humanist vein, Ian Hacking has discussed the philosophical implications of new anti-essentialist ways of thinking about the historical emergence of identities, for example 'the homosexual role'. Hacking concluded that a 'dynamic nominal- ism' would allow us to see the force of historical labels enabling certain identities – but also to regard the individuals concerned as capable of becoming autonomous of them.[49]

A key point in all this is the issue of how to theorise the import- ance of a subjectivity (whether in terms of the self, or individualism or whatever) that we know to be both experientially powerful but historically and culturally circumscribed. Marcel Mauss rightly noted that the particular conception he was discussing of the moral self 'is formulated only for us, among us' – but sunk into startling ethno- centrism when he commented that throughout 'the Orient' ('which has not yet attained the level of our sciences') its value was questioned.[50]

While in more stable societies it was possible to ignore the extent of cross-cultural difference on matters such as identity, subjectivity and the self, the contemporary world – in which one might plausibly suggest that migration is *the* twentieth-century experience – allows no such insulation. The question of ethnic difference poses itself as a major interrogator of the very categories with which 'we' operate and the very objects that 'we' are attempting to study. Clearly, too, differences of gender identity, sexual preference and behaviour, of parenthood and age, serve to mark out the subject in ways that are, as Foucault might have said, both systematic and discontinuous.

This problem is not necessarily fatal. We have to recognise both that the phenomena of which we speak are historically specific, and bound, culturally and in other ways, *and* that they are not by that token any the less immediately important. A parallel problem has existed in thinking about 'art' – than which nothing could be so subjectively or experientially 'moving' for many people but which, as we know, is a relatively recent invention.[51] Peter Bürger has, in fact, lucidly made the connection between these two in reference to Hegel's aesthetics: there is a link between the rise of 'autonomous subjectivity' and romantic art, an art of subjective inwardness and external contingency.[52]

We may decide from these debates that a position such as Luhmann's would be unduly voluntaristic. Steven Lukes has concluded that 'there is an individualist mode of thought, distinctive of modern Western cultures, which, though we may criticise it in part or in whole, we cannot escape. It indelibly marks every interpretation we give of other modes of thought and every attempt we make to revise our own.'[53] Whether an awareness of the relative character of 'our' modes of thought will enable them and us to become genuinely pluralist is still a matter for speculation.

PSYCHOANALYSIS

In thinking about subjectivity – and especially in the context of a critique of universalising theories – the most telling issues of contemporary debate concern psychoanalysis. The debates on Freud's universalism are a good place from which to begin a consideration of psychoanalysis as an account of subjectivity. Andrew Ross has recently suggested that 'both Marxism and psychoanalysis have come to share a similar fate: each has been stripped, finally, of their pseudo-scientific status as discourses of *universality*'.[54] (This is something of a polemic opening shot, however, for Ross goes on to discuss the complex character of Freudianism with regard to rationality and positivism, and inclines generally to a more 'Lacanian' reading of Freud than the quotation implies.)

Psychoanalysis is an extremely contested area on the issue of universalism. One can describe psychoanalysis as highly reductive in its operations – it tends to explain or interpret phenomena in psychic terms even where other explanations are equally plausible and, indeed, psychoanalysis classically 'interprets' any other explanation as 'resistance' to its own truths. (In this sense its *style* of explanation could be compared with Marxism's, which is economically rather than psychically reductionist.) There is, however, considerable tension within psychoanalysis, and between different traditions within psychoanalysis, between a psychically reductionist approach and a more pluralist, or relativist, model.

Several aspects of these debates are relevant to my concern here with subjectivity. Perhaps the easiest to despatch – for the moment – is the traditional debate in the Freudian tradition over the 'universality' of the Oedipus complex: suffice it to say that in these terms the psychoanalytic claim is a fairly universalistic one, and if the configuration can be recast as a cultural or mythic one, rather than a familial one, it still tends to retain a trans-historical aura.[55]

More important, in terms of thinking about the basis of subjectivity, in more general terms, is the debate over what theory or model of 'the subject' psychoanalysis (particularly read in terms of the ideas of its founder, Freud) operates with. Here, psychoanalysis is distinctively antiessentialist and deconstructive of the 'Cartesian subject': the founding insight of the theory being the limitations of reason, rationality and consciousness and the powerful role played in our subjectivity by the unconscious, repressed and irrational material that in our conscious selves we do our best to disguise. Thus one main point that one would want to make of psychoanalysis, in all its variants, in this context, is that it is profoundly demystifying of the concept of a 'subject' as a conscious, 'centred' and fully capable agent. Having said this, however, one could go into considerable debates within and around psychoanalysis and, in particular, within the Lacanian school as to how far this demystification should go. In comparison with Derrida, and other post-structuralists of the anti-humanist anti-subject school of thought, Lacan posits a subject very clearly.[56] As I have suggested elsewhere, a reading of Lacan in which the psyche is cast principally in terms of fluidity, flexibility and fragmentation is a somewhat stretched reading of a thinker yet remains within the general rubric of 'psychoanalysis' (rather than an exponent of the cultural theory of 'post-psychoanalysis').[57]

A plausible position on the status of the subject in psychoanalysis is instantiated in two arguments that I want to refer to briefly here. Cornelius Castoriadis (author of *The Imaginary Institution of Society* and a practising psychoanalyst) has recently suggested that 'the subject has not just returned, for it never left' and in the context of his discussion of this general issue makes a very useful point. He argues that psychoanalysis, as a therapeutic practice, is predicated upon some version (however attenuated) of the subject in that the answer to the analyst's question of 'who hears' the interpretation and makes sense of it must be an analysand with some of the properties of a 'subject'. The analysand presupposed in the analysis, Castoriadis insists, must be viewed neither as the individual ('the citizen, the social individual lying on the couch'), nor as a non-subject ('substrate or immaterial substance'). The invisible subject is *presupposed* as having 'emergent capacity to gather meaning and to make of it something for him/herself'; in these capacities of gathering and reflecting upon meaning the 'subject' in psychoanalysis is congruent with Castoriadis's more general approach to the subject. To the question as to whether one can find more unity to the singular human being than its bodily identity and chronological history he asserts that not only is there a singularity to each psyche, but that there is a unity to which we do and should aim: 'the unity of reflective self-representation and of the deliberate activities one undertakes'.[58] Castoriadis offers here a different and perhaps more useful approach than Foucault's consideration of one's *rapport à soi* (relationship with oneself).

Paul Ricoeur has tellingly described the Freudian subject as a 'wounded Cogito'. Towards the end of his monumental interpretation of Freud Ricoeur writes: 'it is a wounded Cogito that results from this adventure – a Cogito that posits itself but does not possess itself'. Although Ricoeur rescues more of the essential Cogito than one might wish ('a Cogito that sees its original truth only in and through the avowal of the inadequacy, illusion and lying of actual consciousness'[59]) his position is instructive in showing that one may demystify the claims of the universal or transcendent subject without totally abandoning either a capacity for agency or a sense of subjective coherence.

The issue of the 'universalism' of psychoanalysis can be aired in a variety of ways (the universality or historical specificity of the Oedipus complex, the status of the transcendental subject and so on); it is also useful to think in a very general way about psycho-analysis and the issue of epistemological relativism. In chapter 7 I argue that one should, in relation to Marxism and the theory of ideology, try to recast 'relativism' more positively, as a critique of ethnocentrism and cultural boundedness, and at this point it might be helpful to consider the implications of transferring this argument on to psychoanalysis. No doubt this would meet with a certain amount of resistance, but I want to suggest that this relativisation of psychoanalysis could be thought of as a step forward rather than a defensive posture.

In saying this I should make my position clear on two basic points. The first is that the insights of psychoanalysis with regard to the unconscious, repression, fantasy, sexuality and so on are not merely 'within the true' of psychoanalytic discourse but play an important part in the way in which people in contemporary western societies now understand themselves. Giddens has referred to the 'double hermeneutic' in which members of a society use sociological knowl-edge in their decisions and activities,[60] and this idea can be illus-trated in terms of the use that people make of psychoanalysis in their lives. To say that we live in the west in a therapeutic culture, where people interpret, reflect upon and to some extent change their be-haviour in the light of psychoanalytic ideas (and, for some, therapy) is not to say that these ideas are not 'true': it is to understand the contextuality of their truth. So, it is not a case of being for or against psychoanalysis (though if it were I would be 'for'), but of recognising that in certain times and places – and I am now writing from one of them – psychoanalytic concepts are rooted in the culture.

Secondly, it follows from this that psychoanalysis is not simply a set of ideas, which are or are not 'true': it is also a set of clinical practices, professional protocols, social networks and institutions, educational and intellectual projects and a modest publishing indus-try. (As Jean-Jacques Lecercle has mischievously said, 'psychoanaly-sis is the only theory which says you have to spend money to make it work'.[61] If one looks at psychoanalysis *only* from this point of view (as a social institution rather than as also a body of ideas) as Foucault has tended to, and Deleuze and Guattari, one is likely to arrive at a very critical position.[62]

In this context it is interesting to consider the strange relationships now obtaining between psychoanalysis as a clinical practice and what of psychoanalysis has been appropriated in recent years in the academy – a method and agenda for literary and cultural 'reading'. Richard Feldstein and Henry Sussman have pointed out that many literary critics who base their work on psychoanalysis would be horrified if a requirement for their practice was some experience of analytic therapy, since they often view 'the clinic' as 'analytical mastery masquerading as a privileged place of praxis'. These authors refer to this as a gap between 'the mind and the page', between psychoanalysis as an institution in which patients who suffer seek treatment and psychoanalysis (increasingly what they call an 'inchoate poetics' of post-psychoanalysis) as an interest in language and the 'textualisation' of the mind.[63] On the other hand, we also know of many who have gone in the other direction, from an interest in the ideas of psychoanalysis to the pursuit of clinical practice.[64] These trends are indicative of the complex relationship between psychoanalysis in clinical terms and the way it exists outside the boundaries of the therapeutic. But we would do well to take a general cue from Foucault and insist that the 'ideas' cannot be floated away by cultural critics from the institutional presence of psychoanalysis, since to do so is to neglect their imbrication with power.

There are two aspects of a possible 'relativising' of psychoanalysis that I want to mention here, in conclusion of this discussion. The first aspect would be to recognise the need for a greater pluralism in the way in which psychoanalysis operates. Psychoanalysis has tended towards a rather 'colonialist' style of explanation, in so far as it has encoded – whether necessarily or not is a matter of great debate – values into its account of not merely the psyche but questions of sexuality, parenting and so on. In short, Foucault's dismissal of psychoanalysis as a 'normalising' discourse has some substance to it.[65] One can readily give examples of the 'normalising' function of psychoanalysis, some of them rather clichéd, perhaps – but none the less salient political issues. Psychoanalysis as a professional establishment has endorsed the desirability/necessity of heterosexuality to the extreme point that individuals whose sexual choice and practice is homosexual are formally (although not openly) barred from the major training institutions of British psychoanalysis. (A ban that does not apply to other forms of sexual 'perversion'.) This is merely one rather dramatic instance of the 'normalisation' function of psychoanalysis, but one which would point to the desirability of a more pluralist position. Another example that is often given is what Deleuze and Guattari call 'the incurable familialism of psychoanalysis': they suggest that the exclusive emphasis on the Oedipal triangle and the family as the origin of the psyche blinds psychoanalysis to the role non-familial events play in the constitution of the unconscious. In a radical displacement of any known psychoanalytic account of what the unconscious represses (but not, note, a displacement of the concept of the unconscious itself) Deleuze and Guattari say: 'the rise of fascism, Stalinism, the Vietnam war, May '68 – all these things form complexes of the unconscious, more effective than everlasting Oedipus'.[66] The point here, to employ a distinction that Mary McIntosh and I used in *The Anti-social Family*, is not that psychoanalysis overtly preaches 'familism' as a good thing (although it may do on occasion) but that its entire frame of reference is locked into the assumption that all interpretation proceeds from the centrality of 'original' family experiences and thus its operation is deeply 'familialist' in the sense that it cannot imagine anything else.[67]

These two examples, of heterosexism and familialism, are classic ones in debates over the normalising aspects of psychoanalysis. To take a more relativist position on psychoanalysis in the light of them would involve *either* redrawing the relevant concepts and arguments to eliminate or minimise the problem, *or* accepting that this was a political position from which psychoanalysis self-consciously spoke. What one cannot do is to continue to regard a psychoanalysis with such direct allegiances as a neutral discourse.

A second, somewhat more positive, relativising project with psychoanalysis has begun with recent work on how to rethink psychoanalytic ideas about the self in a context that also admitted the salience of the social. Until comparatively recently, when things seem to be shifting somewhat, there has been a tendency to divide up the field, psychoanalysis ceding interpretation of social and economic 'macro' events to social scientists, but hanging on to a purely psychic account of the self. This may have been a reaction against the rather amateurish attempts by Freud in the field of cultural history, sociology and anthropology. In an earlier epoch, however, Freud's ambition to explain psychoanalytically phenomena of a cultural, religious or aesthetic kind was viewed less critically – Ricoeur saw this as the step which lifted Freud's interpretation to a 'global and sovereign . . . world view'. 'After the analogy,' he continues, '. . . the gaze of the eagle.'[68] Psychoanalysis, perhaps because of these rather grandiose earlier projects, has stepped back from such a confident theorising of the social, but it has tended to insist that the self can be understood solely in terms of the psychic. This is now under some scrutiny, as recent work on the self in its social context will indicate.

From the eagle's position within psychoanalysis, this project is, of course, somewhat contaminated by 'sociologism'. I will confine myself to two examples of these new discussions.

Nancy Chodorow has suggested that one can counterpose the 'autonomous self' of classical Freudian analysis with the 'relational self' of object relations theory and practice. In psychic terms she notes that the self reconstructed in object relations theory is not focused on the defences, boundaries, separation and autonomy of the self that concern orthodox Freudianism, but understands an inner core of the self, which is created through 'internalised self-other representations'. This self is not only constructed relationally, it is 'intrinsically social': able to recognise others as selves too and attain 'the intersubjectivity that creates society'. Chodorow notes that the Freudian drive-determined model of the self goes hand in hand with an abstract and universalist view of the self, whereas the relational model 'derives from an appropriation and interpretation of experienced relationships and accordingly varies by individual, culture, period, gender and so forth'.[69] This amounts to a revision of, but from within, psychoanalytic theory, in which the interaction of the psychic and the social is productively acknowledged.

My second example is taken from a different standpoint, and one much less 'within' psychoanalysis. John Brenkman has crisply drawn attention to a central problem with what he sees as Lacan's failure to fully reground Freud's theory of sexuality and sexual identity in a cultural, social framework. The reason for this, suggests Brenkman, is that Lacan 'conceives of *culture* without reference to *society*; that is, he conceives of culture only in terms of language and discourse'. Brenkman himself insists that 'the cultural mediations required for the subject to assume his or her sexual identity and sexual behaviour are bound up with social institutions whose logic and function are tied to the total organisation of society at a determinate historical moment, and bound up with those cultural codes, like the sex-gender system, which are the vehicle of economic as well as sexual domination'.[70]

What is needed at this juncture is a renewed effort to attempt the difficult task of squaring up the claims of a theory such as psychoanalysis with a more social approach. What is not needed is a redoubled theoretical colonialism, in which sociologists deny the power of psychic processes while psychoanalytic theorists claim psychic causes of, for example, economic or military behaviour.

I have concluded with this lengthy epilogue about psychoanalysis for two reasons: first, because it is the place one might reasonably start to correct the lamentable lack of attention paid to subjectivity within Marxism's theory of ideology, and second, because psycho-analysis has shared the universalistic pretensions of Marxism. The project of 'relativising' such discourses, or injecting a more respectful pluralism into them, is not a conservative one. Classical Marxism, and classical psychoanalysis, obviously had – and to a lesser extent still have – an enormous radical force. But, in both cases, their cultural boundedness and failure to recognise their own limitations must be challenged.

Part III

The Politics of Truth

6

History, Discourse, 'Truth' and Power: Foucault's Critique of Ideology

Michel Foucault, in a much quoted response to a question posed by an interviewer, has provided a neat summary of what is wrong with the concept of ideology. Asked whether he thought that behind the concept of ideology lay 'nostalgia for a quasi-transparent form of knowledge, free from all error and illusion', Foucault replied as follows:

> The notion of ideology appears to me to be difficult to make use of, for three reasons. The first is that, like it or not, it always stands in virtual opposition to something else which is supposed to count as truth. Now I believe that the problem does not consist in drawing the line between that in a discourse which falls under the category of scientificity or truth, and that which comes under some other category, but in seeing historically how effects of truth are produced within discourses which in themselves are neither true nor false. The second drawback is that the concept of ideology refers, I think necessarily, to something of the order of a subject. Thirdly, ideology stands in a secondary position relative to something which functions as its infrastructure, as its material, economic determinant, etc. For these three reasons, I think that this is a notion that cannot be used without circumspection.[1]

These three issues will be dealt with in some detail later on in this chapter. For the moment it is enough to note that Foucault rejects the concept of ideology because (1) it is implicated, as the other side of the coin, in unacceptable truth claims, (2) it rests on a humanist understanding of the individual subject and (3) it is enmeshed in the unsatisfactory and determinist base-and-superstructure model within Marxism.

'Post-structuralist' critiques of the theory of ideology, of which Foucault's remarks have now become an exemplar, have commonly developed the concept of 'discourse' as the focus of an alternative theoretical model. Naturally, however, one cannot simply substitute the one for the other, leaving the surrounding ideas and concepts unchallenged: to understand the scope and significance of the shift from ideology to discourse in social theory, one has to assess the developing uses of the term discourse in their broader contexts. This, it may be said, is not necessarily an easier task than that of unravelling the various and contradictory uses of the term ideology (even in the work of one writer, as chapter 1 showed for the case of Marx).

TEXTUALITY

At the outset it is important to clarify two separate tendencies in modern social and cultural theory, whose confusion and conflation has muddied the waters of these debates. For simplicity at this point I shall call these the issues of *textuality* and discursivity. Under the heading of *textuality* one could summon up a movement within literary and cultural theory and in philosophy towards the revaluation and revalorisation of the text *as text* rather than as pale reflection of some prior reality. An emphasis on the importance of the text – its 'writerliness', textuality, sensuality, literarity and so on – can take many forms. Many traditional, as well as recent, forms of literary, art and film criticism concern themselves principally with the object of study as a 'text' to be engaged with in its *own* terms rather than something to be explained with reference to external factors such as historical, social or biographical 'context'. The balance between, and conflicting claims of, 'text' and 'context' has been much debated in such disciplines over the years in a variety of arenas.

It would be hard to dispute that the claims of 'the text' have been raised in recent years, and the most basic point underlying this change is a new apprehension of the character of language. The key figure, as far as cultural theory is concerned, was Roland Barthes. His argument that all writing was text, despite the superficial appearances that led us to recognise 'textuality' only where it paraded itself and to ignore it in writing that claimed the spurious legitimation of the cleric or pedagogue, has been well taken. Hence 'writerliness' (just as 'painterliness') may be a variable aspect of a text, but all forms of writing have a style.[2] At the root of this position lay the understanding that language is not a medium for the transmission of content – it is not 'transparent' in such a way as to convey its contents without interference: on the contrary, language *is* the producer of meaning. This idea has been taken to a more radical conclusion in the work of Jacques Derrida, for whom, for example, there is 'no such thing' as a summary or a translation – merely 'another' text.[3]

As may readily be seen, these arguments are profoundly subversive of traditional knowledge claims, and they challenge conventional distinctions between 'academic' and 'creative' writing and between 'fact' and 'fiction'. Their influence is evident not only in literary critical studies, where the practice of textual deconstruction (unravelling the traces of meaning buried in the text's operations) has become highly popular, but also in disciplines such as philosophy and history. What is sometimes referred to as 'the linguistic turn' in history is clearly allied to the recent movement towards a greater emphasis on textuality: archives are examined as producers of historical, cultural meaning in their own right rather than as 'sources' of information about another, more social 'reality' that is the traditional goal of the historian's labours. Legal documents or medical records are scrutinised as texts in themselves, rather than as conduits to forms of knowledge that can be expressed in terms of a linear historical narrative for which such sources give the 'evidence'. This raises some interesting epistemological problems, to which I will revert later. In philosophy the issue of textuality has been equally subversive, given the conventions (in the 'Anglo' tradition particularly) of subordinating language to the role of the silent vehicle for the clearest possible expression of meaning. Against this, Derrida's philosophical works – in their positive 'untranslatability', their intricate and relentless plays of language, and the visual representation on the page of their writerliness – announce, in what is called the 'performative' aspect of writing, their textuality and hence the contingent nature of any 'truth' contained within them.

Common-sense definitions of 'discourse'   An advantage of making a distinction between a new emphasis on 'textuality' and the realm of the 'discursive' as elaborated by Foucault is that it enables us to see the difficulties of regarding 'discourse' simply as the text, or spoken word, or as language in the sense of communication. These relatively 'common-sense' meanings of discourse come to mind easily from the vocabulary of a 'discourse' or 'treatise' on a particular subject. The *Oxford English Dictionary*, for example, lists the following among the meanings of 'discourse': to talk, converse, discuss; to speak or write at length on a subject; a talk, a narrative. The French is similar – *discours* is given in the dictionary as 'talk, speech, address, dissertation, language' etc. But in relation to contemporary theoretical

debates, these historical meanings of the term are of limited use to us.
The emphasis on textuality in Barthes, Derrida and other writers
(sometimes wrongly or loosely invoked as 'discourse theory') is very
different from the attempts that Foucault and others have made to
describe a theory of discourse, or discursive formations, in a more
social context – but it is important to remember that *neither* of these
schools of thought use discourse in the common sense or 'dictionary'
sense given above.

FOUCAULT'S CONCEPT OF DISCOURSE

Although many contemporary writers and theorists now employ a
vocabulary centred on the concept of 'discourse', it is in the work of
Foucault that we should look for the most original, monumental,
general theory as to why this theoretical lexicon is preferable to that
of ideology, social formation, class and so on. (The irony that
Foucault himself would repudiate most of the words I have used
above should not escape us, but I will return to this problem later.)

In direct contrast to the concerns associated with 'textuality',
Foucault's use of the concept of discourse, and of what we could call
discursivity in general, is very much related to *con*text. Let us take
one example. In drawing a distinction between language and discourse, Foucault writes in such a way as to focus our attention on a
crucial aspect of context: 'The question posed by language analysis of
some discursive fact or other is always: according to what rules has a
particular statement been made, and consequently according to what
rules could other similar statements be made? The description of the
events of discourse poses a quite different question: *how is it that one
particular statement appeared rather than another* [my italics]?'[4] This is,
perhaps, the most important general point to grasp about Foucault's
concept of a discourse: it enables us to understand how *what* is said
fits into a network that has its own history and conditions of existence (albeit very different ones from the categories that historians or
philosophers or other academics have traditionally used). Edward
Said, summarising Foucault's work in a memorial essay, characterises it with the example that 'what enables a doctor to practise
medicine or a historian to write history is not mainly a set of
individual gifts, but an ability to follow rules that are taken for
granted as an unconscious a priori by all professionals'. 'More than
anyone before him,' claims Said, 'Foucault specified rules for those
rules, and even more impressively, he showed how over long periods

of time the rules became epistemological enforcers of what (as well as how) people thought, lived, and spoke.'[5]

Foucault's concept of discourse is formally explained in his major methodological work *The Archaeology of Knowledge*, although his arguments there will probably find more resonances in readers who are familiar with any of his remarkable historical narratives – *The Birth of the Clinic, Madness and Civilisation, Discipline and Punish*, the *History of Sexuality* and so on. Foucault begins by despatching the claims of taken-for-granted categories for thinking about discursive unities – such as book, *œuvre*, tradition, genre or discipline – and insists that the building blocks of analysis must be a 'pure description' of the discursive field, whose most significant units are 'statements', both written and spoken.[6] Naturally there is a certain amount of discussion in the literature as to what is involved in Foucault's 'statements', and Dreyfus and Rabinow, for example, argue convincingly that Foucault is not interested in all statements (what philosophers such as Austin and Searle call everyday speech acts) but only in a subset of statements which have some autonomy and contain truth claims (akin to the notion of 'serious speech acts').[7] Foucault's 'statements' are not propositions, or sentences, and he explains that the *enunciative function* (which is contextual) can differentiate one statement from another even where in grammatical terms its propositional content might be the same. His example of how to think of a statement is much quoted: he suggests that the letter sequence AZERT on a French typewriter keyboard is not a statement, whereas the presentation of this layout in a typing manual, as 'the alphabetical order adopted by French typewriters', is.[8]

Gilles Deleuze has satirically likened the 'Azert' discussion to a story by Gogol, casting Foucault as the 'new archivist': 'He will ignore both the vertical hierarchy of propositions which are stacked on top of one another, and the horizontal relationship established between phrases in which each seems to respond to one another. Instead he will remain mobile, skimming along in a kind of diagonal line that allows him to read what could not be apprehended before, namely statements.'[9] One might, perhaps, gloss this to mean that although *The Archaeology of Knowledge* is a fascinating methodological essay – shot through with characteristically Foucauldian 'surprises' and challenges to the fine details of one's intellectual assumptions – there is a sense in which Foucault's own achievements when 'skimming along' and selecting some statements rather than others remain unexplained by the formal method he outlines.

If 'statements' are the molecular unit, what creates the discursive unity of statements that Foucault would want to call a 'discourse' or, more precisely, a 'discursive formation'? In general, Foucault theorises the discursive field as characterised by 'systems of dispersion' and it is the systematicity of these dispersions that forms the basis of the discursive regularities that he wishes to study. This is explained with reference to the example of a group of statements conventionally called 'medicine', 'economics' or 'grammar'. Foucault speculates about where their unity as a group of statements lies – what makes a statement belong to one group rather than another. He rejects various possibilities – there are no well-defined objects, or definite normative statements, or continuous themes – and concludes that one finds instead various incompatible themes, series with gaps in them, heterogeneous levels of analysis and so on. And hence, he says, follows the idea of studying these dispersions themselves, to discover whether 'one cannot discern a regularity: an order in their successive appearance, correlations in their simultaneity, assignable positions in a common space, a reciprocal functioning, linked and hierarchised transformations'. It is in the discovery of regularities in the dispersions of statements in a discursive field that Foucault locates the concept of 'discursive formation' (often cast more simply as 'discourses'). To quote: 'Whenever one can describe, between a number of statements, such a system of dispersion, whenever, between objects, types of statement, concepts, or thematic choices, one can define a regularity (an order, correlations, positions and functionings, transformations), we will say, for the sake of convenience, that we are dealing with a *discursive formation.*'[10]

It is worth emphasising at this point that although Foucault begins from a critique of conventional 'unities of discourse', stressing the dispersion and discontinuities to be found in the discursive field, ultimately his project was to expose and redraw *different* unities and regularities – as indeed can be seen from the influence his work has had on historical understanding of mental illness, punishment, sexuality and so forth. He is not a theorist of dispersion, contingency and heterogeneity *tout court* and described himself as 'flabbergasted' when the French reference book *Petit Larousse* defined him as 'a philosopher who founds his theory of history on discontinuity'. ('No doubt,' he reflected, 'I didn't make myself sufficiently clear ....')[11] Perhaps one might also add at this point that there is a world of difference between the detailed historical researches that Foucault himself undertook when seeking to recast our understanding of particular discourses (medical, penal, sexual etc.) and the extremely superficial relabelling that often goes on in which, for example, sociology becomes 'sociological discourse' without any substantive elaboration of what the discursive ordering and regularities might be.

Foucault's concept of discourse is embedded in a theoretical system (however anti-systematic) that has at one and the same time involved the explicit rejection of the categories of classical Marxism – particularly the vexed concept of ideology – and offered the most fully elaborated, and deployed, alternative. It is impossible to get the measure of his concept of discourse without relating it to these broader issues, which I propose to treat here under the following headings: (1) issues concerned with the sociological and historical context of discourse, particularly the problem of determinism, (2) issues concerned with epistemology, and the question of knowledge, truth and power, and (3) issues concerned with the definition of the subject, agency, the self and ethics.

It is, of course, no coincidence that these headings take us back (as I shall show) to the specific objections Foucault himself raised against the concept of ideology and it can be seen that this shift from ideology to discourse lies at the heart of a much broader theoretical transformation.

Foucault and the problem of determination

DISCOURSE AND THE NON-DISCURSIVE

Initially, in considering Foucault's position on the issue of determinism, it is clearest to look at an essay where, in response to questions generated by *The Order of Things* (as the English translation of *Les Mots et les Choses* is entitled), he makes a crisp differentiation between three aspects of 'the play of dependencies'. Foucault there distinguishes dependencies which are:

intradiscursive (between the objects, operations, concepts within one discursive formation);

interdiscursive (between different discursive formations, for example, the correlations discussed in *The Order of Things* between natural history, grammar etc.);

extradiscursive (between discursive and non-discursive transformations, for example, the correlations studied in *Madness and Civilisation* and in *The Birth of the Clinic* between medical discourse and a whole play of economic, political and social changes').

In an obvious reference to the determinist base/superstructure model in Marxism, Foucault adds: 'I would like to substitute this whole play of dependencies for the uniform, simple notion of assigning a causality; and by suspending the indefinitely extended privilege of the cause, in order to render apparent the polymorphous cluster of correlations.'[12] Foucault believed that the concept of ideology was irretrievably contaminated by the unilinear economic determinism characteristic of Marxism.

To those who see all forms of 'post-structuralism' as a rampant idealism in which all non-discursive social phenomena are obliterated, one should emphasise here the unequivocal distinction Foucault made between discourse and extradiscursive social practices. The way in which he thought of the relations between the discursive and the non-discursive, and the values he attached to them, are, however, profoundly different from the conventions of Marxism. In *The Archaeology of Knowledge* he elaborated a view that one might summarise, a little polemically, as the production of 'things' by 'words'. Discourses are composed of signs, but they do more than designate things, for they are 'practices that systematically form the objects of which they speak'. In a neat reversal of the classical materialist hierarchy Foucault says that the rules of discursive practice 'define not the dumb existence of a reality, nor the canonical use of a vocabulary, but the ordering of objects'.[13] He wishes to shift attention away from 'things' 'the referent', ('the dumb existence of a reality') and – standing the causal presumption of materialism on its proverbial head – 'To substitute for the enigmatic treasure of "things" anterior to discourse, the regular formation of objects that emerge only in discourse. To define these *objects* without reference to the *ground*, the *foundation of things*, but by relating them to the body of rules that enable them to form as objects of a discourse and thus constitute the conditions of their historical appearance.'[14]

Thus Foucault describes his claim that the 'tight embrace' between words and things can be loosened by attending to the processes that govern the construction of objects in discourse. This is the level of analysis he needs to address problems such as how criminality could become an object of medical expertise, or how sexual deviance an object of psychiatric discourse. To take another example, he differentiates between the 'primary' (or 'real' – a curious regression) relations between family and judiciary in the nineteenth century, the objects of psychiatric discourse, and a third question: what nineteenth-century psychiatrists *could say* about the relations between the family and criminality. This point is drawn out rather nicely in an interview where Foucault was asked whether it would not be useful to create an archaeology of sexual fantasies rather than *The History of Sexuality*. He replied: 'I try to make an archaeology of discourse about sexuality which is really the relationship between what we do, what we are obliged to do, what we are allowed to do, what we are forbidden to do in the field of sexuality and what we are allowed, forbidden, or obliged to say about our sexual behaviour. That's the point. It's not a problem of fantasy; it's a problem of verbalisation.'[15]

There are a number of questions that one might take up with regard to Foucault's concept of discourse. We should note, first, his radical questioning of the hierarchy of determinism found in Marxism. Foucault saw determination as polymorphous rather than unilinear, and he wanted to claim the determinative powers of discourse in constituting practices that are intimately responsible for – as Said put it – 'how people thought, lived and spoke'. Foucault also wanted to challenge the materialist mind-set that sees value only in the mute, grey world of the pre-discursive and treats with disregard the productive creations of discourse. Secondly, it is worth noting at this point that Foucault opposed at every turn the conception of social structure so powerfully present in Marxism, and – of course – restricted it to the role of social class as the backbone of that structure. Foucault developed another and equally general concept, to which I shall return below – that of power. And, in general, the discourses he tended to analyse – medical, legal, sexual and so on – led to considerations quite other than those of class.

HISTORY AND GENEALOGY

Before looking at how the concept of discourse meshes with Foucault's general focus on power, it is important to clarify the links between his rejection of the 'primacy' of the material (as in Marxism) and his rejection of the primacy of a search for 'origins' in history. Just as he elaborated a theory of discourse to repudiate the one, so his concepts of archaeology and then genealogy were designed to repudiate the other. Foucault argues, in the opening pages of *The*

Archaeology of Knowledge, that 'total' history was constituted around a set of linked, and mistaken, assumptions: that one could reconstitute the overall form of a civilisation or principle of a society; that all the phenomena of a period had a shared significance with underlying laws accounting for their cohesion; that systems of homogeneous relations could be established; that networks of causality could be identified; and that the same form of historicity operates across the boundaries of economic, social, mental, technical or political phenomena. 'These are the postulates that are challenged,' wrote the grand mover of this challenge, 'by the new history when it speaks of series, divisions, limits, differences of level, shifts, chronological specificities, particular forms of rehandling, possible types of relation.'[16] A total, or totalising, history tends to draw all phenomena to a single centre; whereas what Foucault calls 'general' history deploys the space of dispersion.

    This theme underlies Foucault's appropriation of the Nietzschean notion of a genealogy, which he saw as a form of decentring that was in opposition to 'the search for an original foundation that would make rationality the *telos* of mankind'.[17] In his essay 'Nietzsche, Genealogy, History', Foucault elaborates the significance of his argument that Nietzsche's concept of genealogy 'opposes itself to the search for origins'. He likens the 'chimeras of the origin' to calling in a philosopher when what one needs is a doctor: 'History is the concrete body of a development, with its moments of intensity, its lapses, its extended periods of feverish agitation, its fainting spells; and only a metaphysician would seek its soul in the distant ideality of the origin.'[18]

    The essay considers critically the usage of various German words by Nietzsche at different times which, while often all translated as 'origin', properly refer to descent (*Herkunft*) and emergence (*Entstehung*) as well as the more usual term for origin – *Ursprung*. Foucault's discussions of these terms illuminate the gulf between his own genealogical historiography and the concerns of a traditional, origins-oriented approach. Recasting origins as 'descent' enables one to think of difference rather than resemblance, of beginnings rather than a beginning, of exterior accident rather than internal truth. Searching for descent is, according to Foucault, the opposite of erecting foundations; it is to disturb the immobile, fragment the unified and show the heterogeneity of what was thought to be consistent. And, finally, the domain of descent is the domain of the body and genealogy is thus situated within the 'articulation' of the body and history.[19] The concept of 'emergence' is equally at odds with the received perspective of origins. Emergence, Foucault says, is not the culmination of historical process (even if things appear so) but merely the 'current episodes' of a series. We should not read a teleological motive into the present moment and thus genealogy seeks to establish *not* the 'anticipatory power of meaning' but the hazardous play of dominations. Quoting Nietzsche: 'the iron hand of necessity shaking the dice-box of chance'.[20]

This theme of hazard or chance is not an easy one to incorporate into a philosophy of history, and few historiographers take on that particular challenge. Foucault, however, in his inaugural lecture (as 'professor of the history of systems of thought') at the Collège de France, noted what he called 'the absence of a theory enabling us to think the relation between chance and thought'. He added the following rider to his exposition of his characteristic approach to the examination of 'discontinuous systematicities': 'Finally, though it is true that these discontinuous discursive series each have, within certain limits, their regularity, it is undoubtedly no longer possible to establish links of mechanical causality or of ideal necessity between the elements which constitute them. We must accept the introduction of the alea [chance] as a category in the production of events.'[21]

Foucault continued by suggesting that chance, the discontinuous and materiality were three elements one needed to include in a history of discourses – allowing a connection between the history of systems of thought and the practice of historians – but commented that for some historians these constituted a 'triple peril' which had to be exorcised by casting history as the unravelling of necessity.[22] Foucault's position has proved extremely contentious among professional historians, not surprisingly perhaps. For he has pushed home a fundamental challenge to the conventions of western historiography, and has had an enormous influence on many younger historians and indeed on a much broader constituency of readers than historical studies usually command. A typical remark in an interview will show the qualities in Foucault which made him so irritating to many historians, whilst at the same time being *right*: 'A few years ago, historians were very proud to discover that they could write not only the history of battles, of kings and institutions but also of the economy; now they are all amazed because the shrewdest among them have learned that it was also possible to write the history of feelings, behaviour and the body. Soon, they will understand that the history of the West cannot be dissociated from the way its "truth" is produced and produces its effects.'[23] The concept of discourse, for Foucault, was closely connected with his concepts of truth, knowledge and power. Let us turn first to Foucault's concept of power and the role this plays in his system of thought as a whole.

POWER

For our purposes here, considering Foucault's work as a critique and alternative to the way determination has been conceptualised in Marxist theories of ideology, the concept of power is an important one. For Foucault developed a concept of power that was truly in sympathy with his concern with the polymorphous play of dependencies mentioned at the beginning of this section. As we shall see, he developed a concept of power that did not locate it in agencies (whether the state, individuals, economic forces etc.) but saw it in terms of 'micro' operations of power and by means of strategies and technologies of power. In general terms, his concept of power is probably the element of his system that is least compatible not only with Marxism but with most modern social science in which paradigms of a determining social structure exist. Hence to understand the significance of what Foucault was challenging with this new concept of power, one has to take on board a background of what Giddens has called the traditional 'skewing' in sociology towards the structure side of a structure/agency duality.[24]

A further difficulty is that Foucault's own development, methodologically speaking, is most complex around that question of power. If there is a significant 'break' in Foucault's work, it is to be located after *The Archaeology of Knowledge*. Hubert Dreyfus and Paul Rabinow suggest that this text, where Foucault reflects on his earlier works (particularly *Folie et déraison: l'historie de la folie à l'âge classique* – abridged in English as *Madness and Civilisation* – *The Birth of the Clinic* and *Words and Things*), is a methodological failure from which Foucault developed in a somewhat new direction. They argue a set of complex related theses on this point, bringing into play a series of debates such as whether Foucault had ever been influenced by 'structuralism', from which one can perhaps extract as central the following points. Foucault, they note, began by understanding discourses as epistemic regimes, in favour of which social and institutional practices were analytically subordinated; this tended to weight theory over practice and, not surprisingly, to cast the 'archaeologist' as phenomenologically and epistemologically detached from the discursive formations studied. But Foucault's subsequent major works, *Discipline and Punish* and *The History of Sexuality*, are predicated upon favouring practice over theory and understand discourse in a framework of 'organised and organising' practices; in this perspective archaeology has given way to genealogy as the principal method and the writer no longer regards himself as detached from the social practices he is studying.[25]

Another way of looking at this shift in Foucault's point of view is simply to say that he discovered the concept of *power*. As he put it himself: 'When I think back now, I ask myself what else it was that I was talking about, in *Madness and Civilisation* or *The Birth of the Clinic*, but power? Yet I'm perfectly aware that I scarcely ever used the word and never had such a field of analyses at my disposal.'[26] His own explanation for his difficulty in formulating the problem of power is a classically Foucauldian one: 'this was an incapacity linked undoubtedly with the political situation we found ourselves in'. Thus the political situation, in terms of his own model of discursive formations, plays a part in what can be thought and said in a theoretical discourse such as his own as much as in political discourse as such. Here, as in many other contexts, it is clear how marked Foucault was by and against the left orthodoxies of his subculture in post-war to 1968 Paris. He suggested many times that the Marxist insistence on the dominance of economic considerations tends to systematically exclude or occlude other considerations of power. Relating this to his own concerns he says: 'To put it very simply, psychiatric internment, the mental normalisation of individuals, and penal institutions have no doubt a fairly limited importance if one is only looking for their economic significance. On the other hand, they are undoubtedly essential to the general functioning of the wheels of power. So long as the posing of the question of power was kept subordinate to the economic instance and the system of interests which this served, there was a tendency to regard these problems as of small importance.'[27]

Foucault's concept of power was, in significant measure, developed as a critique of Marxism's theory of power as an instrument of a class dominance that was understood to originate from economic interest. Foucault saw power, on the contrary, as something that is *exercised* rather than possessed; it is not attached to agents and interests but is incorporated in numerous practices. Power can thus work from the 'bottom up', and Foucault uses the notion of the capillary to describe the operations of power at a micro level. Power is not exclusively negative, either, but produces pleasure and meaning as well as more coercive dimensions – why else, asks Foucault, would power be so seductive and powerful?

This analysis of power is not clear unless fitted into what is now more generally discussed as the critique of 'essentialism' in social theory (discussed earlier in this book in relation to the arguments put forward by Ernesto Laclau and Chantal Mouffe). For Foucault, 'power is co-extensive with the social body; there are no spaces of primal liberty between the meshes of its network'.[28] We are all already regulated, already participants in networks of power, already constituted within the operations of power – and notions such as the 'free individual', on whom power descends from above – are completely meaningless. Foucault did not believe that this position entailed 'seeing power everywhere' or reducing everything to power, just as Marxism had reduced everything to economics, although this criticism is frequently made of his work. He suggested instead that the problem was to understand *how* power operated in specific methods and strategies, *how* major shifts such as the increased disciplining of individuals in modern western society had taken place, and *how* one could show the political and economic dimensions of changes in power.[29]

The word *how* is the key to Foucault's concept of power. He considered that the question of power, in modern western societies where the issue of poverty (and the claims of the economic) had ceased to be of primary importance, had assumed a fundamental status. Yet questions of power – Who is making decisions for me? Who is preventing me from doing this and telling me to do that? – are questions that can *only* be answered when the question *how does it happen* is resolved. Thus, for Foucault, we can only study the 'who' of power – who exercises power – in conjunction with the 'how': 'the strategies, networks, the mechanisms, all those techniques by which a decision is accepted and by which that decision could not but be taken in the way it was'.[30] Foucault suggested that his 'little question' of *what happens?*, the 'flat and empirical' *how* of power, does not pose any ultimate challenge to the metaphysics or ontology of power and is hence not attempting to eliminate the what, who and why of power: it simply allows a critical investigation of the thematics of power. The object of analysis changes from power as an absolute, or in itself, to power in terms of *power relations*.[31]

In examining the 'how' of power, Foucault developed complex, and shifting, distinctions between programmes, strategies and technologies of power.[32] It is, however, because of his brilliant substantive histories of discipline, normalisation and the 'carceral society' that these theoretical elaborations have come to life. *Discipline and Punish*, for example, deals with the extension of the operations of power in Western Europe that can be seen in a change from punishment by exemplary torture to punishment by surveillance. Foucault describes (in gory detail) the tortures, public executions and so on of the period up until the eighteenth century not as barbarism but as a technique of power that was increasingly perceived as inefficient and costly. In its place there developed techniques of surveillance, of which the most quoted example is Bentham's panopticon, a model for the organisation of institutions such as prisons, but also informing the design and philosophy of other institutions such as schools, hospitals, reformatories and so on. The principle was, at its simplest, to expose the prisoner to the gaze of surveillance: 'the principle of the dungeon is reversed; daylight and the overseer's gaze capture the inmate more effectively than darkness'.[33] *Discipline and Punish* explores many themes which have subsequently become more salient and it would be hard to overestimate the influence of this book on a wide range of work. Foucault shows how an internalisation of the surveillance develops, how space becomes recognised as a political problem, how power relations can be heterogeneous rather than simply adversarial and so on.

Most importantly for the present discussion, Foucault shows how the body thought of in Marxism as the 'productive body' – as labour – is *only* that when *also* the 'subjected body' of a system of power: 'it is largely as a force of production that the body is invested with relations of power and domination; but, on the other hand, its constitution as labour power is possible only if it is caught up in a system of subjection (in which need is also a political instrument meticulously prepared, calculated and used)'.[34] Presaging the themes of 'bio-power' that were to be formulated in his later work, Foucault argued in *Discipline and Punish* for an analysis of the 'political technology of the body'. In discussions of the implications of his approach, Foucault agreed that his conception of power took it to be 'consubstantial' with the forces of production, as opposed to 'superstructural', and this may readily be seen in terms of Foucault's disagreement with the determinist ethos of Marxism. At this point it would be useful to attempt to characterise this in such a way as to focus the issues at stake in the ideology/discourse conflict.

FOUCAULT AND MARXISM

Foucault is the most obliging of the post-structuralists on this question, in the sense that in his books, and even more so in the many interviews in which he clarified and explained the theses of his major studies, he often refers back to his disagreements with Marxism. (One frequently voiced complaint against Derrida, for example, is that his 'encounter' with Marxism seems to be being indefinitely deferred.) In a late interview Foucault expressed the desire that there might be an 'unburdening and liberation of Marx in relation to party dogma, which has constrained it, touted it and brandished it for so long.' In response to the question as to whether Marx was 'at work in your own methdology' Foucault added more fuel to the fire of the dispute as to the 'compatibility' between Marxism and his own perspective. With a certain nonchalance in regard to scholarly convention, he replied: 'Yes, absolutely. You see, given the period in which I wrote those books, it was good form (in order to be viewed favourably by the institutional Left) to cite Marx in the footnotes. So I was careful to steer clear of that.'[35]

More seriously, Foucault's disagreements with Marx were profound and extensive. As we shall see in the next section of this chapter, he rejected entirely the 'realist' epistemology on which the ideology/science distinction and the construal of ideology as critique or illusion has been founded. He also rejected outright the notion of the subject, both individual agent and class subject, which Marxism has presumed. In relation to the whole problematic of determinism – and we might here remember Stuart Hall's 'When we leave the terrain of "determinations", we desert, not just this or that stage in Marx's thought, but his whole problematic'[36] – his position is unequivocally challenging. He sidelines the social structures – social class, the state – on which the determinist model is built, stripping their powers of agency away and arguing that 'production' and 'labour' go hand in hand with politics and subjection. Hence one would say that Foucault is working outside the Marxist problematic of determinism, rather than seeking to retrieve a polymorphous model of causality within it. In particular, as we saw earlier, Foucault does not defer to the 'dumb reality' of the pre-discursive. His model of power is not commensurate with the topographical metaphor of base and superstructure in Marxism, which has proved intractable and difficult to dislodge without bringing down the whole theoretical edifice as well. As David Couzens Hoy has interestingly observed: 'In fact, the top-bottom metaphor is unusable, for there is no absolute top or bottom, but rather a grid or network. A linguistic model comes closer to capturing Foucault's conception than a causal, materialist model. Foucault tends to think of the network as being like a grammar, which conditions what can be uttered in a language but does not determine which actual utterances emerge (and when).'[37]

Here we might say, perhaps, that the issue of determinism, posed within the framework of Marxist materialism, is one that is most firmly entangled with the intellectual climate at the time and place of the birth and consolidation of Marxist perspective. Increasingly it is clear – to put it very simply – that the materialist (in practice economic reductionist) premises of Marxism are inadequate as a basis for thinking about political, cultural and social life in a late twentieth-century society whose 'determinations' are so different from those of mid nineteenth-century manufacturing capitalism. Foucault's work is irritating to many Marxists precisely because it draws attention to what is assumed in Marxist theory – to the historical conditions in which Marxism emerged as a discourse – and this is in and of itself subversive of Marxism's claims to 'truth'. Alan Sheridan, indicating the degree of iconoclasm that Foucault has to go in for against the Marxist left orthodoxy prevailing at the time he was writing, quotes from the polemical passage in *The Order of Things*: 'Marxism exists in nineteenth-century thought like a fish in water; that is, it is unable to breathe anywhere else.'[38] As Sheridan observes, Foucault makes clear in that book that 'Marxist thought is irredeemably confined by an *episteme* that is coming to an end'.[39]

Most importantly of all for the specific concerns of this book, Foucault's concepts of discourse and power – and the intimate relation between them – were consistently and repeatedly elaborated as a critique of the concept of ideology. Frequently he moved straight to the issue of ideology when the general question of Marxism was raised. In 1975, for example, he said: 'As regards Marxism, I'm not one of those who try to elicit the effects of power at the level of ideology. ... Marxism considered as an historical reality has had a terrible tendency to occlude the question of the body, in favour of consciousness and ideology.'[40] Perhaps we could summarise his position by connecting both his critique of ideology and his arguments about *discourse* and *power* to his notion of truth. For part of his emphasis on power was, precisely, on what he called 'the politics of truth'. It was essential for and integral to Foucault's constitution of 'the politics of truth' as an object of study that he dismantle Marxism's obsessive interest in ideology or 'the economics of untruth'. Another quotation from Foucault in generalising, if somewhat flippant, mode about his life's work will make the connection abundantly clear: 'If I wanted to pose and drape myself in a slightly fictional style, I would say that this has always been my problem: the effects of power and the production of "truth". I have always felt uncomfortable with this ideological notion which has been used in recent years. It has been used to explain errors or illusions, or to analyse presentations – in short, everything that impedes the formation of true discourse. It has also been used to show the relation between what goes on in people's heads and their place in the conditions of production. *In sum, the economics of untruth. My problem is the politics of truth* [my italics]. I have spent a lot of time dealing with it.'[41]

Foucault thus replaces Marxism's concern with 'the economics of untruth' with his own examinations of 'the politics of truth'. Taking this focus, one of the most interesting discussions of Foucault's relationship to Marxism is that of Barry Smart, who suggests that Foucault's project was – although of course Foucault himself did not use this vocabulary – to show 'the complex multiple processes from which the strategic constitution of forms of hegemony may emerge'.[42] The background to Smart's recent article on the question of Foucault and hegemony lies in his earlier book *Foucault, Marxism and Critique*, in which he sketches out the conceptual limitations of the Marxist model and discusses the possibility that Gramsci's work offers solutions that go beyond the limitations of Marxism.[43] The question as to whether Gramsci can be read as departing from or constrained by the precepts of 'classical Marxism' is a heavily contended one, and the discussion of chapter 4 of this book considered this from the point of view of a detailed commentary on the break Laclau and Mouffe eventually made with Gramsci in developing a model of hegemony that was not class reductionist or essentialist. This is a discussion where there is still considerable room for interpretation; to me the attempt to lift Gramsci out of the classical Marxist tradition, making him the standard-bearer of a nonreductionist Marxism, is looking increasingly strained.

Barry Smart, rightly I think, contrasts Gramsci and Foucault in this regard, closing the balance sheet firmly in Foucault's favour: 'Although it may be argued that Gramsci was sensitive to the limits and limitations of Marxist analysis arising from the cornerstone principle of economic-determination-in-the-final-instance and sought through the conception of hegemony to develop a new approach to the problem of politics and power, ultimately the analysis remains at best ambiguous on the problem of economism and virtually silent on the complex matter of the establishment of forms of hegemony. In contrast, Foucault by virtue of his critical distance from the limits and limitations of the Marxist problematic has been able to transform

the terms of debate from a preoccupation with the ambiguous concept of "ideology" and its effects to a consideration of the relations of
"truth" and "power" which are constitutive of hegemony.'[44]

Whether or not Smart is right to recast Foucault's project in terms
of the language of hegemony (given the mixture of resonances now
carried by the term), we can agree with the underlying theme of his
interpretation: Foucault made a clean exit from the conceptual log-
jam where the concept of ideology is stuck in Marxism but developed
an approach to 'the politics of truth' that was, in a different way,
critical rather than neutral.

Foucault and the problems of epistemology

In this section I want to revert briefly, with regard to the Foucauldian critique of the concept of ideology, to some of the themes that
were considered at the beginning of the book as part of the 'classical
disputes' within Marxism. These concern the nature of knowledge:
there was the debate as to whether ideology should be regarded as
critical or neutral – whether one could adopt the so-called epistemological definition of ideology, and the question of whether a distinction could be drawn between ideology and science. In some ways,
Foucault is an extreme 'position' to select here as he is so far from
the epistemological security that the original debates within Marxism
rested on. Anyone who can describe his project in terms of the
relationship between truth on the one hand and reflexivity and the
self on the other must be found on the sharply ' conventionalist' side
of the debate between realism and conventionalism in epistemology:
'my own problem has always been the question of truth, of telling
the truth, the *wahr-sagen* – what it is to tell the truth – and the
relation between "telling the truth" and forms of reflexivity, of self
upon self'.[45] Anyone who formulates his first objection to the concept of ideology as the problem of 'drawing a line' between scientificity and truth must be such a complete relativist as to make the issue
scarcely worth discussing. Anyone whose own project is to see historically 'how effects of truth are produced within discourses which
are themselves neither true nor false' is, perhaps, beyond the pale
of debates about epistemology. Yet there are, too, reasons why
Foucault cannot be 'written off' in this way: in the first place he
offers a theory of *knowledge*, and the relations between truth and

power and, also, because there is considerable tension between Foucault's polemical general statements about epistemology and the obvious epistemological claims of his more specific essays and historical studies.

Foucault's lecture 'The Order of Discourse' is perhaps the best place to find a serious and sustained consideration of knowledge, discourse, truth and power. There Foucault describes the results of his many years of work researching 'the three great exclusions which forge discourse' in post-medieval western society.[46] These are, first, the *prohibitions* on what we can speak about, on who may speak and when, which interact in complex ways to form what Foucault calls a grid, with looser and tighter controls and exclusions (currently notable in sexuality, and politics, for example) that teach us that discourse is not simply a translation of domination into language but is itself a *power* to be seized. Secondly, Foucault refers to the opposition between reason and madness as another great principle of exclusion, not in this case a prohibition but a division and a rejection. Sheridan summarises Foucault's thesis as to what had occurred between Montaigne and Descartes: '*Man* may become mad, but *thought*, as the exercise of a sovereign subject duty-bound to observe the true, cannot be insane. The experience, so familiar to the Renaissance, of an unreasonable Reason and a reasonable Unreason, is now precluded.'[47] A third principle of exclusion, which Foucault calls the 'will to know' or the 'will to truth', was also historically constituted, in his view, since its emergence can be located in pre-Platonic Greek thought. It involved a shift from seeing truth as a given property of the discourse of those in power to seeing truth as a property of the referent of discourse. From this, argued Foucault, sprang the entire western ethos in which the will to truth is reinforced and renewed, whether in scientific 'discoveries' or the valorisation of the 'vraisemblable' in literature, in the practices and institutions of education, publishing and so on. As a modern example, Foucault gives the case of legal discourse, which has increasingly abandoned a theory of justice as its justification, and moved towards the externally guaranteed 'truth' of sociological or medical knowledge: 'it is as if even the work of law could no longer be authorised, in our society, except by a discourse of truth'.[48]

In this context Foucault gives an account of the role of 'disciplines' in the management of truth, using Canguilheim's distinction between truth and being 'in the true'. No doubt for many readers evoking Kuhn's account of how paradigms shift, Foucault writes: 'Mendel spoke the truth, but he was not "within the true" of the biological discourse of his time . . . .' Disciplines operate within certain rules: 'Within its own limits, each discipline recognises true and false propositions; but it pushes back a whole teratology of knowledge beyond its margins.'[49] For Foucault, science has become institutionalised as *power*, and the 'will to truth' is a key dimension of that historical process.

In considering these arguments a whole range of questions arise. In one sense, Foucault is not disputing the existence of absolute or scientific truth, merely stating his interest in the processes by which effects of truth are secured – which is a different issue. How else can we interpret the following sentence? 'It is always possible that one might speak the truth in the space of a wild exteriority, but one is "in the true" only by obeying the rules of a discursive "policing" which one has to reactivate in each of one's discourses.'[50] But, in another sense, the concession that one could speak the truth outside discourse is fundamentally at odds with his general thesis. On another general question, one might ask what would be preferable to the 'will to truth', of which Foucault is so critical, when its predecessor – according to him – was the assignation of 'truth' on the basis of social power (scarcely a more desirable relationship between discourse, truth and power). Or again, how do we address the 'desirability' of truth? Foucault was asked by an interviewer the blunt question 'Doesn't science produce "truths" to which we submit?' and his reply is characteristically irritating from a rational point of view and yet also provocative in a productive way. He began by linking science and power and then added rather demurely: 'I am only taking up one of the fundamental problems of Western philosophy when it poses these questions: Why, in fact, are we attached to the truth? Why the truth rather than lies? Why the truth rather than myth? Why the truth rather than illusion? And I think that, instead of trying to find out what truth, as opposed to error, is, it might be interesting to take up the problem posed by Nietzsche: how is it that, in our societies, "the truth" has been given this value, thus placing us absolutely under its thrall?'[51] If we go beyond the initial spluttering rationalist response, there are interesting questions to consider. In what circumstances do we choose to tell lies? Use myths? Prefer illusions to the truth? (No doubt even the most rigorous of rationalist philosophers in the Anglo-American school has colluded at times with Father Christmas or the tooth fairy.)

Foucault is difficult to 'pin down' on such issues, and partly because he completely eschews the style of the Cartesian tradition, albeit in a less flamboyant manner than Derrida. One aspect of this is the question of textuality, or the 'writerliness' of Foucault's texts and the effects this has on the way in which his ideas are read. His essay 'What Is An Author?' carries, in its discussion of the 'author function', a different argument from that of Roland Barthes's 'The Death of the Author', but some parallels can obviously be made.[52] Foucault has made it clear that his 'texts' are not to be regarded as correct for all time, they are instead a process of work. Hence he on numerous occasions recorded his awareness of changing his mind, moving on, refusing to be caught under the searchlight of consistency. In a much quoted remark at the end of the Introduction to *The Archaeology of Knowledge* and one which, typically, irks those who think a writer should 'stand by' their earlier work but endears him to a new generation of readers, he wrote: 'Do not ask who I am and do not ask me to remain the same: leave it to our bureaucrats and our police to see that our papers are in order. At least spare us their morality when we write.'[53] Another infraction of the conventions of scholarly texts might be seen in Foucault's remarks about the relationship of his books' titles to their content. Asked if this was a 'game' with the reader, Foucault replied that there was often a 'gap' between a title he chose at the beginning and a new problem he was able to formulate at the end of the book: he described this as the distance he effected in the course of writing.[54]

These issues of writerliness and authorship are not of purely incidental interest – they mark a new style of work and a contempt for the sovereign I of traditional academic writing. The other side of this particular coin – where Foucault writes at length in exegesis of another thinker but is read as speaking for himself – has already caused a certain amount of confusion. Gary Gutting, for example, has pointed out that various critiques (including that of Habermas) of Foucault's supposed relativism are based on passages where 'Foucault is not speaking in his own name' but is giving a lengthy exposition of others.[55]

These issues about 'style' can be formulated in an even more significant way, as they affect the process of argument profoundly. Perhaps we need an epistemology of style. One example of this is the interesting exchange that has arisen over Charles Taylor's critique of Foucault. Paul Bové, in an impassioned Foreword (which is entitled 'The Foucault Phenomenon: The Problematics of Style') to Deleuze's book on Foucault, casts a shadow over Taylor's unremitting and to some highly convincing critique of Foucault's ideas about power, freedom and truth. Bové shows how the passages of Taylor's piece that strike one as most dismissive – Taylor claims that Foucault 'does not make sense', is 'driven by contradictory positions', has 'obscured the issues which count by his mode of expression' and so on – spring precisely from Taylor's own disciplinary truth apparatus. Bové suggests that 'it is naïve for Taylor to approach the text of a leading theoretician of writing, language, literature and style as if his writing were merely a failed attempt at transparently presenting "positions", something merely unfortunately obscure'.[56] Bové also 'interprets' the critique of Foucault found in Frederic Jameson's *The Political Unconscious* in terms of Jameson's anxiety not to see the implications of Foucault's critique of academic disciplines. It results, claims Bové, in 'the politically motivated, too hasty dismissal of Foucault at the cost of what he has to teach us about the positions of intellectuals within power'.[57]

Leaving this aside, we can agree with Richard Rorty that there is a major ambiguity in Foucault on the question of epistemology. He is not relativist in any way – contrary to some misreadings of his work – and his statements about epistemology and truth are themselves loaded to the brim with truth claims. Equally, his historical accounts – of mental illness, crime, sexuality, the rise of the social and so on – manifestly present themselves as claims for a better historical knowledge of their objects. As Rorty puts it: 'he is not content simply to give a genealogy of epistemology, to show us how this genre came into being (something he does very well). Rather, he wants to *do* something like epistemology.'[58] The same issue can be put in the form of Gary Gutting's question: 'Is Foucault's critique of reason self-refuting?' Gutting concludes that it is not, and that Foucault offers a conception of philosophy which, while shorn of the foundationalism and a priorism of traditional philosophy, provides an important intellectual tool for working on normative judgements arrived at elsewhere.[59] For Rorty, Foucault's work was both more troubling and more visionary: 'reaching for speculative possibilities that exceed our present grasp, but may nevertheless be our future'.[60]

Foucault and the problems of the subject

As we have seen at the beginning of this book, the 'problem of the subject' did not exist in classical Marxism's theories of ideology; but it has certainly compensated for its late arrival on the scene in terms of the interest it currently engenders. At stake here are a number of related issues, some of which (the critique of the Cartesian subject, the problem of humanism and so on) were discussed at some length in chapter 5. As far as Foucault is concerned, he insisted that the subject should be thought of as constituted rather than a given, and his interest in the practices constituting that subject (discursive, social and so on) was much broader than that of many other modern theorists. Foucault's approach to subjectivity tended to focus on conscious material, particularly what can be verbalised, but (despite his antipathy to psychoanalysis) he also dealt with that which is not brought to consciousness. It is scarcely necessary to add that Foucault's interest in subjectivity was not primarily oriented towards social class, for indeed his central interest was in other forms of identity. ('I have tried to show how we have indirectly constituted ourselves through the exclusion of some others: criminals, mad people and so on.')[61]

Foucault's perspective on 'the subject' changed over the years partly, perhaps, in response to the charge that his earlier position left little room for 'resistance'. Considerable debate still takes place over this issue with regard to his work, and to the related problem of humanism and anti-humanism. Before looking at these issues in more detail, it is worth remarking that the combination of Foucault's displacement of social class from the theorisation of subjectivity, and his implacable critique of the 'sovereign' subject of humanist discourse, have made him into a post-structuralist whose work has been much used, applied and debated within feminism. As Biddy Martin has appositely remarked about Foucault's critique of humanism: 'feminist analyses demonstrate ever more convincingly that women's silence and exclusion from struggles over representation have been the condition of possibility for humanist thought: the position of woman has indeed been that of an internal exclusion within Western culture, a particularly well-suited point from which to expose the workings of power in the will to truth and identity'.[62] The implications of Foucault's work for feminist analysis will be considered shortly.

In the meanwhile, it is perhaps worth adding that in these debates – about both subjectivity and the correct conception of 'the subject' – there can be no adversarial logic in which if Foucault is wrong the Marxist theory of ideology might be right. The glaring weaknesses of Marxism in this area suggest that should Foucault turn out to offer us no more, even, than what I have described as the 'sorry legacy' of Althusserianism, the classical Marxist problematic will still be woefully inadequate, causing us to look elsewhere for a better approach.

Foucault's changing approach to these questions is often referred to as something like 'the return of the subject in late Foucault'. Towards the end of his life he expressed an increasing interest in the self, and this is seen by many (although not entirely with justification) as some kind of repudiation of his earlier position. Whether or not one wants to make a grand *coupure* or break in his thought is not clear: one can also see continuities and coherences in these succeeding concerns.

In *The Archaeology of Knowledge* Foucault addressed the way in which he thought of the relationship between the subject and discourse, and in one particular passage he clarified eloquently the importance of understanding the discursive construction of the subject – as against the conception of discourse as something appropriated by a fully fledged or *given* subject. He wrote: 'discourse is not the majestically unfolding manifestation of a thinking, knowing, speaking subject, but, on the contrary, a totality, in which the dispersion of the subject and his discontinuity with himself may be determined. ... it is neither by recourse to a transcendental subject nor by recourse to a psychological subjectivity that the regulation of its enunciations should be defined.'[63]

Foucault's critique of the 'transcendental' or Cartesian subject was completely bound into his critique of humanism. In fact, he *defined* humanism as 'subjected sovereignties', saying that 'By humanism I mean the totality of discourse through which Western man is told: "Even though you don't exercise power you can still be a ruler. Better yet, the more you deny yourself the exercise of power, the more you submit to those in power, the more this increases your sovereignty."' Foucault went on to explain that humanism was institutionalised in western civilisation through Roman law which, in an 'elegant exchange', required the property owner to submit to the laws supporting his claim to property whilst at the same time fixing the right to property as the possession of those in power. According to Foucault, the sovereign subject of western culture is thus in reality – and here lies the meaning of 'humanism' – a *pseudosovereign*.[64]

Another example of Foucault's 'deconstruction' of humanism can be given from the same interview. Speaking of the superficiality of dealing with 'rights' of prisoners, he argued that the radical aim of the group in which he was active – GIP (Information Group on Prisons) – was to challenge the distinction between guilt and innocence. 'Our action ... isn't concerned with the soul or the man *behind* the convict, but seeks to obliterate the deep division that lies between innocence and guilt.' This position he contrasts with the characteristic response of humanism to the problem of prisons: 'Confronted by the penal system, the humanist would say: "The guilty are guilty and the innocent are innocent. Nevertheless, the convict is a man like any other and society must respect what is human in him: consequently, flush toilets!"'[65] (Although Foucault is manifestly right about the toilets – currently a topic of much official concern in Britain – his own position is a curiously 'sixties' one.) The article from which I have been drawing was, interestingly, a discussion between Foucault and a group of *lycée* students published in the French magazine *Actuel*. Even in 1971, with Foucault taking a pro-drugs position, carefully explaining to the students that the police campaign against drugs was 'the indirect exaltation of the normal, rational, conscientious, and well-adjusted individual', those bright sixth-formers were much more sober: young 'Serge' thought that drug use was only for drop-outs, and certainly not for politicised students.[66]

In any event, the burden of Foucault's earlier works was undoubtedly to 'ruin the sovereignty of the subject'. In his later work – and the turning-point comes after he had begun the project of *The History of Sexuality* – Foucault became interested in what he termed 'subjectivisation', or 'the procedure by which one obtains the constitution of a subject'.[67] And although most of his previous work had been located in the post-medieval European context, this new interest was to take Foucault back to the writings of Greek and Roman antiquity. Foucault explained that after he had written the first volume of the proposed 'History', he had intended to write a historical sequence going from the sixteenth century onwards but was stopped in his tracks by it 'not working out'. The problem that remained unanswered was to do with morality: 'why had we made sexuality into a moral experience?' The answer he eventually came up with concerned both the moralising of sexual experience in Christianity and a concomitant appropriation of morality by a theory of the subject. In comparison, the ethic of antiquity was one that did not moralise sexuality but took much greater 'care of the self'. And in so far, suggested Foucault, as the package of moralised sexuality and the pseudosovereign ('a moral experience essentially centred on the subject') was no longer satisfactory to us today, certain questions 'pose themselves to us in the same terms as they were posed in antiquity'.[68]

It is these questions that led Foucault to his work on the ethics of the self: 'the kind of relationship that you ought to have with yourself, *rapport à soi*, which I call ethics, and which determines how the individual is supposed to constitute himself as a moral subject of his own action'. As Ian Hacking has unpretentiously put it: 'the sheer stuff that you worry about if you are a moral agent'.[69] Hacking gives a very clear account of the significance of Foucault's move: 'The knowledge/power story has been elaborately illustrated in Foucault's books, but those are outer-directed narratives – what we say about others, say to others, have said to ourselves by others, do to others or have done to ourselves. They leave out the inner monologue, what I say to myself. They leave out self-discipline, what I do to myself. Thus they omit the permanent heartland of subjectivity.' Hacking then notes that 'There is nothing private about this ... The cunning of conscience and self-knowledge is to make it feel private.'[70] Foucault's *The Care of the Self* is perhaps the most interesting elaboration of these new themes: a fascinating discussion of the representation of sexuality in the writings of 'the early centuries of our era' (that is, Greek and Roman texts of various kinds), where Foucault shows the increasing moralisation and anxiety around sex that develops within antiquity and is carried forward in the Christian epoch.[71]

In *Technologies of the Self* Foucault suggested that there are four major types of technologies: technologies of *production, sign systems, power* and *the self* and that he 'wanted to show both their specific nature and their constant interaction'. He argued that the first two – technologies of production and of sign systems – had been most studied elsewhere, whilst his own interest had lain with power and, latterly, technologies of the self.[72] It is important to note that Foucault's approach to the question of the subject and the self is thus one that arises in a very broad context. John Rajchman has elegantly pinpointed the sense in which Foucault's rejection of the myth of the transcendental subject, his anti-humanism and his analysis of individualisation in modern society is quite different from Derridian and Lacanian post-structuralism: 'Foucault preserves one idea: that the subject is constituted. But he rejects the Lacanian thesis that the subject is constituted in *language*.'[73]

This broad perspective, which effectively means that Foucault's insights can be set to work across a whole spectrum of work in historical, textual, sociological and critical debates, is one reason for his popularity. Comparatively speaking, and with some notable exceptions, the influence of Derrida and Lacan has been overwhelmingly concentrated in the areas of literary and film textual criticism, and the attempt to 'import' these thinkers into, for example, history or sociology has been much more vexed than the reception of Foucault ('patchy' even though that has been).[74]

FOUCAULT, FEMINISM, THE BODY AND POLITICS

It is, though, in feminism and in work on sexuality that Foucault's ideas have recently 'taken off'. This is partly because of his emphasis on 'the body', which *again* Foucault contextualises in criticism of the concept of ideology. 'I wonder whether, before one poses the question of ideology, it wouldn't be more materialist to study first the question of the body and the effects of power on it.'[75] The reasons why 'the body' has ceased to be something taken for granted and shot to prominence as an object of social analysis are complex. As I have suggested elsewhere, they are particularly acute issues in feminism, partly because of the importance of the politics of biology (including the implications of recent medical/technological developments) to feminist struggles.[76]

Foucault's focus on 'the body', and the characteristic manner in which he has recast many people's thinking about sexuality, has coalesced with both a major surge of interest in sexual identity and preference (particularly in gay and lesbian studies) and a period of major development in feminist thought. A central aspect of this is the issue of 'essentialism'. As Biddy Martin has pointed out, Foucault's demolition of the notion of 'repression' assisted the resistance of some feminists both to the ontologising of woman as essentially superior to man and to the deference to the 'truth' of women's confessed experience that was at that point becoming popular in feminism.[77] Foucault's work ties in usefully with the tendency within feminism towards an anti-essentialist position, just as it offers a much more sophisticated methodology for providing an account of sexual identity than the traditional 'social construction of gender' models on which feminists have tended to rely.

In saying this, however, one is immediately drawn into the political weaknesses of a Foucauldian approach. The entire burden of Foucault's work is to delegitimate the hypostatising of social structures such as 'the gender order' or 'patriarchy' as explanations but rather to uncover the complex strategies and operations of power, within and beyond the discursive, that result (with some deference to the role of chance) in what we see has emerged. Yet, and this is a repeated criticism of Foucault that I would not want to endorse in the general and vituperative terms in which it is often made, there are difficulties with failing to position *oneself* on these questions. It is one consequence of the tension in Foucault between (as Rorty put it) giving a critical history of how epistemology is as it is, and wanting to do epistemology oneself. Foucault errs on the side of implying that the position from which he speaks, as historian principally, is a neutral one. This can be dealt with by the letter of the law, as in Charles Taylor's claims that Foucault does not 'make sense'.[78] Or one can point out the contradiction in a more positive light, as Nancy Fraser has done in showing, for example, how Foucault's intransigent anti-humanism at a theoretical level is belied by the argument of *Discipline and Punish*, which 'even as it indicts humanist reform for complicity in disciplinary power, depends for its *own* critical force on the reader's familiarity with and commitment to the modern ideals of autonomy, reciprocity, dignity and human rights.'[79]

This curious tension has some odd consequences, some serious, and others of perhaps more anecdotal interest. Biddy Martin suggests that 'To speak from a position of abstract correctness, rather than grounding oneself within the limitations of one's own material and ideological reality, is a privilege that can only reproduce the androcentric and fundamentally humanist universalising "I", this time in the apparent form of the "Not-I".'[80] Martin's comment arose with reference to Foucault's view that rape should be regarded as assault rather than a specifically sexual crime – a view which has been roundly criticised by some feminists, notably Monique Plaza.[81] Foucault's remarks, on this as well as on other matters of policy and law relating to sexuality, are strangely naïve. In the notorious discussion of rape, where Foucault floated the idea that rape should be treated like 'a punch in the face', he keeps reverting with surprise to the reaction of the women present: 'both of you, as women, were immediately upset [indeed, they became incoherent] at the idea that one should say: rape belongs to the realm of physical violence and must simply be treated as such'.[82] Foucault's position does have a respectable feminist pedigree, in fact (in the demystification of rape as a 'sexual' crime rather than one of power and violence), but he expressed it simplistically and without questioning the position from which he spoke – as a man. Similarly, he was very naïve in his speculations around the issue of the age of consent, the sexuality of children and paedophilia: 'the child may be trusted to say whether or not he was subjected to violence' seems particularly feeble given what we now know about the question of power and the sexual abuse of children.[83]

Another aspect of the 'false universalising' of which Foucault seemed strangely unaware is the lack of reflection as to what he meant by 'our culture', 'our civilisation', 'western society' and so on. As Edward Said bluntly put it: 'his Eurocentrism was almost total'. Said points out that this has a substantive bearing on the purchase of Foucault's analyses: 'he does not seem interested in the fact that history is not a homogeneous French speaking territory ... He seems unaware of the extent to which the ideas of discourse and discipline are assertively European and how ... discipline was also used to administer, study and reconstruct – then subsequently to occupy, rule and exploit – almost the whole of the non-European world.'[84]

HUMANISM AND THE PROBLEM OF AGENCY

A somewhat different inflection of these problems can be seen in relation to the place of affect and feeling in Foucault's work, on which a number of comments might be made. Probably everyone notices, as they read Foucault, the imposition of complete silence about emotion or, more accurately, a refusal on Foucault's part to verbalise the emotional content of what is being discussed. Mark Poster refers to 'the great lacuna of Foucault's history of sexuality: a relative and remarkable absence of discussion about the affective nuances of sexual relations'; he also suggests that Foucault's treatment of the family is inadequate because it concentrates on the action of discourses external to the family and ignores the internal constitution of the family, notably through the emotional interaction of its members.[85] Poster attributes this problem to Foucault's antipathy to psychoanalysis in particular and the psychological level of explanation in general, and this no doubt plays a part in the matter. Some aspects of this are illuminated in the rare personal interview Foucault gave, published under the salient title of 'The Minimalist Self'.[86] It is notable, however, that many contemporary anti-humanists suffer from the same syndrome – as if to be caught speaking of emotion would involve a dubious subjectivism. The desire to avoid formulations that smack of vulgar humanism leads to the extraordinarily cerebral and skeletal character of 'the body' in this new discourse.[87]

Terry Eagleton (a recent convert to the relative merits of the human-ist legacy as a weapon against the politically yet worse forces of post-modernism) reads Foucault's emotional flatness as another sign of his conservatism. In a scorching attack on Foucault's ethics of the self he accuses him of completing 'his long trek from the hymning of madness to the public school virtues'.[88]

It is possible, however, to make a less tendentious connection between Foucault's self-denying ordinance in the realm of affect and a more general set of problems with his work on the question of agency. Here it is clear that agency has to be considered in relation to both the agency of individuals and that of groups. Anthony Giddens has described what can be seen as a link between the epistemological ambiguities of Foucault's work and the tortured positions he arrives at in addressing questions of agency. 'Foucault's history tends to have no active subjects at all. It is history with the agency removed. The individuals who appear in Foucault's analyses seem impotent to determine their own destinies. Moreover, that reflexive appropriation of history basic to history in modern culture does not appear at the level of the agents themselves. The historian is a reflective being, aware of the influence of the writing of history upon the determina-tion of the present. But this quality of self-understanding is seem-ingly not extended to historical agents themselves.'[89]

Foucault's odd conception of agency hangs on his theory and vocabulary of power – programmes, strategies, technologies. Of these, it is Foucault's notion of strategy that is most vexing. One can see why Foucault uses the term 'effects', which is initially paradoxi-cal in a thinker who is so deconstructive of the notion of 'cause', by attending to the plurality rather than singularity of effects and to Foucault's insistence on the role of chance – and unintended effects – in his account of history. But Foucault's notion of strategy is more fundamentally puzzling, since the received meaning of strategy (from the Greek *strategus*: commander or magistrate) derives so unambi-guously from the orders of an individual. For Foucault, however, the central aspect of strategy is caught in an apparently oxymoronic statement quoted by Charles Taylor: 'que les relations de pouvoir sont à la fois intentionelles et non subjectives' (power relations are both intentional and non-subjective). Foucault expands on this theme as follows: 'there is no power that is exercised without a series of aims and objectives. But this does not mean that it results from the choice or decision of an individual subject; let us not look for the headquarters that presides over its rationality; neither the caste which governs, nor the groups which control the state apparatus, nor those who make the most important economic decisions direct the entire network of power that functions in a society ... the logic is perfectly clear, the aims decipherable, and yet it is often the case that no one is there to have invented them, and few who can be said to have formulated them.'[90]

Within Marxism, this phenomenon has been dealt with through the proposition that people act in their objectively given interests and where these (as specified in theory) do not coincide with their actual behaviour then the notion of ideology is brought in to bridge the gap. For Foucault, of course, that whole package is a non-starter; but in his own theses on power it is undoubtedly the issue of agency that causes the most scepticism as to whether he has offered a plausible alternative. Charles Taylor comments that 'there are obviously lots of aspects of social life in which this reciprocal play of micro-practice and global structures, each producing (largely unintended) consequences for the other, is the right explanatory model. The problem arises only when one combines this with Foucault's very strong claims to systematicity, in the idea that there are pervasive *strategies* afoot which condition the battle in each micro-context, that "power" can "retreat" or "re-organise its forces". These can only be combined via some account of how actions concatenate systematically. ... But Foucault doesn't even try.'[91]

But the problem for Taylor is that although one would expect him to be right, and certainly he is 'within the true' of modern rationalist social theory in what he says, such concatenations do not necessarily have to be explicable in terms of one of his models. (What logic can be invoked to explain the hideous concatenations of circumstance that pile up in a Thomas Hardy novel but yet have some resemblance to what is possible?) Without lapsing into irrationalism one can still see if we examine the social world in a different way large movements in society that have a systematicity without a clear motive or logic. This is partly because although social theory may traditionally be locked within a rationalist tradition, people do not necessarily behave in a rational way all the time. This is clearest perhaps in considering mainstream economics (and, indeed, the much newer 'rational choice theory'), where one can easily point out that the so-called 'rational individual' which is the methodological cornerstone of the model is subject to many contradictory pressures on his/her behaviour. One could take many examples, from the trivial to the major, of social changes that are hard to 'explain' in a systematic way but within themselves have a certain force and coherence. How does one 'explain' world-cup fever? Why is illegitimacy not the social stigma it was? How has religious fundamentalism become articulated as of major political significance in relatively secularised countries like Britain? One way of illustrating the point is to think about the effects of groups and crowds, which often result in individuals be-having in ways they retrospectively regret or – at least – can be very surprised by. The power of example, of a pressure to conform, is legendary. In contemporary politics we can see that politicians have now learnt the lessons of the theorists of hegemony – issues are taken up and run with for just as far as they will go, electorally speaking, and dropped when the tide of opinion starts to drift against them. Banal as some of these points are, they address a sense of the predictable/unpredictable element in movement in history. Although Foucault's views about agency were undoubtedly curious, they none the less reveal the weaknesses of the comforting assumptions about historical necessity made in 'total' history; equally, he insisted on the existence of patterns of power and tendencies of historical move-ment, against those who constitute everything in terms of chance and the logic of contingency.

Foucault: discourse and the critique of ideology

Let us revert to Foucault's objections to the concept of ideology in the light of his own arguments about society and history. On the issue of determinism, Foucault is right to side with those who see the whole topographical base-and-superstructure model of Marxism as unhelpful, and he is right to displace the primacy of social class and the economic in his conceptualisation of power in society. In addition to making arguments analogous to the 'post-Marxism' of Laclau and Mouffe, Foucault has provided his own provocative and illuminating analyses – limited by his Eurocentrism it is true – of power in just the areas (insanity, medicine, sexuality etc.) where Marxism has been so weak and in which many of us are now so interested. As far as epistemology is concerned, Foucault's arguments are merely another nail in the coffin of the scientistic definition of ideology; his own focus on the politics of truth a positive improvement on Marxism's obsession with the illusions of 'the economics of untruth'. On the third count – that of ideology presupposing the notion of a 'subject' – the legacy of Foucault is more problematic and remains the source of continuing debate. Undoubtedly his insistence on the materiality of the body has led one way forward; his account of technologies of the self and the ethics of selfhood can be appropriated in a variety of ways; his thinking about agency remains contentious and puzzling. Underlying some of these difficulties, as I shall suggest in the final chapter, is the unresolved problem of humanism.

7

Conclusion: Post-Marxism and the Concept of Ideology

It makes sense to begin these concluding remarks by reverting to the original themes of the book, and recapitulating the arguments elaborated in earlier chapters. The first part of the book looked at how classical Marxism had formulated the issues around a theory of ideology. Chapter 1 surveyed the varying, and not entirely compatible, ways in which Marx himself had used the concept of ideology. Although it is a theory of enormous resonance and power – such that often it is scarcely possible to think of another word to put in the place of ideology – the root of the main problems with the Marxist theory of ideology could be said to lie in Marx's somewhat chaotic formulations: ideology as illusion, ideology as base and superstructure, ideology as commodity fetishism and so on. Of the various meanings of the term in Marx, the one of most general usefulness is that of mystification. At the beginning of the book I suggested that a consensual definition of ideology in Marxism (and beyond, to some extent) would be that of 'mystification that serves class interests'; I shall suggest below that the problem with this arises not so much with the general idea of mystification, but with the exclusive and functional connection to social class.

Marx's various formulations about ideology set the pattern for a debate, within the classical Marxist tradition, whose boundaries were extraordinarily wide. Chapters 2 and 3 of this book sought to show just how little consensus there had been on the fundamental issues on which the usefulness of the theory of ideology would depend. In practice, the most important has been the issue of whether to think of ideology in a critical or a neutral sense: to think of ideology as by definition involving an element of illusion or distortion (as being ineluctably opposed to truth or knowledge) or whether to see ideology as the expression of a historical consciousness whose strengths and limitations would be understood outside the ideological. 'Classical

Marxism' (which I take to stop at Gramsci in terms of new ideas, but which flourishes e'en now in the repetition of its old truths) had difficulty with this problem. Although the dominant tradition has been to follow what one might call the balance of Marx's opinions in adopting the 'critical' or 'epistemological' definition, there has been enough of a minority view to cause considerable lack of coherence.

The other major disputed issues within the classical tradition of Marxist thought concerned the distinction between 'ideology and science' and the highly charged problematic of determinism. A difficulty with the first of these is that our knowledge of 'science' exists now in a much more generally reflexive and critical perspective than could have been the case for Marx in the nineteenth century. The post-atomic popular understanding of science has had to deal with science as knowledge of that which cannot be seen, and we are now much better informed of the ways in which 'science' houses contradictory and puzzling truths. This is *not* to say that there is not such thing as scientific knowledge or universal truths of science which cannot be disputed, but it is to insist that the context of these knowledges is relevant to our understanding of the content. Reading Marx now, his naïve 'scientism' can be interpreted as no more and no less than the product of the 'triumphalist' approach to science characteristic of that moment of European confidence and assertiveness.

The issue of determination is a more complex one. This is because debate about the concept of ideology, couched within classical Marxism in terms of the intransigent and intractable metaphor of 'base and superstructure', triggers the much more general issue of Marxism's materialism. That is, it triggers the question of what status to attach to things at the 'level' of resources, production, and the economic (regarded as material), and – second layer – the state and politics, and – third storey of this model – philosophy, culture, religion and ideology. This model is problematic for more reasons than I can go into now, but fortunately I do not have to. This is because there is another, perhaps more local but in my view definitive problem with the determinist approach to ideology within Marxism: this is the issue of class as the material determinant of ideology. Here I think one can stand full square and confidently upon the lessons of feminism, anti-racism and our political understanding of post-colonialism and say that if a theory of ideology were to be useful it would most certainly have to be applicable to understanding the cultural, ideational and subjective experiences of people in terms other than – if additional to – those of social class. There can be no doubt that people's experiences of migration, for example, or sexual preference, or varying situations with regard to their employment and responsibility for children and other relatives, form part of their subjectivity and their decisions and actions. Hence I would incline to shelve the larger issue of determinism and materialism – which has been and continues to be a major source of debate within Marxism – and suggest instead that the more serious problem in terms, specifically, of a theory of ideology is the problem of social class as the hypothesised and hypostatised determinant.

Here I would make a break after the theoretical problems about ideology that were thrown up by consideration of Marx's work and within the classical Marxist tradition and which formed the basis of my discussions in the first part (chapters 1 to 3) of the book. For two major issues have come to light subsequent to that classical moment, and it is they that have constituted a newer set of problems *with* rather than within the classical model. Part II of the book was concerned to examine the nature of these fundamental problems of the Marxist model, as far as its theory of ideology was concerned. The two problems I would identify here are, first, the issue of social class and whether ideology should be seen as 'class belonging' and, second, the issue of what theory of the subject is or is not in play in any theory of ideology and what implications this has for understanding human agency. These two problems were the central focus of chapters 4 and 5, which aimed to show that taking these newer problems seriously has proved very difficult within the framework of a theory that is recognisably 'Marxist'. Chapters 4 and 5, therefore, are a discussion of what I call 'internal strain' in the Marxist model – the point at which the problems it has thrown up from within the theoretical paradigm cannot be resolved internally but have to be (as Ernesto Laclau put it) superseded in the development of a new theory.

I understand Gramsci and Althusser to represent this cracking, or train, of the Marxist model as in their different ways they recognised and sought to transcend the limitations of the theory. As far as Gramsci is concerned, opinion varies on how far his work is to be read as ultimately reproducing the economism of classical Marxism or whether one might see his analysis of 'hegemony' as the basis for a new and non-reductionist theory and politics. In relation to the work of Laclau and Mouffe, it is clear that in so far as one breaks with the 'class-belongingness' of ideology one is logically led to a break with Marxism in general and it is also clear, I think, that Gramsci himself remained quite unequivocally on the 'Marxist' side of this gulf.

Althusser's work raises a number of other issues, partly because his bombastic scientism and grandiose theoreticism are so out of tune with the modest pragmatism of today. With regard to ideology, however, he raised – as no one within Marxism had done with the same vigour and effect before – the twin problems of humanism and of how to think of 'the subject' as constituted rather than given a priori. Retrospectively, I suggested, it was surprising that Althusser had been so influential in some alternative radical theoretical circles when his account of social reproduction was very class reductionist, his anti-humanism bankrupt in its implications and his appropriation of Lacan partial and contradictory. Nevertheless, Althusser's work contributed to a productive interrogation of complacent assumptions about individual political agency and a recognition – however inadequate – that modern psychoanalytic ideas had a role to play in thinking about ideology and subjectivity.

One can see in the work of Gramsci and Althusser, and in the problems that have exercised their many respective followers and commentators, an agonised struggle with impossibly impacted theoretical difficulties in the area of ideology. One of the features of post-structuralism is the claim that it offers a critique of, and alternative to, the entire framework of assumptions and conventions in which such epistemological problems have got stuck. Thus, for example, it can be said that 'Derrida has no objection to a reductive formula such as "philosophy is the ideology of the western ethnos", except for the fact that to say it is impossible. The formula is essentially meaningless ...'. Descombes explains why this should be so: that for Derrida the discourse of a critique of ideology is simply a means of expanding the sway of rationalism within a position that is as much bounded by the 'philosophical' as the one being criticised.[1]

Post-structuralist theory in general is very critical of the theory of ideology in any form, and one could expand the theme in a variety of different contexts. In part III of this book, however, I have chosen to represent these arguments through the work of Foucault: since he is helpfully explicit in his critique of Marxism and particularly the Marxist concept of ideology; since his own work comprises a set of alternative substantive social and historical analyses which can be used to measure the implications of his methodological positions; and since his insistence on the political character of knowledge and truth made him – rarely among post-structuralists – an overtly politicised thinker in the tradition of radical social thought. Foucault's work provides us, in my view, with an approach to discourse and power in society and history that matches Marxism in its sweep and scope, draws attention away from some overplayed themes and focuses it on to topics of great, but neglected, significance. His emphasis on the body was timely and has been highly influential; his arguments about knowledge and truth were not so much relativist, as highly politicised. Foucault was, however, thought by many to be relatively weak on the question of agency and 'the subject' and to this one might add that his work also shows up the adverse implications of an inflexible anti-humanism. These points are brought out very clearly in Habermas's critique of Foucault's general position, and I shall return to this debate a little later.

Theoretical universalism   In the meanwhile, it would be helpful to draw out the implications of the arguments that I have been pursuing through the various discussions of the book. A central theme has been the problem of *theoretical universalism*. In chapter 5 I discussed this problem in some detail in relation to the explanatory claims of psychoanalysis, whose universalistic tendencies are on a par with those of Marxism. Marxism, which has represented itself as a universal discourse of emancipation, has been shown to speak with a very particular historical voice. Classical Marxism may have enabled bourgeois men to analyse society from the point of view of the industrial proletariat but it has subsequently been shown to have occupied a position that was both masculinist in content and Eurocentric in context. Here one might comment that the position of 'western feminism' is a contradictory one – caught between pointing out the false universalisings from the masculine to the general characteristic of Marxism, but vulnerable, at the same time, to the eloquent charge of black women that western feminist discourse has itself spoken (in the name of an entire sex) only for the aspirations of certain specific groups of women.

Consideration of the difficulties of a theory of ideology within Marxism has brought forward the more general issue of how to dampen down the universalistic pretensions of theories without making a complete surrender to particularism. In the context of the issues at stake in the debate over ideology I would identify three general issues on which we can move forward. These are (1) the need to rethink old prejudices about relativism, (2) the need to develop a clearer, more self-conscious, interpretative stance and (3) the need to counter mechanical anti-humanism with a more adequate account of agency and subjective motivation.

RELATIVISM

We need a different conception of the old problem of 'relativism'. As Richard Rorty points out, nobody thinks of themselves as a relativist:[2] like ideology, relativism is something that other people suffer from. Yet if we are to take seriously the criticism that supposedly universal discourses of emancipation must, *de facto*, be spoken from a certain historical and social position and always in practice encode the experience of their creators, this must lead us to a different and more positive understanding of what used to be castigated as relativism. There are several ways of looking at this. One way in is to look at the problem of who 'we' are when we speak: this is the problem that Derrida has drawn attention to in relation to the logocentrism of western philosophy. It is also the central point in, for example, Edward Said's critique of 'orientalism' in western thought, which includes Marxist and social science conceptions of 'Asiatic' modes of production and domination.[3] The problem of the enunciating pronoun has been put at its most extreme by Meaghan Morris, who says we are choking on the utterance act: 'The roar of battle surrounds the pronoun: "I" spells a host of sins from the humanist horror of talking heads to the simple vulgarity of claims to authenticity; "one" has been written into the masculine, and as for "we", that embarrassing macro-binary constraint from the days of unity and solidarity, whatever is to be done with "we"? How many disparate and displacing "you"s and "I"s are being dispossessed?'[4]

One of Foucault's most useful contributions was to recast this anxiety in a positive direction, which he did by associating knowledge and power. This might enable us to displace somewhat the battle between realism and conventionalism or relativism, in which the lines have become drawn between discourse on the one hand and the 'real world' on the other. In discussing Foucault's concept of discourse I went to some lengths to show that Foucault himself argued that discourse was only one of a variety of practices, and indeed that some of his own studies were organised around the relationship of discourses to extradiscursive social practices. Taking that model, one can adopt a somewhat different stance to the problem raised by Terry Lovell about what she terms the 'discursive relativism' of Hindess and Hirst. The example she gives is an important one: 'A history of the Third Reich which made no mention of the murder of six million Jews would be felt by most people to be seriously inadequate. Is this only because we are erroneously comparing this discourse about the Third Reich with other discourses which happen to contain among their objects "extermination camps", "gas chambers", "pogroms" etc.? Or is it because such discourses and their objects are quite properly referred to a world of real objects in which these things really existed, and not just internally to their own logic?[5] It is not necessary to dwell on the methodological difficulty that we all share in getting accurate knowledge of social historical reality, which is of a somewhat different order from knowing (the classic philosophical realist example) facts about the natural world that are independent of human existence and agency.[6] Presumably we can all agree that it would be impossible or unlikely that all our sources for knowing that the Holocaust had happened should die out or be destroyed (although this is theoretically possible, as time goes by). But the problem of the relationship between discourse and the non-discursive 'real' world takes on a completely different light if we consider Foucault's arguments. There is now a revisionist scholarship which seeks precisely to redefine the Holocaust, both denying the scale of the existence of it and the culpability of those responsible: it is precisely this type of discursive development that Foucault's ideas on the *power* axes of discourse can help to illuminate. In a general sense, I would suggest that Foucault's linkage between discourse/truth/knowledge and power has a profoundly politicising effect rather than a negative or conservative effect.

CRITICAL HERMENEUTICS

A second general theme that I would like to mention briefly here, in relation to the fading charms of universal discourses such as Marxism, concerns the recent revaluation of the hermeneutic tradition in social theory. Many have contributed to the restoration of interest, in the humanities and social sciences academic subjects and in social and political thinking generally in this perspective, and the writings of Gadamer have undoubtedly had the greatest influence. Hans-Georg Gadamer's work has lifted the study of hermeneutics into a modern, critical mode in which the historicity of both interpreter and object of interpretation has been productively recognised, and recent interest in the implications of his work has generated a significant debate about interpretation in a variety of contexts.[7]

It is worth noting here that Foucault has made little contribution to the problem of explicating an adequate interpretative stance. Jürgen Habermas's extensive critique of Foucault's general theoretical and methodological position is persuasive on this point. Habermas has articulated an unease that many of us have in reading Foucault as a problem that he rather curiously labels as 'presentism'. Foucault's historiography dismisses the attempt to make the actors' behaviour and thoughts comprehensible in terms of either the understanding of the historian or within their own self-understanding. Rather, Foucault's method, as we saw in the explication of *The Archaeology of Knowledge*, was to uncover the underlying discursive regularities that made such individual instances meaningful. The interpretation is consistently from the outside, rather than a Gadamerian fusion of the frameworks of interpreter and actor. This concept of history where, as Habermas rather unkindly puts it, 'discourses emerge and pop like glittering bubbles from a swamp of anonymous processes of subjugation',[8] thus has no theory of interpretation or understanding. Although this absence of a hermeneutic is, of course, a strategy on Foucault's part to avoid subjective bias, it results according to Habermas in the worst excesses of subjectivism. Habermas points out that in practice Foucault not only makes comparisons between different technologies of power rather than taking them as free-standing entities, but also implicitly refers his epochal schemas to the *present* age. Habermas concludes that 'Foucault is aware of the aporias raised by a procedure that wants to be objectivistic but must remain diagnostic of its time – but he does not provide any answer to them.'[9]

To say, however, that Habermas's critique of Foucault in this area is persuasive is not to endorse Habermas's own position on the hermeneutic enterprise. In many ways, Foucault's critique still remains unanswered in the Habermasian perspective. John Brenkman, in an extremely thoughtful attempt to select and combine the best of Marxism, psychoanalysis and hermeneutics, has recently recast Gadamerian hermeneutics in a more reflexive vein, suggesting that the ideal of universality residually present in both Gadamer and Habermas be abandoned in favour of stressing the plural, constructed heritages of the modern world over the notion of 'preserved-transmitted' traditions.[10]

HUMANISM AND AGENCY

Thirdly, the issue of humanism and anti-humanism must decisively be reopened in the light of the issue of agency. In chapter 5 I suggested a number of reasons why a blanket hostility to humanism was misplaced: it does not follow from a critique of the excesses of the humanist tradition and nor has it enabled any better theory of agency and the subject to emerge. Indeed, one could say that as the problem of agency has been raised, in response to the unilinear anti-humanism of Althusser, early Foucault and so on, so certain previously 'contaminated' elements of humanism have come creeping back in. For anti-humanism in its very strong forms, as well as pulling the rug from under the possibility of political action, has also found it impossible to cope with the entire realms of affect, emotion, sensuality, identity as experienced, or – for example – with issues of art or religion. This enables us to continue with a theoretical rhetoric that has (mercifully) little bearing on the way in which we spend our time and live our lives.

A point that Paul Ricoeur has made in relation to Althusser is worth emphasising in more general terms here: that we need a language of motivation to understand political agency, and Althusser's consigning of all political *will* to the category of ideology was both contradictory and counter-productive.[11] Here, as I suggested earlier, Gramsci's 'optimism of the will' is a far better formulation.

In relation to post-structuralism the issue of agency and anti-humanism is a yet more complex one. Although 'theoretical anti-humanism' is probably the one and only point of contact between Althusserian Marxism and post-structuralism, it is nevertheless a somewhat disabling position from which either might speak: it generates considerable doubt about the authorial subject position and point of enunciation. In the last chapter I raised some of these problems in relation to Foucault but they are, if anything, more obvious in the Derridian tradition of post-structuralist thought. This is particularly apparent if we consider issues of political significance rather than textual interpretation.

As has been widely pointed out, Derridian deconstruction has been extremely effective as an instrument of critique and subversion; the first move of reversing and displacing the hierarchies of dominant binary oppositions has been successfully transgressive. The second move, of transformation, has however been far more difficult to effect – and precisely because (as Derrida himself has made clear) the first move tends to deconstruct the very categories of power that a second move must change. Commenting on this problem in relation to feminism, Derrida noted: 'In a given situation, which is the European phallogocentric structure, the side of the woman is the side from which you start to dismantle the structure. ... But as soon as you have reached the first stage of deconstruction, then the opposition between women and men stops being pertinent. ... We need to find some way to progress strategically.'[12] The dilemma is one that feminists influenced by Derrida's work have also expressed, and it is now folded into the feminist variant of the more general debate on 'essentialism'.[13] Feminists recognise that the 'naming' of women and men occurs within an opposition that one would want to challenge and transform, yet political silencing can follow from rejecting these categories altogether. So it is an issue of whether one wants, speaking as a feminist, to deconstruct or to inhabit the category of 'woman'.

Some Marxists as well as feminists have tended to be rather scathing of these deconstructive manifestations of existential *angst*, and there certainly is an interesting abandonment of authorial responsibility that arises from the tendency in deconstruction to privilege the text so massively over the author. In Derrida's own case it is striking that the two texts in which he has chosen to speak as an individual, on highly politicised matters, differ in style from his other writings in which authorship is more distant or even refused. In his lengthy reflection following the posthumous discovery of Nazi collaborationist texts by his friend and colleague Paul de Man, and in his tribute to Nelson Mandela, Derrida has written with significantly more 'accessibility' than is usually the case: the address to the reader is more direct, there is far less textuality and writerliness and more overt privilege accorded to the content of the argument. In short, although these texts certainly have their equivocations and authorial absences, Derrida has something to say and uses language more as a medium than an end in itself: these are pre-eminently 'translatable' texts.[14]

Even so, there is no mileage in saying that post-structuralism has been caught with the shirt-tails of agency hanging out, for Derrida himself can account for this better than anyone. And if the post-structuralist critique of humanism results in an empty soap-box where once the unreflexive certainties of ethnically and gender bound Marxist correctness had once been expounded, then so much the better. For if post-structuralism's anti-humanist abandonment of individual agency and responsibility is ultimately no answer, it has at least effectively undermined the presumption of correctness and universal applicability in its predecessors.

IDEOLOGY

In the light of these more general considerations, what can we conclude about the concept of ideology itself? There is, in my view, a useful set of meanings that the term ideology can capture well;

they cluster around processes of mystification. The retrievable core of meaning of the term ideology is precisely this: discursive and significatory mechanisms that may occlude, legitimate, naturalise or universalise in a variety of different ways but can all be said to mystify. In such a usage, the term ideology is clearly a general term referring to mystification: it refers to a function or mechanism but is not tied to any particular content, nor to any particular agent or interest. On this definition, ideology is not tied to any one presumed cause, or logic, of misrepresentation; it refers to a process of mystification, or misrepresentation, whatever its dynamic.

To define ideology in this way is to both lower the epistemological profile of the concept and broaden its practical applicability. Decisively, such a usage of ideology is post-Marxist: any Marxist theory of ideology coalesces around the point of class interest as the dynamic force behind mystification and this is simply inadequate, for all the reasons that have been brought forward in this book. Hence the concept of ideology that I would propose applies equally to processes of mystification that arise around other (non-class) social divisions and other forms of social power and domination. Furthermore, this definition of ideology (ideology = mystification) unequivocally frees the concept from the framework of social structural (usually economic) determinism within which it has been locked in Marxist thought. This would open the way for a far more flexible exploration of cultural and subjective phenomena and allow them to be given the weight they deserve.

In this book I have confined myself to the Marxist model of ideology – its internal inconsistencies and the eventual collapse of the paradigm, and to the post-structuralist critique of Marxism on this point as represented by Foucault. I have argued here that the Foucauldian critique of the theory of ideology has considerable force, whatever reservations one may have about Foucault's alternative approach. (One does not have to become a Foucauldian to accept many of his points of critique of Marxism.) At the end of the day, then, it will be obvious that if the distinctively Marxist definition of ideology (ideology = mystification serving class interests) is untenable, the residual meaning of the term as a shorthand for mystification brings it much closer to the tradition of 'critique' of the Frankfurt School and its successors. Thus it is very clear that the 'post-Marxist' concept of ideology is also one with a long 'not Marxist' history, from the work of Karl Mannheim onwards.[15] To engage with 'critical theory' in the detail that would be required would have been the task of a different book and one which I am not qualified to write. But I will make one last point, that may be read in this context too. The definition of concepts, like the definition of everyday words, is partly a matter of usage: one cannot legislate against other people's uses of terms and one cannot with any confidence lay out a new meaning of a term and expect it to stick. It is much easier to coin new terminology than to redefine old. The old meanings adhere, and Foucault's insistence on the political nature of all knowledge, discourse and 'truth' confirms our understanding of this. This is particularly salient in the case of ideology, whose meaning has played such an important part in social critique and politicised debate. The connotations of simplistic illusion or 'false consciousness', however inaccurate, are difficult to shake off. The implication of an 'infra-structure' is always there. The 'explanation' in terms of class is never really forgotten. In some ways, the work undertaken by the concept of ideology is often too shallow and too easy, by virtue of the history of the usage of the concept. Better, perhaps, that we point with more accuracy to an instance that might previously merely be labelled ideological: a partial truth, a naturalised understanding or a universalistic discourse, for example. Better, perhaps, that we oblige ourselves to think with new and more precise concepts, rather than mobilising the dubious resonances of the old.

Notes

1 Marx: Inheriting Contradictions

1 For those who want *un peu d'histoire* about the concept in its pre-Marxist days, Jorge Larrain has traced the term back to Machiavelli. Larrain interprets the development, from the sixteenth century onwards, of a scientific as opposed to a religious style of thought as the major factor in the philosophical background of the concept. Both Larrain and Raymond Williams, who has also provided a useful sketch of the history of the concept, agree that Destutt de Tracy was the first person to use the term *idéologie*. De Tracy, writing in France in the 1790s, sought to specify under this new term a rationalist science of ideas that would cut away the old metaphysical thought.

This relatively favourable (in 'modernist' terms) use of the concept was rapidly eclipsed by the pejorative meaning of the term as used by Napoleon Bonaparte, who, 'disillusioned with his former friends, ... who could not accept his despotic excesses, turned against them and labelled them "ideologists", with the derogatory meaning that they were unreasonable and doctrinaire intellectuals ignorant of political practice'. Raymond Williams points out that this ushered in the dominant modern meaning of the word, where *ideologues* tended to be those (frequently democrats or revolutionaries) whose policies were derived consciously from social theory. Jorge Larrain, *The Concept of Ideology* (London, Hutchinson, 1979); Raymond Williams, 'Ideology', *Keywords* (London, Fontana, 1976).

2 Karl Marx and Frederick Engels, *The German Ideology*, ed. C. J. Arthur (London, Lawrence and Wishart, 1974), p. 47.

3 John Plamenatz, *Ideology*, Key Concepts in Political Science series (London, Macmillan, 1979), pp. 23–5.

4 David McLellan, *Ideology* (Milton Keynes, Open University Press, 1986), p. 18. For confirmation of this interpretation see Jorge Larrain, *Marxism and Ideology* (London, Macmillan, 1983). See Terrell Carver, *Marx and Engels: The Intellectual Relationship* (Brighton, Wheatsheaf, 1983).

5 Karl Marx and Frederick Engels, *Selected Correspondence*, 3rd edn (London, Lawrence and Wishart, 1975), p. 434.

6 Martin Seliger, *The Marxist Conception of Ideology: A Critical Essay* (Cambridge University Press, 1979), pp. 31, 33.

7   Marx and Engels, *German Ideology*, p. 47.
8   Karl Marx, 'Toward a Critique of Hegel's *Philosophy of Right*', *Early Texts*, trans. and ed. David McLellan (Oxford, Basil Blackwell, 1971), p. 115.
9   Larrain, *Marxism and Ideology*, p. 13.
10 Ibid., p. 8.
11 Joe McCarney, *The Real World of Ideology* (Brighton, Harvester, 1980), p. 140.
12 Ibid., pp. 80, 92.
13 Ibid., pp. 3–4, 86.
14 Ibid., p. 95.
15 Ibid., p. 127.
16 George Lukács, *The Historical Novel* (Harmondsworth, Peregrine Books, 1969).
17 McCarney, *Real World*, p. 127.
18 See Allen Wood, *Karl Marx* (London, Routledge and Kegan Paul, 1984), pp. 117–20; Bhikhu Parekh, *Marx's Theory of Ideology* (London, Croom Helm, 1982), pp. 10–13. (Wood identifies historical idealism, functional ideology and ideological illusion, Parekh idealism and apologia.)
19 Marx and Engels, *German Ideology*, p. 64.
20 See, for example, Judith Williamson, *Consuming Passions* (London, Marion Boyars, 1986); Rosalind Coward, *Female Desire* (London, Paladin Books, 1984); Ien Ang, *Watching Dallas* (London, Methuen, 1985); Janice Radway, *Reading the Romance* (Chapel Hill, North Carolina University Press, 1984; reprinted London, Verso, 1987).
21 Dale Spender, *Man Made Language* (London, Routledge, 1980), *Women of Ideas – and What Men Have Done to Them* (London, Pandora Press, 1982) and *For the Record* (London, Women's Press, 1985).
22 For a definitive critique see Maria Black and Rosalind Coward, 'Linguistic, Sexual and Social Relations: A Review of Dale Spender's *Man Made Language*', *Screen Education*, 39 (1981); see also Alison Assiter, 'Did Man Make Language?', in Roy Edgeley and Richard Osborne (eds), *Radical Philosophy Reader* (London, Verso, 1985).
23 See Charles Husband (ed.), *White Media and Black Britain* (London, Arrow Books, 1975); Stuart Hall, 'The Whites of Their Eyes: Racist Ideologies and the Media', in George Bridges and Rosalind Brunt (eds), *Silver Linings: Some Strategies for the Eighties* (London, Lawrence and Wishart, 1981); Cecil Gutzmore, 'Capital, "Black Youth" and Crime', *Race and Class*, vol. 25, no. 2 (1983).
24 Marx and Engels, *German Ideology*, pp. 65–7.
25 Ernesto Laclau, *Politics and Ideology in Marxist Theory: Capitalism, Fascism, Populism* (London, New Left Books, 1977).
26 Parekh, *Marx's Theory*, p. 47.
27 Goran Therborn, *The Ideology of Power and the Power of Ideology* (London, Verso, 1980), p. 9.
28 Karl Marx, 'Preface to a *Contribution to the Critique of Political Economy*', in Marx and Engels, *Selected Works*, 1 vol. (London, Lawrence and Wishart, 1973), p. 182.

29 Ibid., p. 181.
30 Stuart Hall's article, in a collection now unfortunately out of print, provides an exemplary discussion of the development of Marx's thought on questions of the determination of ideology: 'Rethinking the "Base and Superstructure" Metaphor', in Jon Bloomfield (ed.), *Class, Hegemony and Party* (London, Lawrence and Wishart, 1977).
31 Hall, 'Base and Superstructure', p. 60.
32 Louis Althusser, 'Contradiction and Overdetermination', *For Marx*, trans. Ben Brewster (Harmondsworth, Penguin Books, 1969); Louis Althussser and Etienne Balibar, *Reading 'Capital'* (London, New Left Books, 1977).
33 John Mepham, 'The Theory of Ideology in *Capital*', in John Mepham and David-Hillel Ruben (eds), *Issues in Marxist Philosophy*, vol. 3: *Epistemology, Science, Ideology* (Brighton, Harvester, 1979), pp. 151–2.
34 See also on this point Larrain's *Marxism and Ideology*, p. 8.
35 Ben Fine writes: 'Commodity fetishism is the simplest and most universal example of the way in which the economic forms of capitalism conceal underlying social relations ... It establishes a dichotomy between appearance and concealed reality (without the former necessarily being false) which can be taken up in the analysis of ideology' (Tom Bottomore et al. [eds], *A Dictionary of Marxist Thought* [Oxford, Basil Blackwell, 1983], p. 87).
36 Mepham, 'Theory of Ideology', pp. 150–1; in this connection see Hall's discussion of *Darstellung* (the theory of representation in *Capital*), 'Base and Superstructure', pp. 61–3.
37 Mepham, 'Theory of Ideology', pp. 167–8.
38 Quoted in ibid., p. 152.
39 Larrain, *Concept of Ideology*.

2 Ideology: Critique or Description?

1 Jorge Larrain, *The Concept of Ideology* (London, Hutchinson, 1979) and *Marxism and Ideology* (London, Macmillan, 1983).
2 From Larrain's entry on ideology in Tom Bottomore et al. (eds), *A Dictionary of Marxist Thought* (Oxford, Basil Blackwell, 1983), p. 223.
3 Terry Lovell, *Pictures of Reality: Aesthetics, Politics and Pleasure* (London, British Film Institute, 1980), pp. 51–2.
4 Ibid., p. 53.
5 Louis Althusser, 'Ideology and Ideological State Apparatuses', *Lenin and Philosophy and Other Essays*, trans. Ben Brewster (London, New Left Books, 1971; originally pubd France, 1970), pp. 147–8.
6 For a full-blown critique of 'Althusserianism', including on these grounds, see E. P. Thompson, *The Poverty of Theory* (London, Merlin Press, 1978).
7 Nicholas Abercrombie, Stephen Hill and Bryan Turner, *The Dominant Ideology Thesis* (London, Allen and Unwin, 1980).

8   See David Held, 'Power and Legitimacy in Contemporary Britain', in Gregor McLennan, David Held and Stuart Hall (eds), *State and Society in Contemporary Britain* (Cambridge, Polity Press, 1984), p. 331.

9   Abercrombie, Hill and Turner, *Dominant Ideology Thesis*, p. 153.

10 V. I. Lenin, 'What Is To Be Done?', *Selected Works in Twelve Volumes* (London, Lawrence and Wishart, 1936), vol. 2, p. 62.

11 Georg Lukács, *Lenin: A Study in the Unity of His Thought* (London, New Left Books, 1977), p. 24.

12 See Georg Lukács, *The Historical Novel* (Harmondsworth, Peregrine Books, 1969) and 'On Modernism', *The Meaning of Contemporary Realism* (London, Merlin Press, 1972).

13 Georg Lukács, *History and Class Consciousness* (London, Merlin Press, 1971), p. 50.

14 Gareth Stedman-Jones, 'The Marxism of the Early Lukács', in New Left Review (eds), *Western Marxism: A Critical Reader* (London, Verso, 1983; originally pubd in *New Left Review*, 70 [1971]). This article is a comprehensive critique of Lukács's position and I have only extracted one theme in this discussion. It was written from an 'Althusserian' perspective, subsequently to be criticised by its author in Gareth Stedman-Jones, 'The Rise and Fall of French Marxism', in Lisa Appignanesi (ed.), *Ideas from France: The Legacy of French Theory* (London, Institute of Contemporary Arts, 1985).

15 Stedman-Jones, 'The Early Lukács', p. 25.

16 Ibid., p. 37.

17 Agnes Heller, 'Lukács's Later Philosophy', *Lukács Revalued* (Oxford, Basil Blackwell, 1983), p. 177. Heller's collection is a recent sympathetic reappraisal of Lukács in general; for an earlier set of essays see Istvan Meszaros (ed.), *Aspects of History and Class Consciousness* (London, Routledge, 1971).

18 Karl Korsch, *Marxism and Philosophy* (London, New Left Books, 1972), pp. 72–3.

19 Ibid., pp. 71, 73.

20 Larrain, *Marxism and Ideology*, p. 78.

21 Ibid., pp. 78–9.

22 Antonio Gramsci, *Selections from the Prison Notebooks*, ed. Quintin Hoare and Geoffrey Nowell-Smith (London, Lawrence and Wishart, 1976), chap. 1.

23 'Even in Gramsci's mature works we find numerous effects of historicism,' writes Nicos Poulantzas in *Political Power and Social Classes* (London, New Left Books, 1976), p. 138.

24 John B. Thompson, *Studies in the Theory of Ideology* (Cambridge, Polity Press, 1984), pp. 130–1.

25 John Mepham, 'The Theory of Ideology in *Capital*', in John Mepham and David-Hillel Ruben (eds), *Issues in Marxist Philosophy*, vol. 3: *Epistemology, Science, Ideology* (Brighton, Harvester, 1979).

26 Jürgen Habermas, 'Ideology', in Tom Bottomore (ed.), *Modern Interpretations of Marx* (Oxford, Basil Blackwell, 1981; originally pubd in Habermas, *Toward a Rational Society* [1970]), p. 166.

27 Thompson, John B., *Theory of Ideology*, p. 131.

28 Goran Therborn, *The Ideology of Power and the Power of Ideology* (London, Verso, 1980), p. 2.
29 Ibid.
30 Ibid., pp. 3–4.
31 See, for contemporary trends, the publications of Free Association Books (London).
32 Alex Callinicos, *Marxism and Philosophy* (Oxford University Press, 1983), pp. 151, 134–5.
33 Ibid. p. 153.
34 Richard J. Bernstein, *The Restructuring of Social and Political Theory* (London, Methuen, 1979), p. 107.
35 For a UK example see *Feminist Review*, 31 (1989), particularly the articles by Mary Louise Adams and Pratibha Parmar; for a US instance see Bella Brodzki and Celeste Schenck (eds), *Life/Lines: Theorizing Women's Autobiography* (Ithaca, Cornell University Press, 1989).

3 Problems of Science and Determinism

1 Karl Marx, Preface to the French edn, *Capital* (London, Lawrence and Wishart, 1970), vol. 1, p. 21.
2 See William Outhwaite, *New Philosophies of Social Science: Realism, Hermeneutics and Critical Theory* (London, Macmillan, 1987); Ted Benton, *Philosophical Foundations of the Three Sociologies* (London, Routledge, 1977), esp. pp. 165–9; Russell Keat and John Urry, *Social Theory as Science* (London, Routledge, 1975); Derek Sayer, *Marx's Method: Ideology, Science and Critique in 'Capital'* (Brighton, Harvester, 1979); Gregor McLennan, *Marx and the Methodologies of History* (London, Verso, 1981).
3 Louis Althusser, 'On the Young Marx', *For Marx*, trans. Ben Brewster (Harmondsworth, Penguin Books, 1969), p. 84.
4 Jorge Larrain, *Marxism and Ideology* (London, Macmillan, 1983), pp. 9–10.
5 Althusser, *For Marx*, p. 231.
6 Ibid., p. 233. It should be noted that Althusser subsequently rejected the theoreticism of some formulations in *For Marx*.
7 Ibid., pp. 231–6.
8 Louis Althusser, 'On the Materialist Dialectic', *For Marx*, pp. 182ff.
9 Pierre Macherey, *A Theory of Literary Production* (London, Routledge, 1978).
10 Colin Sumner, *Reading Ideologies: An Investigation into the Marxist Theory of Ideology and Law* (London, Academic Press, 1979), p. 172.
11 Terry Lovell's discussion is based on Louis Althusser and Etienne Balibar, *Reading 'Capital'* (London, New Left Books, 1977), as well as *For Marx*. See *Pictures of Reality: Aesthetics, Politics and Pleasure* (London, British Film Institute, 1980), pp. 34–6.
12 Lovell, *Pictures of Reality*, p. 36.
13 Nicos Poulantzas, *Political Power and Social Classes* (London, New Left Books, 1976), p. 206.

14 Louis Althusser, 'Marxism is not a Historicism', in Althusser and Balibar, *Reading 'Capital'*, pp. 119ff.

15 Poulantzas, *Political Power*, p. 205.

16 Larrain, *Marxism and Ideology*, p. 86.

17 Jacques Rancière, 'On the Theory of Ideology – Althusser's Politics', in Roy Edgeley and Richard Osborne (eds), *Radical Philosophy Reader* (London, Verso, 1985), p. 116.

18 See Sebastiano Timpanaro, *On Materialism* (London, Verso, 1980).

19 Lovell, *Pictures of Reality*, p. 15.

20 Ibid., pp. 32–43; Ted Benton, *The Rise and Fall of Structural Marxism: Althusser and His Influence* (London, Macmillan, 1984), p. 181.

21 Althusser, *For Marx*, p. 230.

22 Anthony Cutler et al., *Marx's 'Capital' and Capitalism Today* (London, Routledge, 1977), vol. 1; see also Paul Hirst, 'Althusser and the Theory of Ideology', *Economy and Society*, vol. 5, no. 4 (1976), and *On Law and Ideology* (London, Macmillan, 1979). Of the various general critiques available, perhaps the best is Andrew Collier's 'In Defence of Epistemology', in John Mepham and David-Hillel Ruben (eds), *Issues in Marxist Philosophy*, vol. 3: *Epistemology, Science, Ideology* (Brighton, Harvester, 1979).

23 Cutler et al., *Marx's 'Capital'*, pp. 214ff.

24 Lovell, *Pictures of Reality*, p. 37.

25 John B. Thompson, *Studies in the Theory of Ideology* (Cambridge, Polity Press, 1984), p. 97.

26 Larrain, *Marxism and Ideology*, p. 190.

27 Michel Foucault, 'Truth and Power', *Power/Knowledge: Selected Interviews and Other Writings, 1972–1977*, ed. Colin Gordon (Brighton, Harvester, 1980), p. 118.

28 Alex Callinicos, 'Postmodernism, Post-structuralism and Post-Marxism?', *Theory, Culture and Society*, vol. 2, no. 3 (1985), p. 96.

29 Stuart Hall, 'Rethinking the "Base and Superstructure" Metaphor', in Jon Bloomfield (ed.), *Class, Hegemony and Party* (London, Lawrence and Wishart, 1977), p. 52.

30 Franz Jakubowski, *Ideology and Superstructure: In Historical Materialism* (London, Allison and Busby, 1976), p. 37.

31 Ibid., p. 46

32 Karl Korsch, *Marxism and Philosophy* (London, New Left Books, 1972), p. 84.

33 Althusser, *For Marx*, p. 113.

34 Hirst, *Law and Ideology*, pp. 18–19.

4 Ideology, Politics, Hegemony: From Gramsci to Laclau and Mouffe

1 Antonio Gramsci, *Selections from the Prison Notebooks*, ed. Quintin Hoare and Geoffrey Nowell-Smith (London, Lawrence and Wishart, 1976), pp. 376–7.

2 Ibid., pp. 325–6.

3 Ibid.
4 Antonio Gramsci, *Selections from Cultural Writings*, ed. David Forgacs and Geoffrey Nowell-Smith (London, Lawrence and Wishart, 1985).
5 Perry Anderson, 'The Antinomies of Antonio Gramsci', *New Left Review*, 100 (1976–7).
6 Stuart Hall, Bob Lumley and Gregor McLennan, 'Politics and Ideology: Gramsci', in Centre for Contemporary Cultural Studies, *On Ideology* (London, Hutchinson, 1984; originally pubd in *Working Papers in Cultural Studies*, 10 [1977]). I am indebted in this account to the exposition of Gramsci in this admirably clear essay.
7 Anderson, 'Antinomies', p. 49.
8 Jorge Larrain, *Marxism and Ideology* (London, Macmillan, 1983), chap. 2.
9 C. Mouffe (ed.), *Gramsci and Marxist Theory* (London, Routledge, 1979), p. 178.
10 Stuart Hall, 'Rethinking the "Base and Superstructure" Metaphor', in Jon Bloomfield (ed.), *Class, Hegemony and Party* (London, Lawrence and Wishart, 1977), pp. 65–6.
11 Ernesto Laclau, *Politics and Ideology in Marxist Theory: Capitalism, Fascism, Populism* (London, New Left Books, 1977) and *Hegemony and Socialist Strategy* (London, Verso, 1985).
12 See the discussion of reductionism as a major problem in Marxist 'explanations' of women's oppression in Michèle Barrett, *Women's Oppression Today: The Marxist/Feminist Encounter*, 2nd edn with new Introduction (London, Verso, 1988), pp. 23ff. A more recent trend is to clear away the entire problem of reductionism, by abandoning the focus on pre-given interests characteristic of classical Marxism; see, for example, Barry Hindess, 'The Problem of Reductionism', *Politics and Class Analysis* (Oxford, Basil Blackwell, 1987), and Les Johnstone, 'Class and Political Ideology: A Non-reductionist Solution?', *Marxism, Class Analysis and Socialist Pluralism* (London, Allen and Unwin, 1986).
13 Laclau, *Politics and Ideology*, p. 113.
14 Ibid., p. 142.
15 Ibid., p. 135.
16 Ibid., pp. 108–9.
17 Colin Mercer, 'Fascist Ideology', in James Donald and Stuart Hall (eds), *Politics and Ideology* (Milton Keynes, Open University Press, 1986), p. 237.
18 See Stuart Hall and Martin Jacques (eds), *The Politics of Thatcherism* (London, Lawrence and Wishart, 1983), and especially Hall's 1979 essay 'The Great Moving Right Show'; Stuart Hall, *The Hard Road to Renewal* (London, Verso, 1988).
19 Hall, 'Great Moving Right Show', p. 29.
20 Stuart Hall, 'Authoritarian Populism: A Reply', *New Left Review*, 151 (1985), p. 119.
21 Bob Jessop et al., 'Authoritarian Populism, Two Nations and Thatcherism', *New Left Review*, 147 (1984).
22 Hall, 'Authoritarian Populism', p. 120.

23 Laclau, *Politics and Ideology*, pp. 60–1.
24 See, for example, Ellen Meiksins Wood, *The Retreat from Class: A New 'True' Socialism* (London, Verso, 1986); Norman Geras, 'Post-Marxism?', *New Left Review*, 163 (1987).
25 Laclau and Mouffe, *Hegemony and Socialist Strategy*, p. 2.
26 'In the sense given to this term by Jacques Lacan (and generally used substantively): one of the three essential orders of the psycho-analytic field, namely the Real, the Symbolic and the Imaginary....'. For further exposition of the concept see J. Laplanche and J.-B. Pontalis, *The Language of Psycho-Analysis* (London, Hogarth Press, 1973), p. 210.
27 Laclau and Mouffe, *Hegemony and Socialist Strategy*, p. 67.
28 Ibid.
29 Ernesto Laclau, 'The Impossibility of Society', *Canadian Journal of Political and Social Theory*, vol. 7, nos 1 and 2 (1983).
30 Laclau and Mouffe, *Hegemony and Socialist Strategy*, p. 111; Jacques Derrida, *Of Grammatology*, trans. G. C. Spivak (Baltimore, Johns Hopkins University Press, 1974), p. 158.
31 Laclau and Mouffe, *Hegemony and Socialist Strategy*, p. 111.
32 John Urry, unpublished talk at the University of Surrey, 1990.
33 Paul Hirst, 'Ideology, Culture and Personality', *Canadian Journal of Political and Social Theory*, vol. 7, nos 1 and 2 (1983), p. 125.
34 Laclau and Mouffe, *Hegemony and Socialist Strategy*, p. 105.
35 Donna Landry and Gerald Maclean, 'Reading Laclau and Mouffe' (forthcoming).
36 Laclau and Mouffe, *Hegemony and Socialist Strategy*, p. 88, n. 1.
37 Ibid., p. 112; Jacques Derrida, 'Structure, Sign and Play', *Writing and Difference* (London, Routledge and Kegan Paul, 1978), p. 280.
38 Laclau and Mouffe, *Hegemony and Socialist Strategy*, p. 112.
39 Ibid.
40 Ibid., p. 152.
41 Ibid., p. 159.
42 Ibid., p. 162; see also Jacques Donzelot, *The Policing of Families* (London, Hutchinson, 1980).
43 Laclau and Mouffe, *Hegemony and Socialist Strategy*, p. 163.
44 Ibid., p. 164.
45 Ibid., p. 155.
46 Ibid., p. 156.
47 Ibid., p. 151.
48 Johanna Brenner and Maria Ramas, 'Rethinking Women's Oppression', *New Left Review*, 144 (1984), pp. 68–9.
49 Richard Wright, review, *Rethinking Marxism*, vol. 1 no. 2 (1988), p. 170.
50 Barrett, *Women's Oppression Today*, p. x.
51 See Stuart Hall's work, especially *Politics of Thatcherism*; Gill Seidel (ed.), *The Nature of the Right* (Amsterdam, John Benjamins, 1988); Ruth Levitas (ed.), *The Ideology of the New Right*; and Michèle Jean et al., 'Nationalism and Feminism in Quebéc', in R. Hamilton and M. Barrett (eds), *The Politics of Diversity* (London, Verso, 1986).

52 Laclau and Mouffe, *Hegemony and Socialist Strategy*, pp. 160ff.
53 Ibid., p. 161.
54 Donzelot, *Policing of Families*; Leonore Davidoff and Catherine Hall give a different account of the gendered character of the 'private sphere' in *Family Fortunes* (London, Hutchinson, 1987).
55 Landry and Maclean, 'Reading Laclau and Mouffe'.
56 Wood, *Retreat from Class*, p. 59.
57 Ernesto Laclau and Chantal Mouffe, 'Post-Marxism without Apologies' (A Reply to Norman Geras), *New Left Review*, 166 (1987), p. 82.
58 Laclau and Mouffe, *Hegemony and Socialist Strategy*, p. 154; see also Richard Rorty, *Consequences of Pragmatism* (Minneapolis, Minnesota University Press, 1982), pp. 166–7.
59 Laclau, 'Impossibility of Society', p. 24.
60 See Sebastiano Timpanaro, *On Materialism* (London, Verso, 1980).
61 Ernesto Laclau, 'Psychoanalysis and Marxism', *The Trials of Psychoanalysis*, ed. Françoise Meltzer (Chicago University Press, 1988), p. 143.
62 Ibid., p. 142.
63 Ibid., p. 144.
64 Charles Jencks, *What Is Post-modernism?* (London, Academy Editions, 1986), p. 7.

5 Subjectivity, Humanism, Psychoanalysis: Beyond Althusser's Lacan

1 Vincent Descombes, *Modern French Philosophy* (Cambridge University Press, 1980), pp. 134–5.
2 Gareth Stedman-Jones, 'The Rise and Fall of French Marxism', in Lisa Appignanesi (ed.), *Ideas from France: The Legacy of French Theory* (London, Institute of Contemporary Arts, 1985), p. 32.
3 Terry Eagleton, *Criticism and Ideology* (London, New Left Books, 1976).
4 In 1980, Althusser, in one of the recurrent bouts of psychotic depression to which he was subject and for which he was from time to time hospitalised, strangled his wife Hélène Althusser, and has subsequently been under permanent psychiatric care. The tragic character and consequences of this are obvious, but one has some reservations about the euphemistic terms in which Marxist writers on the subject tend to refer to it. The tragedy cannot, however distressing, be of quite the same order as a tragic accident, since from a feminist point of view one could ask why the 'desperate act' (Elliott, p. 9) should take this particular form.

    See K. S. Karol, 'The Tragedy of the Althussers', *New Left Review*, 124 (1980), for an account very sympathetic to both the Althussers; Gregory Elliott, *Althusser: The Detour of Theory* (London, Verso, 1987), p. 9, for a more 'awkward' reference. At a recent conference on Althusser it was, interestingly, Etienne Balibar (Althusser's co-author and close friend) who broke the heavy silence on this issue.

5 Louis Althusser, *For Marx*, trans. Ben Brewster (Harmondsworth, Penguin Books, 1969), and 'Ideology and Ideological State Apparatuses', *Lenin and Philosophy and Other Essays*, trans. Ben Brewster (London, New Left Books, 1971; originally pubd France, 1970).
6 Louis Althusser, 'Marxism and Humanism', *For Marx*, p. 233.
7 Ibid., pp. 231–4.
8 Ibid., p. 227.
9 The classic, extreme instance being E. P. Thompson's *The Poverty of Theory* (London, Merlin Press, 1978); see also Perry Anderson's attempt to balance the two sides in *Arguments within English Marxism* (London, New Left Books and Verso, 1980).
10 Althusser, 'Marxism and Humanism', p. 229.
11 Ibid., p. 223.
12 Ibid., p. 234.
13 Ibid., p. 230.
14 Paul Ricoeur, *Lectures on Ideology and Utopia*, ed. George H. Taylor (New York, Columbia University Press, 1986), p. 132. Ricoeur's thesis will be discussed further in the final chapter of this book.
15 Paul Hirst and Penny Woolley, *Social Relations and Human Attributes* (London, Tavistock, 1982), p. 110.
16 One widely cited study disputes Althusser's reading of Marx as an anti-humanist: Norman Geras, *Marx and Human Nature: Refutation of a Legend* (London, Verso, 1983). On 'triumphalism' see Raymond Williams's review of Sebastiano Timpanaro's *On Materialism* (London, Verso, 1980), entitled 'Problems of Materialism', *New Left Review*, 109 (1978).
17 Frantz Fanon, *Black Skin, White Masks* (New York, Grove Press, 1967); Simone de Beauvoir, *The Second Sex* (Harmondsworth, Penguin Books, 1974).
18 Raymond Williams, *Keywords* (London, Fontana, 1976), p. 135.
19 Terry Eagleton, *Literary Theory* (Oxford, Basil Blackwell, 1983).
20 Francis Mulhern, 'English Reading', in Homi Bhaba (ed.), *Nation and Narration* (London, Routledge, 1990), p. 263.
21 See Geras, *Marx and Human Nature*.
22 Hirst and Woolley, *Social Relations and Human Attributes*; Stephen Horigan, *Nature and Culture in Western Discourses* (London, Routledge, 1988).
23 E. P. Thompson, *Poverty of Theory*; Simon Clarke et al., *One Dimensional Marxism: Althusser and the Politics of Culture* (London, Allison and Busby, 1980); Paul Hirst, 'Althusser and the Theory of Ideology', *Economy and Society*, vol. 5, no. 4 (1976); Anthony Cutler et al., *Marx's 'Capital' and Capitalism Today* (London, Routledge, 1977); Stedman-Jones, 'Rise and Fall'; Ted Benton, *The Rise and Fall of Structural Marxism: Althusser and His Influence* (London, Macmillan, 1984); Descombes, *Modern French Philosophy*, chap. 4.
24 Paul Hirst has pointed out that Althusser is in error in conflating the division of labour with the relations of production – see 'Althusser', pp. 390ff.

25 Richard Johnson, 'Histories of Culture/Theories of Ideology', in Michèle Barrett et al. (eds), *Ideology and Cultural Production* (London, Croom Helm, 1979), p. 74.

26 See particularly the essays in Annette Kuhn and AnnMarie Wolpe (eds), *Feminism and Materialism* (London, Routledge, 1978); Maxine Molyneux, 'Beyond the Domestic Labour Debate', *New Left Review*, 116 (1979); Veronica Beechey, 'On Patriarchy', *Feminist Review*, 3 (1979); also the discussion of these issues in Benton, *Rise and Fall*, chap. 6.

27 See Michèle Barrett, *Women's Oppression Today: The Marxist/Feminist Encounter*, 2nd edn with new Introduction (London, Verso, 1988), pp. 19–29, xvi–xxiii.

28 Althusser, 'Ideology', p. 171.

29 Ibid.

30 Ibid., p. 137, n. 8.

31 Ibid., p. 155. John Fletcher has pointed out to me that the notion of ideology as 'address' was present in Barthes's *Mythologies* (1957).

32 Althusser, 'Ideology', p. 163.

33 These definitions are based on the translator's note (Alan Sheridan) in Jacques Lacan, *Écrits* (London, Tavistock, 1977; reprinted London, Routledge, 1989), pp. ix–x, and on Bice Benvenuto and Roger Kennedy, *The Works of Jacques Lacan* (London, Free Association Books, 1986), pp. 80–2.

34 He views 'The mirror stage as formative of the function of the I as revealed in psychoanalytic experience' (*Écrits*, p. 2).

35 Louis Althusser, 'Freud and Lacan', *Lenin and Philosophy*, p. 201.

36 Althusser, 'Ideology', p. 166.

37 Benvenuto and Kennedy, *Works of Jacques Lacan*, p. 53.

38 Althusser, 'Freud and Lacan', p. 197.

39 Althusser, Publisher's note to ibid., pp. 177–8.

40 Lacan, *Écrits*, p. 7.

41 Hirst, 'Althusser', p. 406.

42 For an informative account of Lacan's role in the institutions of psychoanalysis see chapter 11 of Benvenuto and Kennedy, *Works of Jacques Lacan*.

43 See Michèle Barrett, 'The Concept of Difference', *Feminist Review*, 26 (1987), pp. 36–9, and *Women's Oppression Today*, pp. xxixff.

44 Jacqueline Rose, *Sexuality in the Field of Vision* (London, Verso, 1986), p. 89.

45 See particularly Juliet Mitchell and Jacqueline Rose, *Feminine Sexuality: Jacques Lacan and the École Freudienne* (London, Macmillan, 1982); David Macey, *Lacan in Contexts* (London, Verso, 1988), chap. 6, presents a detailed case for regarding Lacan as a writer who 'reproduces a basic heterosexism and a trivialisation of feminism' (p. 207).

46 For a useful review of the different schools of thought in this area see Nancy J. Chodorow's recent essay, 'Psychoanalytic Feminism and the Psychology of Women', *Feminism and Psychoanalytic Theory* (Cambridge, Polity Press, 1989).

47   Marcel Mauss, 'A Category of the Human Mind: The Notion of
     Person; the Notion of Self', in Michael Carrithers et al. (eds), *The
     Category of the Person* (Cambridge University Press, 1985), pp. 1–25.
48   Niklas Luhmann, 'The Individuality of the Individual', in Thomas C.
     Heller et al. (eds), *Reconstructing Individualism: Autonomy, Individuality
     and the Self in Western Thought* (Stanford University Press, 1986),
     p. 324.
49   Ian Hacking, 'Making Up People', in Heller et al., *Reconstructing
     Individualism*, p. 33.
50   Mauss, 'Category of the Human Mind', p. 22.
51   See Janet Wolff, *The Social Production of Art* (London, Macmillan,
     1981).
52   Peter Bürger, *Theory of the Avant-garde* (Minneapolis, Minnesota Uni-
     versity Press, 1984), p. 92.
53   Steven Lukes, Conclusion to Carrithers et al., *Category of the Person*,
     p. 298.
54   Andrew Ross, 'The Politics of Impossibility', in Richard Feldstein and
     Henry Sussman (eds), *Psychoanalysis and . . .* (New York and London,
     Routledge, 1990), p. 113.
55   See the entry 'Oedipus Complex' in J. Laplanche and J.-B. Pontalis,
     The Language of Psycho-Analysis (London, Hogarth Press, 1973),
     pp. 282–7.
56   See Charles Larmore, 'The Concept of a Constitutive Subject', in Colin
     McCabe (ed.), *The Talking Cure* (London, Macmillan, 1981). My
     thanks to Kate Nash for discussion of this point.
57   See the discussion of 'post-psychoanalysis' in chapter 4 of this volume;
     Barrett, 'Concept of Difference'; and 'Words and Things: Materialism
     and Method in Contemporary Feminist Analysis', in M. Barrett and
     A. Phillips (eds), *Destabilizing Theory: Contemporary Feminist Debates*
     (Cambridge, Polity Press, 1992).
58   Cornelius Castoriadis, 'The State of the Subject Today', *Thesis Eleven*,
     24 (1989), pp. 7, 37.
59   Paul Ricoeur, *Freud and Philosophy* (New Haven and London, Yale
     University Press, 1970), p. 439.
60   Anthony Giddens, 'What Do Sociologists Do?', *Social Theory and
     Modern Sociology* (Cambridge, Polity Press, 1987), pp. 18ff.
61   Jean-Jacques Lecercle, *Philosophy through the Looking-glass* (London,
     Hutchinson, 1985), p. 179.
62   Gilles Deleuze and Felix Cuattari, *Anti-Oedipus: Capitalism and Schizo-
     phrenia* (London, Athlone Press, 1984), with Preface by Michel
     Foucault.
63   Feldstein and Sussman, *Psychoanalysis and . . .* , pp. 1–8.
64   For example, Juliet Mitchell, Nancy Chodorow.
65   Michel Foucault, *Power/Knowledge: Selected Interviews and Other Writ-
     ings, 1972–1977*, ed. Colin Gordon (Brighton, Harvester, 1980), p. 61.
66   Deleuze and Guattari, *Anti-Oedipus*, p. 97.
67   Michèle Barrett and Mary McIntosh, *The Anti-social Family* (London,
     Verso, 1982).
68   Ricoeur, *Freud and Philosophy*, p. 258.

69 Nancy Chodorow, 'Toward a Relational Individualism: The Mediation of Self through Psychoanalysis', *Feminism and Psychoanalytic Theory.*

70 John Brenkman, *Culture and Domination* (Ithaca, Cornell University Press, 1987), pp. 187–8.

6   History, Discourse, 'Truth' and Power: Foucault's Critique of Ideology

1   Michel Foucault, 'Truth and Power', *Power/Knowledge: Selected Interviews and Other Writings, 1972–1977*, ed. Colin Gordon (Brighton, Harvester, 1980), p. 118.

2   See John Sturrock, 'Roland Barthes', *Structuralism and Since* (Oxford University Press, 1979), for a discussion of Barthes's account (in *Writing Degree Zero*) of lucidity (*la clarté*) in this context.

3   Jacques Derrida, *Dissemination*, trans. Barbara Johnson (Chicago University Press, 1981).

4   Michel Foucault, *The Archaeology of Knowledge*, trans. A. M. Sheridan Smith (London, Routledge, 1972), p. 27.

5   Edward Said, 'Michel Foucault, 1926–1984', in Jonathan Arac (ed.), *After Foucault* (New Brunswick, Rutgers University Press, 1988), p. 10.

6   Foucault, *Archaeology of Knowledge*, pp. 21–7.

7   Hubert Dreyfus and Paul Rabinow, *Michel Foucault: Beyond Structuralism and Hermeneutics* (Brighton, Harvester, 1982), pp. 45–8.

8   Foucault, *Archaeology of Knowledge*, pp. 85–6.

9   Gilles Deleuze, *Foucault* (Minneapolis, Minnesota University Press, 1988), p. 1.

10 Foucault, *Archaeology of Knowledge*, pp. 37–8.

11 See the interview with Fontana and Pasquino in Foucault, *Power/Knowledge*, p. 111. Later, Foucault was to revert to this misunderstanding, arguing that he saw discontinuity in history 'as a problem to be resolved' (interview with Boncenne, 'On Power', in Lawrence Kritzman [ed.], *Michel Foucault: Politics, Philosophy, Culture* [New York and London, Routledge, 1988], p. 100).

12 Michel Foucault, 'Politics and the Study of Discourse' (trans. from an article in *Esprit*, 1968), *Ideology and Consciousness*, 3 (1978), pp. 7–26.

13 Foucault, *Archaeology of Knowledge*, p. 49.

14 Ibid., pp. 47–8.

15 Kritzman, *Michel Foucault*, p. 8.

16 Foucault, *Archaeology of Knowledge*, pp. 9–10.

17 Ibid., p. 13.

18 Michel Foucault, 'Nietzsche, Genealogy, History', in Paul Rabinow (ed.), *The Foucault Reader* (Harmondsworth, Peregrine Books, 1986), p. 77.

19 Ibid., pp. 80–3.

20 Ibid., pp. 83–6, 89.

21 Michel Foucault, 'The Order of Discourse', trans. Ian McLeod, in

Robert Young (ed.), *Untying the Text* (London, Routledge, 1981), p. 69. 'Aleatory' is defined as 'dependent on the throw of a die' (*Oxford English Dictionary*).

22 Foucault, 'Order of Discourse', p. 69.
23 Kritzman, *Michel Foucault*, p. 112.
24 Anthony Giddens, *Central Problems in Social Theory* (London, Macmillan, 1979), pp. 253ff.
25 See Dreyfus and Rabinow, *Michel Foucault*, chap. 4.
26 Foucault, *Power/Knowledge*, p. 115.
27 Ibid., p. 116.
28 Ibid., p. 142.
29 Kritzman, *Michel Foucault*, pp. 104–5.
30 Ibid., pp. 103–4.
31 Michel Foucault, 'The Subject and Power' (Afterword), in Dreyfus and Rabinow, *Michel Foucault*, pp. 217, 219.
32 For discussion of these distinctions see Foucault, 'Subject and Power', and Colin Gordon's Afterword to Foucault, *Power/Knowledge*, p. 251.
33 Michel Foucault, 'The Eye of Power', *Power/Knowledge*, p. 147.
34 Michel Foucault, *Discipline and Punish: The Birth of the Prison* (Harmondsworth, Peregrine Books, 1979), p. 2.
35 Kritzman, *Michel Foucault*, p. 46.
36 Stuart Hall, 'Rethinking the "Base and Superstructure" Metaphor', in Jon Bloomfield (ed.), *Class, Hegemony and Party* (London, Lawrence and Wishart, 1977), p. 52.
37 David Couzens Hoy, 'Power, Repression, Progress: Foucault, Lukes, and the Frankfurt School', *Foucault: A Critical Reader* (Oxford, Basil Blackwell, 1986), p. 142.
38 Alan Sheridan, *Michel Foucault: The Will to Truth* (London, Tavistock, 1980), p. 70.
39 Ibid., p. 73.
40 Foucault, *Power/Knowledge*, pp. 58–9.
41 Kritzman, *Michel Foucault*, p. 118.
42 Barry Smart, 'The Politics of Truth and the Problem of Hegemony', in Hoy, *Foucault*, p. 160.
43 Barry Smart, *Foucault, Marxism and Critique* (London, Routledge, 1983), pp. 38–42.
44 Smart, 'Politics of Truth', p. 161.
45 Kritzman, *Michel Foucault*, p. 33.
46 Foucault, 'Order of Discourse', pp. 52–5.
47 Sheridan, *Michel Foucault*, p. 23.
48 Foucault, 'Order of Discourse', p. 55.
49 Ibid., p. 60.
50 Ibid., p. 61.
51 Kritzman, *Michel Foucault*, p. 107.
52 Michel Foucault, 'What Is An Author?', in Rabinow, *Foucault Reader*; Roland Barthes, 'The Death of the Author', *Image-Music-Text* (London, Fontana, 1977).
53 Foucault, *Archaeology of Knowledge*, p. 17.

54 Kritzman, *Michel Foucault*, p. 251.
55 Gary Gutting, *Michel Foucault's Archaeology of Scientific Reason* (Cambridge University Press, 1989), pp. 274–7.
56 Paul Bové, 'The Foucault Phenomenon; The Problematics of Style' (Foreword), in Deleuze, *Foucault*, p. xiii.
57 Ibid., p. xxvi.
58 Richard Rorty, 'Foucault and Epistemology', in Hoy, *Foucault*, p. 43.
59 Gutting, *Foucault's Archaeology*, p. 285.
60 Rorty, 'Foucault and Epistemology', p. 48.
61 Michel Foucault, *Technologies of the Self*, ed. Luther H. Martin et al. (London, Tavistock, 1988), p. 146.
62 Biddy Martin, 'Feminism, Criticism, and Foucault', in Irene Diamond and Lee Quinby (eds), *Feminism and Foucault* (Boston, Northeastern University Press, 1988), p. 13.
63 Foucault, *Archaeology of Knowledge*, p. 55.
64 Michel Foucault, *Language, Counter-memory, Practice*, ed. Donald Bouchard (Ithaca, Cornell University Press, 1977), pp. 221–2.
65 Ibid., p. 227.
66 Ibid., p. 226.
67 Kritzman, *Michel Foucault*, pp. 252–3.
68 Ibid., pp. 253–4.
69 Ian Hacking, 'Self-improvement', in Hoy, *Foucault*, p. 237.
70 Ibid. p. 236.
71 Michel Foucault, *The Care of the Self* (New York, Vintage, 1988).
72 Foucault, *Technologies*, p. 18.
73 See John Rajchman, *Michel Foucault: The Freedom of Philosophy* (New York, Columbia University Press, 1985), p. 36.
74 A notable exception is the feminist historian Joan Wallach Scott's *Gender and the Politics of History* (New York, Columbia University Press, 1988).
75 Foucault, *Power/Knowledge*, pp. 58–9.
76 Michèle Barrett, *Women's Oppression Today: The Marxist/Feminist Encounter*, 2nd edn with new Introduction (London, Verso, 1988), pp. xxvi–xxviii.
77 Martin, 'Feminism', p. 15.
78 Charles Taylor, 'Foucault on Freedom and Truth', in Hoy, *Foucault*.
79 Nancy Fraser, *Unruly Practices: Power, Discourse and Gender in Contemporary Social Theory* (Cambridge, Polity Press, 1989), p. 57.
80 Martin, 'Feminism', p. 17.
81 Monique Plaza, 'Our Costs and Their Benefits', *m/f*, 4 (1980).
82 Kritzman, *Michel Foucault*, p. 204.
83 Ibid., p. 284.
84 Edward Said, *The World, the Text, and the Critic* (London, Faber and Faber, 1984), p. 222; Edward Said, 'Michel Foucault', pp. 9–10.
85 Mark Poster, 'Foucault and the Tyranny of Greece', in Hoy, *Foucault*, pp. 214, 219.
86 Kritzman, *Michel Foucault*, pp. 3–16.
87 This comment is elaborated in Michèle Barrett, 'The Place of

Aesthetics in Marxist Criticism', in Cary Nelson and Lawrence Grossberg (eds), *Marxism and the Interpretation of Culture* (Illinois University Press, 1988), pp. 700–1.

88 Terry Eagleton, *The Ideology of the Aesthetic* (Oxford, Basil Blackwell, 1990), p. 395.

89 Anthony Giddens, *Social Theory and Modern Sociology* (Cambridge, Polity Press, 1987), p. 98.

90 Taylor, 'Foucault', p. 85; the quotation from Foucault is from *La Volonté de savoir* (Paris, Gallimard, 1976), p. 124; Michel Foucault, *The History of Sexuality* (New York, Vintage, 1980), vol. 1, pp. 94–5.

91 Taylor, 'Foucault' p. 88.

Conclusion: Post-Marxism and the Concept of Ideology

1 Vincent Descombes, *Modern French Philosophy* (Cambridge University Press, 1980), p. 137.

2 Richard Rorty, 'Pragmatism, Relativism, Irrationalism', *Consequences of Pragmatism* (Minneapolis, Minnesota University Press, 1982), p. 166.

3 Edward Said, *Orientalism* (London, Routledge, 1978).

4 Meaghan Morris, *The Pirate's Fiancée: Feminism, Reading, Postmodernism* (London, Verso, 1988), p. 53.

5 Terry Lovell, *Pictures of Reality: Aesthetics, Politics and Pleasure* (London, British Film Institute, 1980), p. 37.

6 See Roy Bhaskar, *The Possibility of Naturalism: A Philosophical Critique of the Contemporary Human Sciences* (Brighton, Harvester, 1979), and William Outhwaite, *New Philosophies of Social Science: Realism, Hermeneutics and Critical Theory* (London, Macmillan 1987).

7 Hans-Georg Gadamer, *Truth and Method* (London, Sheed and Ward, 1975). For commentary on Gadamer see William Outhwaite, 'Hans-Georg Gadamer', in Quentin Skinner (ed.), *The Return of Grand Theory in the Human Sciences* (Cambridge University Press, 1985), and Georgia Warnke, *Gadamer: Hermeneutics, Tradition and Reason* (Cambridge, Polity Press, 1987). The revival of interest in hermeneutics, which includes the work of Habermas, Ricoeur, Gadamer, Karl-Otto Apel and earlier philosophers including Dilthey, Droysen and Schleiermacher, is best explicated in Josef Bleicher, *Contemporary Hermeneutics* (London, Routledge, 1980), and can be sampled in Kurt Mueller-Vollmer (ed.), *The Hermeneutics Reader* (Oxford, Basil Blackwell, 1986).

8 Jürgen Habermas, 'Questions Concerning the Theory of Power: Foucault Again', *The Philosophical Discourse of Modernity*, trans. Frederick Lawrence (Cambridge, Polity Press, 1987), p. 268.

9 Ibid. p. 278.

10 John Brenkman, *Culture and Domination* (Ithaca, Cornell University Press, 1987).

11 Paul Ricoeur, *Lectures on Ideology and Utopia*, ed. George H. Taylor (New York, Columbia University Press, 1986), pp. 103ff.

12 Jacques Derrida, 'Women in the Beehive: A Seminar with Jacques Derrida', in Alice Jardine and Paul Smith (eds), *Men in Feminism* (London, Methuen, 1977), p. 194.

13 See, for example, Gayatri Chakravorty Spivak, 'Feminism and Deconstruction, Again', in Theresa Brennan (ed.), *Between Feminism and Psychoanalysis* (London, Methuen, 1989); Denise Riley, *Am I That Name? Feminism and the Category of 'Women' in History* (London, Macmillan, 1988); Joan Wallach Scott, *Gender and the Politics of History* (New York, Columbia University Press, 1988).

14 Jacques Derrida, 'Like the Sound of the Deep Sea within a Shell: Paul de Man's War', *Critical Inquiry*, vol. 14 (1988); Jacques Derrida, 'The Laws of Reflection: Nelson Mandela, in Admiration', in Jacques Derrida and Mustapha Tlili (eds), *For Nelson Mandela* (New York, Seaver Books, 1987). My thanks to Morag Shiach for drawing my attention to this text.

15 See John Thompson's work for the most sophisticated contemporary exponent of the critical theory tradition as it applies to ideology and also taking on board the ideas of theorists such as Bourdieu, Pecheux, Giddens and Castoriadis and Lefort: John B. Thompson, *Studies in the Theory of Ideology* (Cambridge, Polity Press, 1984) and *Ideology and Modern Culture* (Cambridge, Polity Press, 1990).

Index